Memoirs of A Hippie Girl in India

BY ANN BeCoy

Toronto, 2013

Memoirs of a Hippie Girl in India
BeCoy, Ann (1953–)
ISBN 978-0-9920383-0-4

BeCoy Publishing
153 Spadina Road
Toronto, Ontario
Canada M5R 2T9
www.annbecoy.com

Contents

Preface

WHILE OTHER TORONTO KIDS MY AGE were in college or grad school, I spent my nineteenth and twentieth birthdays in jail, getting a different kind of education. After pursuing a sudden and passionate romance, I quickly found myself becoming a world traveler and teen-aged drug smuggler. And that is an education in itself.

This story recounts my journey through the Middle East to India, then to Europe and back to India again. From the hippie beach in Goa, it brings you into the female side of India's prison system and my personal transformation during three months in Bombay jails. Then the journey takes you to ashram and village life in rural India, to Simla and the Himalayas in northern India, and later to Kathmandu in Nepal.

I went from jail to ashram to jail to ashram. And I saw there wasn't a lot of difference between the two. As Baba Ram Dass said in *Be Here Now*, it's all a question of perception.

In writing this piece of my life adventure, I wanted to portray a time and place unique in history, a place that was magical for a while. I feel blessed to have seen a side of India that no longer exists – an India with 19th-century quaintness but largely free of Western culture. In other words, India when it was still Indian.

For young Westerners the early 1970s was a golden era when they could travel from Europe overland to India. People came in busloads, crossing without hassle through Turkey, Iran, Iraq, Afghanistan and Pakistan. By the hundreds they explored the mysticism of India and Nepal, pursued philosophy, learned Sanskrit or classical Indian music or dance, smoked hashish and opium, and slept naked.

So the story is about more than my adventures. I include other real characters from the scene, some of them known around the world, and real political events and the social climate of that time. But recalling events from forty years ago is difficult. Luckily, I had some notes, journals and photos, and others who were there at the time provided more. To the best of my ability, I recount actual facts and truths about the circumstances and the times. I have tried to be honest without embellishing the story. Indeed, as truth is sometimes stranger than fiction, this story really needs no embellishment.

But to fully evoke the time, place and events – to accurately recreate the feeling of India and Nepal in the early 1970s – I have told the story with a little imagination. Some people call this Creative Nonfiction; I just call it story telling. Because that's what I'm doing ... telling a story without literary pretensions. In so doing I took some license. For example, some names are fictitious, to protect those whose current status I know nothing about. For the most part, however, I have used real names and real places and events, drawn from memory, my scant notes and writings of the period, and from recollections of other people who were there.

Any factual mistakes are entirely my own, and I apologize for them.

I have had the pleasure of support from a wonderful editor who helped research facts when I had only vague recollections, who corrected factual errors and clarified the story as well as fixed typos, punctuation and grammar. I could not have finished this project without his great assistance and insights.

Many would ask what possessed me to do some of the things I did. To which I answer: growing up a certain way I became a tremendous risk-taker. In so doing, I learned to survive a variety of difficult circumstances. In effect the metamorphosis I went through between 1972 and 1974 was a yoga of purification. But it was my foundation and my point of departure into a life fraught with further misadventures, and it gave me strength to endure some even greater hardships later.

Glossary

acha ... yes, I see

Acharya ... "Divine one?"

ahimsa ... non-violence

Allahabad ... holy city and site of Khumba Mela

Brahma ... Creator of the Universe; Supreme God; head of the Trinity

Brahmacharya ... pure one/celibate

baba ... (loosely) old one, uncle

bhakti ... yoga of absolute devotion

Bhagwan ... Supreme Lord

Bhagavad Gita ... sacred scripture recounting Krishna dialogue with Arjuna on the battlefield

burqa/burka ... Muslim women's garment completely covering the body, face and head

chillum ... conical pipe used to smoke hash

chillum baba ... one who smokes hash

charas ... hashish

Chandra ... moon goddess

chai ... milky spicy tea

coolies ... porters (who carry bags and luggage)

dhotara ... two-stringed drone instrument

Durga ... major Hindu goddess

Diwali ... festival of lights

ek ... one

ektara ... one-stringed drone instrument

Farsi ... of Persian descent

fakir ... wandering mendicant, usually an entertainer

ghee ... clarified butter used in cooking and ceremonies

harmonium ... wind and key instrument similar to accordions

Hanuman ... a humanoid monkey god

harem ... (Arabic) women's quarters

Hoogley River ... in Calcutta

Howrah Bridge ... famous bridge spanning the Hoogley River

Jai (as in Jai Ram) ... praise (e.g., to Ram, or Jai Krishna: Praise to Krishna)

-ji ... suffix denoting fondness/ familiarity as in Mahara-ji, Mata-ji, Sunanda-ji

Kali ... fierce black warrior goddess

Kama Sutra ... yoga of erotic tantric sex

kapalubhati ... intense yoga breathing technique

kartel ... Indian temple bells (brass)

Kashatriyas ... caste designation second to Brahmins

kundalini ... subtle snake-like energy that travels up the spine through the chakra system

kurta ... men's long-sleeved loose shirt-like garment

kriya yoga ... yoga of deep introspection

lathi ... brass-tipped wooden baton used by police

lingam ... (as in Shiva lingam) phallic symbol

Leela ... the illusory play of life

lunghi ... men's wraparound garment worn like a skirt

Maharaja ... Great King

Maharanee ... Great Queen

Maharishee ... Great Saint

Mahavatar ... Great Soul

Meher Baba ... a popular living guru in 1972

mehta ... chief/prince; high-caste Brahmin (loosely "respect")

mudras ... yoga hand symbols (used in classical dance)

namaste ... greetings, hello (literally "I salute the light within you")

Pondicherry ... home of Sri Aurobindo and the Mother (also name of a city)

prasad or prasadum ... vegetarian food offered to Krishna and blessed

Ram ... seventh avatar of Vishnu (followed by Krishna)

Rajasthan ... place of Rajas before British occupation/princely states

rajput ... prince

samosa ... deep-fried potato-filled snack sold everywhere in India

Sarada ... female saint; chaste partner of Sree Ramakrishna of Santinikitan

Santinikitan ... sacred site of Kali Temple near Calcutta

Shiva ... third god in the trinity: Brahma, Vishnu, Shiva

Simla ... beautiful Himalayan region in the north in Himachel Pradesh

siddhis ... miraculous powers

tantra ... yoga of extreme indulgence and austerities

Tat Wala Baba ... wandering saint in Rishikesh (see photo page 153)

Vedas ... holy scriptures more than 2,000 years old

Vishnu ... Sustainer of the Universe; second in the triad of Brahma, Vishnu, Shiva

Vrindavan/Brindivan ... holy city sacred to Krishna

Dedicated to

NEEM KAROLI BABA and BABA RAM DASS,
whose teachings have informed and inspired my life,

and to my two kids, AURIEL and SARAH

CHAPTER I

Meeting Donny

Ann as a Toronto high school student in 1970.

MY BRIEF CRIMINAL CAREER as a teen-aged drug smuggler began when I met Donny in early February 1972. Though mid-winter, it was an unusually still, warm night, when everything was covered in delightful snow that fell almost in slow motion with giant flakes that stuck to my nose. There was a hush all over the landscape, as cars slushed by slowly and distant sounds were muffled. I was walking about a kilometer to a friend's house. Living in Toronto's suburbs, I had to walk everywhere so I was quite used to it. I got to Laura's house and found the usual assortment of kids from my high school gang.

But then there was Donny. He was different from the boys I knew at high school. For one thing, he was dressed all in black when everyone else was in paisley shirts, striped pants or multi-colored, tie-dyed tee shirts. He had a cool vibe. He was kind of laid-back, and I noticed he mostly just observed the situation and people around him. Unlike most of the high school boys, he didn't guzzle back copious amounts of beer but instead drank cognac. Maybe that seems affected, but back then it impressed me. He looked like a quiet, measured man who didn't waste time on nonsense talk. He listened more than he spoke. His posture exuded confidence, basically saying 'I don't really care what you think about me.' So naturally I was intrigued.

1

I watched him ever so gently lean against the bar and light a cigarette in a fancy cigarette holder. When someone offered him a joint he politely refused, and I overheard something about not "sharing joints." He kept studying the room and the people scattered there, taking note of who was with whom and who was solo. Pretty soon his gaze landed on me. He smiled, his eyes twinkled and something clicked inside me. I was struck for a moment. Most of my girlfriends were hitched up with steadies, but I was single and in legitimate territory: I could have walked over and struck up a conversation. But I lost my nerve, turned around and went to the bathroom, a woman's refuge at any party.

I asked my hostess, "Who's the new guy, the cutie with the big brown eyes and those lashes! Wow!" Laura smiled. "Oh he's a friend of Rick's brother Alistair, a guy he knows from Yorkville."

Rick was Laura's boyfriend, and his brother was a little bit older than our crowd – it's funny how when you are eighteen you think twenty-four is so mature. Anyway, I got to talking to Alistair, and soon he introduced me to Donny. In no time I discovered a really interesting guy; one who seemed mature, well read and well informed. I felt a bit awkward in his presence, not knowing what to say. He seemed so worldly and clever, and I'd never been anywhere.

"Tell me more about Morocco," I begged eagerly. He suggested, "Why don't we go outside and blow a joint, and we can check out the sky? I think there's a full moon tonight."

So we stole away from the crowd and stepped out onto her patio and looked at the moon. The evening light cast a shadow on his eyes that made his lashes look even longer, and his thick and shiny hair blew gently up against my face. He had his arm around me and pulled me gently towards him. He smelled faintly of patchouli.

Soon we were animatedly talking about life, philosophy and our dreams and ambitions. I didn't really have any concrete ambitions at that point in my life, but craved some adventure. Donny said, "Man, travelling is the best way to learn about the world. You end up trying new things, pushing your boundaries a little. Like the time I told you I did this weird psychedelic tea with a shaman I met in Mexico. Something very strange happened then."

The night was dreamy and Donny, mindful of decorum, was courteous and attentive. He drifted off into a dreamscape for a few moments. I was quiet and just looked at the giant moon in front of me. Low on the horizon, it was a glorious pale yellow disc. Is it possible, I wondered that the moon is really that big?

In the washroom meeting place I told Laura, "I think I really like this guy Donny. He sure has lots of ambition, and he's planning to make a lot of money and buy a farm." Laura said, "Watch out for these really smooth types, okay? Talk is talk – let's see what he's got to offer. I'd say "go for it." Brenda agreed. "Yeah, he's kinda cute. Anyway, what've you got to lose ... your virginity?" We all had a good laugh at that.

I defended myself. "Well, he loves to travel and says I should travel too – he says it's the only way to get a real education. And you know what? I think he's right. I've never been anywhere really." Brenda interjected, "it's fine to want to travel but how do you pay for it?" Laura said. "I'm going to be an airline stewardess." Brenda, leaning over the sink with her generous buttocks protruding for anyone to notice, was applying a new shade of lipstick. "How will your hot-shot traveller finance his travels? Don't tell me he's got an inheritance or something."

"No, he said first he would use the profits of his business to buy a farm Then he could use the farm to grow pot and travel on the proceeds, and he'd always have a place to come home to in Canada." I thought that sounded pretty smart. Most guys I knew didn't have any plans at all. All they thought about was partying. But here was Donny making plans ... to make sure he could keep the party happening.

Pretty soon Donny and I were intimate. I guess you could say he was my boyfriend then, and it was cool because he lived downtown in the famous Rochdale College right near Yorkville.

Now a high-priced boutique district, Yorkville was a hippie haven in Toronto for a brief period, in the late six-

Trooper Drooper, the concierge at Rochdale, 1970.

ties through the early seventies. Rochdale quickly picked up a hippie tenancy, as it was nearby and had a radical approach to education, providing a free school and residences for liberal arts students – a kind of cool college/free school. In the early seventies, combining artists and LSD led to some pretty psychedelic artistic stuff. Every inch of Rochdale's interior walls, ceilings, elevators and floors was covered in crazy, psychedelic art, visions of heaven and hell, poetry or anarchistic rantings and political rhetoric.

The first time I went to Rochdale to score had been two summers before that, in 1970. A great travelling rock festival (travelling by train, no less) called Festival Express was coming to town, and some of my friends and I wanted good drugs for the three-day concert. Or, as my Hare Krishna friend used to call them, "benedictions." He said psychedelics are not drugs because they brought us to a divine state of peace, harmony and love; he believed they were really a kind of sacrament.

Anyway, we were going to see Janis Joplin and the Grateful Dead, The Band, Ten Years After, Mountain and many other favorite bands performing live right in Toronto – and we wanted to get blasted.

An ashram room in Toronto's Rochdale College, 1970.

Where else to get good drugs but Toronto's biggest known non-secret? Rochdale!

In those days Rochdale was in its glory. The place was so unregulated and laid-back that people shared meals, accommodations, clothes, drugs and lovers just like that, and rarely even locked their doors. And no one paid rent. There was a vegetarian restaurant, and if you were hungry they'd feed you even if you couldn't pay. Those were idyllic times … it was really like a commune in an apartment building. There was even a guy living in a tent on the roof.

Back then you'd be greeted at the doorway by an acid-brained hippie, a kind of friendly concierge who would check out your vibe, and if you knew the right people he'd let you in. Of course, he knew all the dealers, the artists, the "management," the runaways and the hangers-on. I went with some girlfriends from high school.

"So what are you kids looking for?" he asked, advising us "There's MDA and some good acid and some magic mushrooms at Bill's place on the fifth floor. Some great Lebanese hash on the eighth floor at Skimpy's. And Hairy Guy's got some nice peyote and native stories and rituals and stuff if you're into that." My friend Joanne said, "native stories??"

Without really trying to impress us, he ran off the list like a waitress reciting the evening's menu. "Oh yeah," he went on. "There're some films showing at Reg's place too; I think there's an Andy Warhol film. Oh yeah, the Hare Krishnas got some kind of music thing happening later. And you know Boots? The Acrylic man, have you seen his work? Out of this world man … he did the elevator doors on the ninth floor … anyway he's in #907 … and he's got some of the best Acapulco Gold man, that's what I smoke … wanna hit?"

We each took a hit and agreed with the concierge: as anyone who's ever smoked real Acapulco Gold knows, it was wicked stuff. "So what'll it be?" I said, "we're looking for some good psychedelics." He told us, "J.J.'s got Orange Sunshine and Windowpane and, believe it or not" – here he leaned forward and whispered conspiratorially – "Gerry's lady, Flower Girl? She's got some amazing Purple Microdot." We all cried in unison, "Purple Microdot!" There was no doubt we'd go for that. Nothing less for Janis Joplin.

Now, two years later, I was going out with a guy who lived in Rochdale. That was so cool.

Etherea vegetarian restaurant in Rochdale, also a front for hashish dealers.

Donny and I were out dancing one night. We went to Grossman's Tavern on Spadina and heard the Downchild Blues Band. Toronto in those days was a real blues city, and good live music could be heard at nearly any downtown bar. The band was playing a slow blues tune. As we danced Donny crooned in my ear, gently caressing my hair and singing softly under his breath, and I was smitten. I could have made out with him right there on the dance floor. I had been single for over six months, and that was a long time in the life of a teenage girl. But of course we would never do such a thing ... not in proper Toronto. We took a break, and as we sat over drinks and cigarettes he told me he had to leave soon on a business trip.

"Where are you going?" I asked a little stunned at this sudden news. "India," he replied. "India? What gives? What are you going to do there?" I stubbed the cigarette out aggressively as this news made me nervous. He said, "You know I buy art and other things to bring back. It's for my import/export business. Remember, I told you a bit about that before." He had, but I wasn't too interested at the time. Now that he was about to leave, it seemed very serious indeed.

MEMOIRS OF A HIPPIE GIRL IN INDIA

"Oh, Donny! That's a bummer. I mean we're kind of just getting to know each other and it feels pretty mellow. How long will you be gone, do ya think?"

"I don't know, really. It depends on how long things take over there. Say ... why don't you come over with me and hang out in India? It could be fun."

The thought had never occurred to me. "But Donny, I was saving my money to go to California. I hadn't thought about going halfway around the world. Anyway, what the heck would we do in India?"

"You know, there's all kinds of really neat architecture ... palaces and stuff. There are gorgeous tropical beaches and jungles with wild animals, there's some really wicked and dirt-cheap hash."

Palaces, beaches and cheap hash. It was already starting to sound attractive. "But Donny, isn't it dangerous ... I mean, what about diseases and stuff like that? And snakes — what about snakes?"

"Oh you silly ... don't worry about stuff like that. You think we don't have poisonous snakes in Ontario? Anyway, we would be mostly staying in the city, in a hotel ... it's not like the jungle is everywhere. So what do you think? You want to think about it? You should let me know soon, 'cuz I'm leaving in two weeks."

Two weeks! There was no way I could get my shit together in that amount of time. "Donny, there's no way. First, it won't be easy to break it to my parents. You have no idea what control freaks they are." He laughed easily and said, "Wait a minute. I know they're immigrants, but surely they must know that the law changed just last year. You're eighteen, right? You are a legal adult now; they can't stop you."

He was right. When I turned eighteen the summer before, Ontario had changed the legal age of consent from twenty-one to eighteen. Now eighteen-year-olds could drink booze, and that summer, by coincidence, Alice Cooper came to town and played his famous song "I'm Eighteen." I remember shouting out the lyrics along with a thousand other people at an amazing outdoor concert, and it felt like the whole world was celebrating being eighteen. We were empowered and liberated, and felt like the whole world was ours for the taking. And it was!

Donny's persuasion worked. In no time at all I planned to join him in India, but it would have to be a few weeks later. Donny said all I had to do was come up with the airfare, and he (or his business) would take care of the rest. I already had a passport and almost enough cash saved

Rochdale family gathering on the roof, 1970.

– if I worked a few evening shifts at the local A & W fast food joint, I could make the rest. I knew I'd have no problem getting a part-time job, as my friend Joanne had recently mentioned they were looking for someone right away.

For three weeks I worked my ass off at two jobs and pined for my distant love. I lived for postcards and letters (at that time long distance calls were expensive and out of the question). Donny's first letter said he missed me a lot. He described Bombay a little (it was dirty), and basically said he was eagerly awaiting my arrival and hoped all was going well with the plan.

A postcard the next week came with a little poem and a drawn kiss, and then a letter with a special request. It seemed Donny needed me to bring over some money, but I would have to do it discreetly. I wasn't sure what this meant. But he gave me contact info for a friend of his, J.P., who lived in Rochdale.

It was mid-March and spring approached as I went to Rochdale the night before my departure. I met up with my contact there, and we arranged the set-up. J.P. (I never learned his real name) was a tall, long-haired, sandy blond with the rugged, outdoorsman face of the Marlboro man. J.P. didn't talk much; he mostly smoked hash and drank herbal tea. This much I learned: he was a borderline alcoholic but had just enough sense to stay away from booze. However, based on the drug paraphernalia I saw around him, it seemed he made up for it with just about every other drug or stimulant he could get. And he was stoned out of his tree. And he was a dealer. But I didn't learn much more about him, as in his line of business the fewer people know about you the better.

It was obvious that J.P. was the main guy who was financing Donny's import business. The plan was that he would hold onto the money until we got to the airport. He would escort me there and casually hand me the special envelope. I would then use the bathroom and hide it in a discreet part of my underwear. The envelope would have twenty thousand American dollars, a lot of cash in 1972.

"I don't get it! Why do I have to smuggle money into India?" J.P. told me it had to do with the black market there. "What's that?" He explained it. "You see, in India there is an inherently corrupt system, and many people in India who were anxious to leave the country couldn't just leave. They are obliged to more or less bribe their way out." He told me.

"But why do they need dollars? Why don't they use their own money?" He laughed and said, "Indian rupees are worthless anywhere else in the world. I mean, have you ever heard of a 'rooo-peee'? So, you see, most bribes have to be paid in foreign cash. And American dollars are always preferred."

"Oh, I see." I was just about to ask more when he said, "Don't ask too many questions, okay? Just do like we said: hide the money on your body somewhere and be cool."

I wondered about being searched, and he said not to worry. He had been to India and knew that the Indian customs officials were too polite to pat down a female, especially a foreign lady. In those days it was true. India really did not have a tourism industry then, and its only experience of foreigners was with

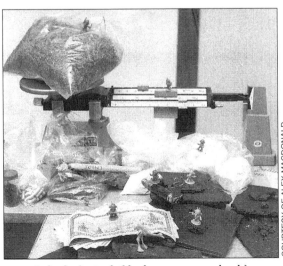

A dealer's stash (dark squares are hash).

diplomats and the British, who had colonized and helped shape their country. Unfortunately, some Indians still fell victim to the subservient mentality in relation to the colonists. J.P. told me, "The Indians are very class-conscious. They will treat you like a wealthy foreign lady; just play the part and they won't dare pat you down."

So it would be easy to pull off. I didn't really understand about the black market, but I figured it should be no big deal. After all, if I wanted to carry my money on my own person, who could really question my right to do so? But I wasn't stupid, either. I knew this money was going to finance a drug deal.

CHAPTER 2

Leaving on a Jet Plane

J.P. LIT UP A CIGARETTE and said, "We have a bit of a problem – we don't quite have all the scratch. I was hoping to get the last of it by now, but it's not looking too promising between now and morning. So ..." He paused to snort a line of coke he'd been chopping on a mirror on a messy table littered with ganja pipes, ashtrays, lighters, incense burners, postcards and candles with melted-down wax dripping off their holders. He offered me the mirror and I snorted a line. It was clean stuff and a good rush.

"So you'll just have to take $16,000 and tell Donny that I'll send the rest by wire. I'll send him a telegram later. There was a problem with one of the partners. I can't go into specifics."

I nodded in agreement and sat back to enjoy the coke buzz. J.P. put on a record. It was Santana's *Abraxus*, one of my all-time favorite albums. He seemed pretty cool and not too worried. His vibe was comfortable enough that I spent the next few minutes looking through his album collection. In those days you could tell a lot about a person from their collection of music and books; it was my habit to check out someone's albums when visiting.

We were both silent for a time. I wasn't used to that. J.P. seemed pre-occupied and I thought I should split. "Do I need to know anything else, J.P.?" He said, "No, I'll see you at the airport tomorrow. There'll be a cab at your house at 8:30 a.m. You got everything packed? You're good to go? Have fun at your party, man. Sorry I can't come ... you know, for *obvious* reasons."

As I left and walked east on Bloor Street I looked at the sculpture behind me and was happy to be leaving the place without inci-

Tourist map in 1972.

dent. I had arrived alone and left alone. I was fairly skipping down the street with excitement now. Tomorrow, tomorrow, I would be leaving on the most exciting trip of my lifetime! My body tingled with excitement, my heart was racing (or was that the cocaine?) and I wanted to scream to the whole world, "I'm free, I'm free! Watch out folks, here I come." I was going to become an International Traveler and would be meeting my boyfriend in Bombay! How cool is that? I felt proud and excited and had already told the whole world I was going to India. For two weeks it was all I could talk about. Most people looked at me strangely. "India? Why India?"

To be honest, I didn't really have much interest in India then. In my mind India was just an inconvenient stop for a few weeks before heading off to really exotic places I'd dreamed of: Paris, Rome, Barcelona. I was so thrilled that I purchased a special outfit for my travels: bright red suede miniskirt, a white halter top, and matching white short jacket, and shoes. Outrageous shoes: rainbow-colored suede platform shoes and white stockings with lacy little butterflies traveling up the side. I had a great figure and I really wanted to show off. In retrospect it was a totally ridiculous outfit for where I was going, but in those days that was the fashion and I didn't think I looked that much out of place. Excited, stepping out into the big world alone for the first time, my heart was racing with excitement, and my mind was restless and fired with the enthusiasm of a child going to the circus. I fantasized that I was a fashion model and imagined this must be the kind of life they would live.

I was a bit nervous because of the secret envelope with cash hiding in my underwear. What would I do if they *did* find it? I figured I could easily get away with it, though. It would not be that hard to act cool. In my crazy, dysfunctional family I had already learned how to be a good actress; it was my survival strategy. Call me foolish or brave, but I was fearless. Anyway, soon enough, I would be running into Donny's arms and everything would be okay. He would take care of me and we would create our own life adventure. Yet, before I even left Malton Airport (as Pearson was then called) I was jolted into a rude awakening, one of many such jolts in the journey that changed my life.

THE PRIEST

I was sitting on the plane, gazing at the dirty grey patches of winter's last remaining snow and visualizing myself on a beach among sun-drenched palm trees. It was March 29 and it had been a long, dreary winter. The plane had to be de-iced before taking off, so there was a delay.

I reflected that this was only my second time on an airplane. Back in 1969 I had flown with my mother to visit relatives in Holland; my stepsister was getting married. That trip was neat because John Lennon and Yoko Ono were having their famous week-long "bed-in" at the Amsterdam Hilton. I happened to be right in the market square just outside the Queen's palace and their hotel, where a huge, excited crowd had gathered. But my mom wouldn't let me stay on my own, and dragged me back to my auntie's house. I wanted to run back to the square and hang out with the hippies, having a terrible feeling that I was missing out on an historic moment. But that was three years earlier, and now I was going halfway around the world, by myself.

I had greedily grabbed the window seat. I wanted to gaze out at the clouds and wonder at one of the greatest engineering feats of mankind: the miracle of flying. Next to me was a priest. I barely looked him in the eye, but gave what I thought was a respectfully pious nod. Next to him in the aisle seat was a nondescript fortyish businessman with his nose buried in the financial pages. I mentally prepared myself for this journey; it was going to be long: at least 18 hours, with several stopovers through several time zones. I didn't know how I'd endure such a long flight, as I was exhausted from the late-night going-away party held in my honor the night before. Now I laid my head back against the seat and closed my eyes waiting for take-off, drifting off. Jimi Hendrix's "Hey, Joe" played over and over in my head, indeed had played over and over the night before as I drifted off in a hash cloud and dreamed of my future. I began to dream in a state of peaceful surrender, but was suddenly jolted by the icy touch of a stranger's hand on my thigh.

Oh my God, the priest! So stunned was I by this brazen intrusion that I simply gasped, and then my body went rigid with fear. Any woman in her right mind would have immediately slapped his hand or said something to deter him. But I was not in my right mind. In my terror I was like the proverbial deer stunned by headlights, literally unable to move. My heart beating so quickly and loudly, and my blood rushing through my veins, made me intensely aware of my body. So I just sat there cold and stiff, and pretended not to have noticed his hand while I tried to figure out what to do.

We've all heard of the fight-or-flight defense mechanism. But what is often not mentioned is that it is fight or flight or freeze. And this time I just froze. I dared not think, dared not move. I was afraid even to breathe. My mind raced with conflicting thoughts. "A priest! How could he? Why me? What if someone sees? This is so embarrassing," I thought – concerned more for him than for me. You can see that I was used to abuse.

His hand started slowly crawling along my thighs, and it felt creepy. Still, I just sat there like an idiot, frozen with fear and trying to ignore it and desperately hoping it would just go away. I reverted back to being a frightened little girl who desperately wanted someone to help me. I was certain that sooner or later the priest had to realize the enormous risk he was taking doing this so openly. I figured soon he would stop. Surely, surely.

Sitting absolutely still and practically not breathing for several very long seconds, I scolded myself: "It must be my fault." Like many young girls, I had fallen victim to the fashion of the times; miniskirts and halter tops were all the rage. And like many young girls, I was foolishly testing my sex appeal and unrealistically expecting that most men would just look, not touch. I know: it's an absurd and incredibly naive notion that many young girls are truly convinced of. All I could think was, "Maybe I shouldn't have worn the miniskirt."

Of course, I thought it was my fault. It was always my fault. I was already half-forgiving the fallen priest in my thoughts: "I guess even a priest can be given to temptation; after all he is a man." Still, something in me argued, "not this kind of man, who smiled at me like a father?" I actually thought religious men had higher morals. How could he do this to me?

Just as I'd decided to forgive him, to really forgive him with all my heart ... his fingers started crawling again, this time with more determination and quite aggressively trying to wedge his fingers between my tightly clasped thighs. I realized with horror, "My God, he's going straight for my crotch!"

Indeed, the horny priest stubbornly refused to acknowledge my forgiveness. How could he know? In retrospect, I think he was probably emboldened by my lack of response. He knew perfectly well that I knew what he was doing, and probably figured that my total passivity and then squeezing my thighs together was a signal that I enjoyed it and was playing a little game. But I was truly scared out of my wits and not enjoying it at all. "Please let someone come," I prayed. Let the stewardess or someone, anyone come along and offer us something, anything. Then the priest would take away his hand and be profoundly embarrassed and immediately repent of his sin.

But this did not happen. Slowly, almost imperceptibly, his fingers began crawling again until I nearly went out of my mind with fear. I think I gasped again. Still frozen with fear and too afraid to deal with this intrusion, I squeezed my thighs together as hard as I could and held my breath. Now he was getting more aggressive and his fingers insisted on prying my thighs apart. This was going on far too long, and he would not stop.

Just as his hand nearly touched my crotch, I abruptly and dramatically shifted my body and loudly cleared my throat to indicate I meant business. Instantly his hand jerked away, and I breathed an enormous sigh of relief. The priest promptly changed his seat (thank God), and mercifully got off at our first stop, London.

The rest of the flight was pretty uneventful, until we got to Cairo.

A BEAUTIFUL DAY IN CAIRO

The plane had to refuel in Cairo, and passengers were told there would be a two-and-a-half-hour stopover. It was three o'clock in the morning when we arrived and I sleepily looked around the plane. Suddenly I was aware of being surrounded by strange foreign faces, which I'd failed to notice had subtly increased after the previous stop, while the number of white Europeans had diminished. Everywhere around me the color of people and their clothing had changed.

A stunningly elegant Indian woman was dressed in a green and gold silk *saree* and adorned with numerous gold ornaments, most strikingly a gold-encrusted diamond stud that bejeweled her nose. I'd never seen such proud beauty as in this woman's demeanor, her black-lined, deep brown eyes and a nose that dared to sport a diamond. She looked like a queen. There were also swarthy men with mustaches in dark suits, possibly Turks; plus Egyptians, Jordanians in white robes, Pakistani women in magnificent *salwar kamis* (traditional dresses), and Sikhs sporting turbans and ritual silver daggers.

This was all new and strange to me, but I decided I really liked these colorful people all around me. Besides which, I reminded myself, I must have looked quite the colorful peacock – for they regarded me with equal curiosity. I decided then and there that one day, I too would get my nose pierced just like the beautiful Indian lady. I was vain enough to want to acquire some of this exotic beauty; I couldn't wait to get to India and start shopping.

I braced myself for the long wait in the Cairo airport, consoling myself with the thought that Bombay was only a few more hours away. It was hard to be cheery after fourteen hours journeying, and passing two hours in another airport did not appeal to me. Even if it was Cairo, it was 3 a.m., and I knew I wouldn't get to see the Pyramids or anything else of the city.

The plane engines shut off and the door opened. In the pre-dawn fog I could faintly make out steps leading down onto the tarmac. I was instantly struck by the quality of the air, heavy and humid; air that smelled slightly putrid and felt hot and sticky to the skin. Then my eye caught what appeared to be two sculpted stone sentries at the foot of the stairs. But soon I realized these were real soldiers with real bayonets. How frightening-looking they were! Growing up in Canada, I had never seen armed soldiers on the street except in parades.

I regarded the rigid soldiers with trepidation and shuddered as I approached them, because I thought all soldiers were killers. As a flower child I was a total pacifist, and naively thought they had chosen to become soldiers and therefore must like killing. I had a lot of fear around that issue. The soldiers, however, were completely oblivious to me and everyone else. The piercing bayonet blade shining in the light caught my eye. I had never seen one this close. In fact I realized I'd never even seen any gun or weapon so close – only in movies. Now I was seeing the real thing, and I realized that my life itself was fast becoming much like a movie. Still, I also felt strangely removed, as if I was involved in all the scenes but also just watching and observing.

Because I was staring so intensely at the two soldiers I lost my balance and nearly tripped on the last stair. Neither soldier budged; in fact no one seemed to notice. I regained my composure and tried to act cool. I felt I had no choice but to act cool because I was so completely out of my element.

Entering the fluorescent-lit airport terminal, I suddenly realized how ridiculous and out of place I looked. My fashionable Western clothes were far too racy for a Muslim country. No one had told me how to dress for this part of the world, and I knew absolutely nothing about the Far East. I did not even know what a Muslim was, so how could I know how to dress? The sum total of my experience was growing up in a sheltered suburban family in WASP (white Anglo-Saxon Protestant) Toronto.

Now people were staring at me with unabashed, penetrating and even unfriendly eyes, which made me feel extremely self-conscious. I tugged at my miniskirt in a useless attempt to make it longer, and searched desperately for a washroom in which to hide. Not a woman in sight. Where did all the women go?

Where was the washroom? I looked at the signs and discovered to my dismay they were all written in a foreign script … Arabic? This was before there were universal symbols for washrooms. I suddenly became aware of the most peculiar and out-of-place music softly playing over the airport speakers. Was I really hearing "It's a Beautiful Day," by the group of the same name?

I felt more and more as if I was under the influence of LSD now. Like I was tripping – but I wasn't tripping. I wasn't on any drug; this was for real. Finally I spotted a woman, dressed in black from head

to foot with only her work-worn hands and wrinkled old face showing through. She had a tattoo on her forehead and a few gold teeth.
We looked at each other with equal puzzlement. I soon realized that
she was the washroom attendant and quickly ducked inside. I tried to
stay in the smelly washroom for the entire two-hour wait. But I could
not sit there holding my nose for two hours. I cursed the fact that I had
nothing decent to change into. I was sure my boyfriend, Donny, would
be mad at me to see me in such a ridiculous outfit in India. But I had
had no idea.

As I stepped out of the washroom I heard a new and unusual
sound, a moaning begging pleading sound through a muted mega-
phone. What a strange sound. It was human but very distorted. It was
what I later learned was the Muslim call to prayer, the words "*Allah ho
Akbar, Allah ho Akbar, la illah il Allah. God is Great, God is Great, there is
no God but God.*" Then the sight of dozens of bums in air greeted me, as
devout Muslims threw themselves down and prayed.

I was shocked. At five in the morning they stop to pray? In the
middle of an airport? Tip-toeing through a sea of raised rumps, I found
a spot on a bench and sat primly on the edge, trying not to disturb the
sanctity of the moment. "What a strange custom," I thought. Then I
glimpsed a spectacular sunrise through the glass doors of the airport
terminal. Absorbed, I didn't move from this spot until it was time to
board the plane again.

After leaving Cairo, I breathed a tremendous sigh of relief. Soon,
soon! I would be with my sweet Donny in Bombay.

CHAPTER 3

Bombay at Last

FLYING INTO BOMBAY, I was shocked at how small and primitive the airport looked with its little neglected, ramshackle buildings. The moment I stepped off the plane my senses were assaulted. The air was thick and warm and humid. It smelled of strange vegetation and humans.

We entered the terminal building, whose interior looked like an old bank with clerks and customs officials behind wood and glass cages in calico uniforms, with only an electric fan and a bare lightbulb suggesting modernity. Confronted by a mass of brown bodies, I saw that I was the only white person in the whole damn airport. Now I knew what it felt like to be a highly visible minority. Hordes of bare-footed, red-turbaned coolies (unskilled laborers) with golden earrings competed to take my bags; beggars tragically mimed their suffering and asked for "just a pittance"; children offered to be my tour guide; and crowds of hungry, desperate faces stared at me as if I'd just arrived from outer space. It was frightening to encounter such a mass of un-friendly faces, again mostly shocked and hostile to my ridiculous attire and my brazen intrusion into their culture.

India did not get a lot of tourists back then, and hippies were even more of a rarity. So it was easy enough to spot a foreigner in the crowd, and pretty soon I found Donny and waved. Once through customs I was whisked away in a taxi. Leaving the airport and cuddling up to him, I finally felt safe, secure and comfortable. Exhausted but too excited to sleep, I gazed dreamily out of the window while snuggling up to Donny in the comfort of his body.

Now I caught glimpses of early morning life in Bombay. All along the highway were poor people living in huge concrete cylinders, dirty-faced children playing in the mud, women washing the few rags they had in water collected from puddles, some tending to pathetic little fires that barely started for lack of adequate fuel. "Who are these people and why are they living like this?" I asked the cab driver. "Hindu refugees from Pakistan," he answered as if I knew the rest. "Why?" I asked Donny. "Don't you know? India is at war with Pakistan, dumbbell!"

We got to the hotel and Donny asked for the envelope. When he saw it had only $16,000, he freaked. "What the fuck is this bullshit?" I told him exactly what J.P. had said: he would wire another $4,000 within a week. "But I've already ordered a whole shitload of product. And I owe money everywhere. This really sucks." Donny fumed pacing back and forth. Trying to lighten the mood, I said, "But Donny, I thought you said we could live here cheap," to which he replied, "Yeah, well, nothing's *that* cheap." But he could do nothing about it except wait for the missing money from J.P.

My first day in Bombay was fun. We were staying in Colaba in the Fort district right near the famous Gateway to India. I was surprised at how civilized and cultured and really Victorian the city looked. In fact, I found a *National Geographic* magazine from ten years earlier that claimed Bombay was one of the last truly Victorian cities. But now high-rise buildings were starting to pop up, and a mixture of old and new were oddly juxtaposed. In

MEMOIRS OF A HIPPIE GIRL IN INDIA

Beautiful examples of Bombay's Victorian architecture seen in the early 1970s. Opposite page: the Victoria Terminus train station.

retrospect, I think that of all the cities I saw in India, I liked Bombay the best. Soon I would learn a lot about this fascinating city, India's biggest (now called Mumbai).

Donny asked me what I wanted to do and proposed several activities. One was to take a horse and buggy to see the city and go along the harbor, and later explore the silver bazaar. I always loved silver jewelry, and was eager to discover some treasure. It was said that Indians sold silver only by weight and often did not consider the craftsmanship or age of a piece, so real bargains could be found.

We were staying at the Sea Palace Hotel, a fairly new and upscale hotel on the harbor, within view of the Gateway to India and walking distance from the five-star Taj Mahal Palace Hotel. There was a pleasant morning breeze, and so we walked a distance in the avenue oddly named Apollo Bandar and had our breakfast at the Taj. Donny wanted to show off, and ordered a bloody feast. It was crazy how much food there was, and I later realized the price we paid probably would have fed an entire Indian family for a month! But by Canadian standards and the extremely good exchange rate he got on the black market, it wasn't that big a deal. Besides, Donny liked to steal the toilet paper there. A few foreigners did this because it was the only place in the whole city you could find such a luxury. You either learned to do your toilet Indian-style washing (with water) or you searched frantically for any kind of disposable paper.

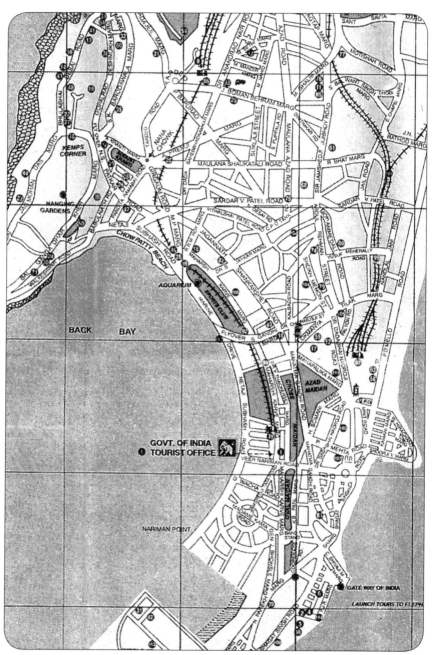

Bombay's tourist area, where hippies tended to congregate.
The Gateway to India and Taj Mahal Hotel, near my hotel, are at lower right
in The Fort district (Colaba Place), Chowpatty Beach is at the top of Back Bay,
and beyond it is the tony Hanging Gardens/Malabar Hills area.

We left the Taj and found a horse and buggy waiting, and oh, didn't they make a ceremony of our mounting the buggy. I was awkward in my skin-tight pants and halter top, and the poor liveryman had no idea where to touch me or how to assist me. But we got in the buggy and trundled through the streets of Bombay.

Paul, another Canadian and new friend of Donny who was also staying at the Sea Palace, was going to join us later as he had an interest in visiting the Muslim bazaar. It was near his favorite opium den, and he invited us along afterward. Paul was pretty cool. He had been in India for a few months and knew a bit about the culture. He was from Vancouver and had a kind of West coast "chill" vibe. I didn't mind him being there as it was convenient that he spoke a few words of Hindi. Besides, I was curious about visiting an opium den. What would that be like?

It was a beautiful sunny day, and the streets were alive with people and noise and exotic smells and activities. As a newcomer I was surprised to see how many animals roamed the streets. In some areas cows wandered about grazing through the garbage, claiming the same right to scavenge as any city dog might have. I was shocked by all the poor people too: the beggars and hungry, dirty children.

On one corner when we were stopped at a light, I was tapped on the shoulder and turned around to see a face that was not a face; where there should have been an eye there was nothing but a mass of pinky-white mottled flesh with thin bluish-white skin stretched taught over the eye socket. And instead of a nose I saw a knobbly mass of flesh that looked like it had been chewed by a dog. No real hair was visible. I did notice a stub in place of an ear on the same side of his face.

I screamed in fear at the hideous apparition that was suddenly close to my face. Then an arm with no hand ... just a stub ... touched me to get my attention. I asked the driver "what was that?" He said, "just a leper" as casually as if it were a dog. A leper! I thought this disease was from biblical times and didn't know it still existed. My God, lepers on the streets ... still?

This world, so new to me, was in fact a very old world, and it assaulted me now with its raw truth. Here for the first time I was exposed to life in all its ugly reality: the blind, the crippled, the orphaned, the diseased, the wounded, the maimed, the mentally unstable. All were out on the streets, wandering, begging, surviving. Not hidden

Child vendor in Bombay's Crawford Market, early 1970s.

away in some institution as in Canada. All of humanity's suffering was there to see and confront and deal with every day. And feel guilty about: why am I so lucky?

We got to the bazaar, which happened to be in the Muslim quarter. "What's a Muslim?" I asked. The guys should have known they were in trouble right then, but, frankly, they hardly knew much themselves. To them, Muslims were strange people who worshiped some god called Allah and did a lot of praying, and whose women wore veils. Neither Paul nor Donny had any real interest in learning about the local culture.

Ah, we three naive, tuned-out dumb Canadians. Two hippie guys and a young girl in the most outlandish dress, traipsing through the Muslim quarter in all our garish bravado. But we thought nothing of it, and off we went. By now I was beginning to get used to being stared at. I was told that Indians stare a lot; they actually glare at you. You just ignore it.

We got off near Shuklaj Street to enter the bazaar on foot, as no vehicles could penetrate the older quarters of the city. The Muslim quarter was a colorful, exotic and interesting place to shop and also had the hashish and opium dens. And the metalware, glass and silver market. I was eager to see the reputed treasures, and asked, "Would you guys mind if we stopped at a silver shop first? I'd really like to have a look." No problem," they assured me. Paul led the way.

RIOT IN THE BAZAAR

We soon found ourselves squatting in a circle as a shopkeeper spread a cloth before us and laid out his magnificent, dazzling wares. The shop was typical of many others I saw in the bazaar. A crude affair; raised about three feet from the street, always overstocked, dusty and poorly lit. There was no furniture but I adapted to the squatting position easily.

The merchant, though dirty and unshaven – possibly an opium addict – was expert at his job. "Look at these beeeyuuutiful trrrreasures," he said, smiling that strange Indian smile (hiding their tongue behind their teeth as they talk). All the riches of India were on display. Gigantic rubies, emeralds and pearls, and a sterling silver arsenic ring, which had a decorative box with a hidden hinge that could open discreetly to poison someone's drink. It was so intriguing that I bought that arsenic ring right on the spot. Luckily it did not stay with me long, as bad karma was probably attached to such a thing as it probably had been responsible for a death. Then there was dazzling filigree silver imported from Indonesia, and some stunning gold pieces.

But this merchant's specialty was silver. I felt as if I had dropped into Ali Baba's cave. Jars of jewels kept opening before me, and it seemed each piece had a romantic story. This ruby belonged to a great Rajput prince who lost his kingdom when the British came. The jewel was stolen by a disgruntled servant and later removed from its identifying setting and reset in this new altered piece created by one of the most famous silversmiths of the 18th century. The merchant had us enthralled with stories, and soon we were offered tea, pipes of hashish and sweets. He could have kept us there all day. He was a good entertainer and, besides, he could easily smell money. He knew we were going to spend a few hundred dollars, and in local currency that would be a good sale.

I had become totally absorbed in the dazzling display of gorgeous jewelry, particularly a pair of anklets that had belonged to a former princess. The merchant showed me her initials engraved in the silver, and I was so fascinated by the story that I failed to hear the murmur of a restless crowd quickly gathering behind me. Donny noticed it first.

As I was squatting, my hip-hugging velvet pants were exposing more of my backside than I had intended. And my backside was facing the street. A massive crowd had gathered around the shop, and they

Street scene in a poor part of Bombay, typical of most cities in India.

Memoirs of a Hippie Girl in India

were all staring at me with angry faces. Clearly they were offended by the mode of dress of this half-naked white lady. Donny urged me to change places with him so that my backside was no longer exposed, and we continued to inspect the treasures.

But the crowd did not disperse; in fact, it increased. We quickly purchased some jewelry and prepared to leave, only to discover that we could not leave. We were facing such a dense crowd of people that they completely blocked our way. Shoulder to shoulder, they seemed a turbulent sea of angry, hostile faces. Hungry, lusty men all offended – and equally aroused – by this display of a half-naked white woman in the Muslim bazaar. It was just too much. I thought they were ready to stone me or beat me or …. There was no way out.

"Holy shit!" I gasped, shocked to face the gathering of several hundred, maybe even a thousand people. All men and boys. Not a woman in sight, although I'm sure many were peeping through their upstairs harem screens. As we prepared to step down from the shop, the crowd did not move to let us pass. Instead they crowded in more densely and heaved towards us. The situation was impossible and I felt very nervous and began to shake uncontrollably. Fear had me in its iron grip and I felt helpless.

The shopkeeper shouted in Hindi, "Go away, get lost – let my customers pass. Move, move away," but not one person budged. He screamed louder, gesturing and trying to part the crowd with a long curtain rod he'd improvised as a weapon, but still not one person moved. The crowd became even more agitated, and argued with the shopkeeper. We got a rough translation. "What is that slut doing in our neighborhood? We have children, families here. It is an offence." Others shouted, "Why do you do business with the foreign slut?" and pressed on towards the shopkeeper. He kept shouting, "Forget it. Just go home. Everything is just fine, they are leaving. Just let them leave."

But no one budged. The crowd got louder and angrier and heaved toward the shop. I kept backing away, hiding behind Donny and Paul and the shopkeeper. The shopkeeper said something to Donny, and he handed me a roll of brown wrapping paper. I wrapped some brown paper around myself to hide some of my nakedness.

Finally a policeman came to see what was causing all the excitement. The shopkeeper signaled to the police officer for help and the policeman slowly worked his way through the crowd, beating people with his *lathi* (metal-tipped wooden baton on a chain) blowing his whistle, or shouting and pushing them out of his way. He finally arrived at the shop.

He quickly ascertained what was happening and began dialoguing with the shopkeeper. Meanwhile, the crowd was shouting complaints to the police officer, and he too could not calm them down. After some discussion it was suggested we could exit with a single-file escort through the crowd, with the policeman in the lead, then Donny directly in front of me, and Paul and the shopkeeper following. We were pressed so close together that we stepped on one another's feet.

In Bombay, the average street cop did not have a gun; his weapons were a baton and a whistle. So the policeman screamed at the crowd, beating them with his baton and blowing his whistle incessantly, while the shopkeeper started pushing the crowd with a bamboo rod, his authority condoned by the policeman. They managed to create enough of an opening that the policeman was able to lead the way into the crowd. Both the policeman and the shopkeeper were shouting at the crowd, "Go home – everything is under control. We are taking them away. Go home, go home. *Chelo chelo.*" They were constantly beating or poking people in the crowd if they got too close. Walking through that mass of bodies was the scariest thing I have ever done.

The policeman kept pushing his way through, warding off aggression with shouts and waving his baton, and slowly we made our way out of the dense slum. Still, it was obvious that we were only five against thousands. At any moment the crowd could have gone nuts and crushed us. My blood felt as if it had turned to ice in my veins and I actually shivered as I moved through the crowd, closely hugging Donny and with Paul almost embracing me from behind. It was the longest walk I had ever taken. Each minute dragged on forever as we negotiated our way through the dense crowd. The policeman continued shouting and blowing his whistle, while Donny and Paul aggressively pushed people away and told them "chelo, chelo" – go away.

Yet the crowd barely moved and certainly did not disperse. They barely parted enough to allow us to pass in single file. I kept my eyes staring downward at the ground and their feet. I could feel the warmth of their breath on me, and could hear their vile curses and insults in Hindi, some in English. "Dirty whore, dirty hippies go home!" I dared not look at any of their faces. Their body language, foul curses and trembling bodies made it clear they were barely able to control their rage.

I was sobbing quietly now, huddling as close as possible to Donny and begging him under my breath "please tell the cop to hurry." Still I could hear the men hissing. One of them spit on me and his filthy saliva trickled down my arm, but I did not react. I felt that at any moment they might pounce on me and tear me to pieces. It seemed to take forever to go only a few feet. Finally the policeman got within sight of the boulevard, and managed to flag down some pedestrians, who quickly got a taxi.

The moment we got into the safety of the cab the crowd went crazy. They began beating and pounding on the car with their fists, and shouting obscenities and spitting on the windows. Their vile saliva, bright red from chewing betel nut, oozed down the window pane. So much hatred I'd never seen, and it was all directed at me. I screamed hysterically at the driver, "Drive faster, get us out of here!" but the density of the crowd would not let him pass. The policeman jumped on the hood of the taxi, blowing his whistle and shouting along with the shopkeeper, telling everyone to calm down and go home. But the crowd did not disperse, and it took another twenty minutes for our taxi to crawl through the narrow streets of the Muslim quarter. Finally we were into the modern boulevards of central Bombay, gratefully speeding towards our hotel. Donny yelled at me the whole way. Of course it was all my fault.

TIME TO GET A SAREE

Obviously we didn't get to the opium den that day. One thing I learned for certain is that I would have to dress more modestly to survive in India. I threw out the offensive Western clothes and bought some long skirts and loose-fitting *kurtas* (long shirts) and a few sarees. Shopping for clothes was an interesting experience. For one thing, India didn't have much in the way of ready-made clothes in those days. But tailors abounded everywhere. Women wore either sarees or *salwar kameez* (lady suits) that had to be tailor-made. Shopping for fabrics was a delight, especially because gorgeous silks and brocades were cheap. I chose a peacock-blue material with splashes of navy, silver, ivory and green to turn into a salwar kameez, my favorite mode of dress.

One time I was at a tailor to fit a saree top. The shop, with sewing machines and tailor paraphernalia, was dimly lit and dusty. In the change room, a little cubbyhole with a flimsy door, I was trying on lovely peacock green silk and admiring myself in the dusty mirror, thinking yes, it works with my green eyes. Just as I was naked from the waist up I spotted in the door keyhole the glaring eyeball of a man staring at me. I was shocked, feeling humiliated and insulted. Why was this happening to me? It seemed there was no safe place for a beautiful and naive young white girl alone in India, at least not in those days.

For the rest of my time in India I dressed in Indian fashion, obliging me to learn a new way to walk. In my Western clothes I was used to the freedom of jeans and loose skirts, in which I could take large strides. But the elegant saree with its petticoat underneath forced me to take smaller steps. Ultimately I found I was walking in a more dainty and perhaps feminine way. The main benefit was that afterwards I experienced only a few groping incidents in crowds, nothing major.

Thinking back on the silver shop incident of the previous week, I remembered that women had been largely absent in the streets in the Muslim quarter. The few women I did see were covered head to foot in a *burqa*, with a black screen sewn into the veil, out of which the frightened eyes of a young woman or girl or even an older woman would gaze. I noticed they moved quickly and surreptitiously, clinging to the walls almost like shadows, and rushing through the streets as though shopping was a great sin and it was dangerous to be out – even in broad daylight. I did not really understand this strange culture, but it certainly frightened me.

THE OPIUM DEN

A few days later we visited an opium den, and this time I made sure I was appropriately dressed. It was my first experience in an opium den. What a strange world.

Opium dens, technically illegal, were often hidden behind a residence or upstairs over a shop. Crude affairs, they were dimly lit, sparsely furnished and full of opium smokers both Western and Indian. I remember the creepy feeling of trying to quietly climb the creaky, filthy, broken staircase that led to a darkened hallway. Mice were running everywhere, and I was in sandals; I could feel them brush

Man with an opium pipe.

against my feet. A short way down the hall I saw the outline of a door dimly lit from behind: the opium den. We entered a cloudy, hazy room full of people in various stages of reclining. Men and women, old and young, Eastern and Western, all sharing the silent ceremony of opium euphoria. There was no furnishing to speak of, no décor. Nothing but a silent dark, den like an attic in an old house with rafters exposed and a small window.

As far as I remember nothing else was offered there, except of course, *chai* (tea) and an ashtray or spittoon.

Preparing the opium and lighting the pipe involved a great ceremony. A pipe *wallah* (servant) dressed in the local poor man's *lunghi* (a *sarong*-type garment) and undershirt was the master of ceremonies. Our pipe wallah seemed like an ordinary enough man, friendly without being talkative. He gestured for us to lie down on our side, and we were each given a wooden block or tin can to support the head. Another wallah massaged our feet and brought chai.

Your every comfort is considered. If you are a man, you will be offered a prostitute. The opium master cleans the pipe and prepares the opium by heating it over a gas flame until it is the right consistency and forms a gooey mass. Once it is properly cooked, he turns it into a little ball by constant twirling at the end of a long stick. It takes a long time and some expert twirling to achieve the perfect temperature to form a ball, and he must be careful not to burn it. Once the ball is formed and the right temperature, the opium master puts it in your bowl and lights it. After a couple of puffs you enter a blissed-out, dreamlike state of peace.

There was little conversation in the den, and no music as far as I can remember. Few people paid attention to us, even though Donny and I were obviously new patrons. The opium master knew Paul, though, as a regular. I was a complete novice, of course, and for some reason thought I had to prove how much I could smoke. I couldn't keep up smoking with the boys, although I tried. I kept smoking more and more bowls (it was, after all, dirt cheap), and got so high at the end of the night that I don't remember how we got home. The next day I was sick as a dog for twelve hours, vomiting and excreting black goop. I realized this stuff really didn't agree with me and swore off opiates forever.

The scene in Bombay in those days was pretty mellow, considering we were living in a huge metropolis. The hippie scene, mostly concentrated in the Fort district, was beginning to integrate into the wide Bombay community. Some people had lived there for months and even years. They assured me that travelers quickly adapt to or left. With India, they said, you quickly learn to either love it or hate it.

I had to get used to the climate, hot and humid just before the monsoon season. But the biggest adjustment for me was that India had only one speed: slow. You just had to get used to it. Everything was done steadily and calmly, as in a meditation. Even the simplest task, such as making *lassi* (a yogurt drink) was done with a deliberately slow, mindful attitude. Sometimes it was maddening, especially to foreigners like me, and I found myself wondering, "Don't these people know how to do more than one thing at a time?" Then I realized I'd gotten caught up in my Western culture and expectations of immediate gratification.

You cannot be impatient in India. The whole experience of India is first and foremost a lesson in patience. So whatever your task might be, whether ordering breakfast or purchasing a train ticket, or even buying heroin over the counter from a local pharmacy, you have to be prepared to wait. India and the third world in general just seem to operate like that.

CHAPTER 4

Boat Ride to Goa

WE QUICKLY GOT BORED with the scene in Bombay, and I really wanted to go to a beach. We'd heard of pristine beaches in Goa a few hundred miles south of Bombay. And it seemed all the hippies in Bombay had either been or were going to Goa. Goa had an interesting history and was still in transition from a former Portuguese colony to a recently acquired Indian territory (by armed force, only eleven years earlier). Back then no roads went to Goa. We could have flown, but that was rather expensive and Donny discovered that he would have to pay full fare for me and resented that I didn't have a student card. We were trying to save money, so we decided to go by boat, which is how nearly everyone went anyway. We were told it was a beautiful journey, hugging the coast, and took 20 hours to cover the 300 miles.

The boat was indeed slow. We booked second-class passage and huddled together with the locals and all their luggage – and their chickens, goats and other animals prepared for a boat ride as cargo. We were not assigned seats, as I recall, but sat huddled in the bow of the boat and slept amongst the bundles and livestock. People ate boiled eggs and dry *chapati* (flatbread), and also had pre-cooked lentil and chickpea curries. I was amazed at what food could be produced on a boat with no proper kitchen. But the baggage that local people travelled with always contained food and preparation utensils. Indians didn't have instant take-out type food stations along the way, so they came prepared.

We landed in the port town of Panjara, now renamed Panjim, which was only ten miles from Calangute. All the locals knew Calangute because it was the only beach with a fancy hotel and was near

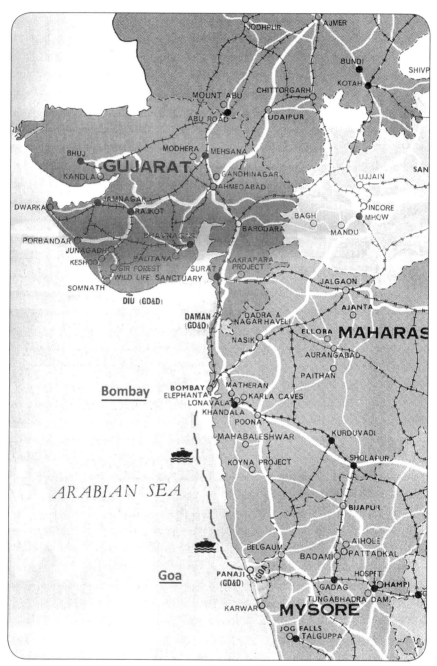

*Western India from a 1972 tourist map, showing Bombay and Goa.
Most hippies travelled between them by steamer.*

MEMOIRS OF A HIPPIE GIRL IN INDIA

Anjuna, which already had a hippie scene. Only the wealthiest Indian tourists, movie stars and film people could afford to stay at such a luxury hotel. Still, the beach beside it was completely undeveloped and mostly unpopulated, having only an occasional fisherman's hut. It was a two-mile walk to Anjuna Beach, where some of the best parties were.

However, we decided we wanted a quieter beach rather than hang out at trendy Anjuna, though Donny was not quite ready to give up his creature comforts of the West. We rented a little hut on the beach in Calangute for about twelve rupees a week, about a dollar. These dwellings didn't have electricity or running water, but one could easily manage with candles, and all the water you wanted could be brought to the house for pennies a day. But in Calangute we had access to a "civilized" hotel, including its running water, showers and decent food – a luxury in this remote and undeveloped piece of the northern Goa coast.

In the tropics the sun always rises early and you don't mind getting up early, because by 7 or 8 a.m. it is hot! I used to wake up at the crack of dawn, just before 6, to enjoy the sunrise. I loved to watch the fishermen hauling in their nets. They had primitive-looking boats made out of wood. It made me feel like I had landed in another time/place ... it seemed so unearthly. The beauty of tropical vegetation all around and the amazing edible fruits – pineapples, coconuts, bananas and cashews – that were available right off the trees.

Watching the fishermen haul in their boats was fascinating and a perfect example of teamwork and cooperation. I was amazed to watch these slight men maneuvering 30-foot boats. With no real leader they still knew exactly what to do. They fastened long oars perpendicular to the boat, several of these along the length of the boat. Then they'd line up four on each side and four rows deep, and all at once lift, heave and start running, their skinny little legs working furiously as they ran in unison like some giant insect with many legs carrying the boat. It was quite a sight. But they brought those boats in securely.

The fishermen were friendly and invited us to go fishing with them one day, but I was too frightened of the high seas and their wooden boats looked so primitive I did not think them seaworthy. But it did sound romantic: "Wooden ships on the water ... very free" from a Crosby, Stills and Nash song came to mind. Donny had no interest in the fishing boats, so we missed out on a fantastic opportunity. But we sure enjoyed their fresh fish.

Pristine Anjuna Beach circa 1972.

Calangute Beach was pretty deserted, with few foreigners, so we walked along the coast to Anjuna Beach to see who we might meet. Joe Bananas, a local hippie, told us where to look up some cool people. We left early in the morning because it would be unbearably hot by 11 a.m. En route we stopped at a famous 16th-century Portuguese church at Baga, where we had lunch on the cliffs overlooking the Arabian Sea.

Only in 1961 had India reclaimed the territory of Goa from Portugal, by invading it. Since the 1500s it had been a Portuguese colony, and its largest city is named after explorer Vasco da Gama. St. Francis Xavier, co-founder of the Society of Jesus (Jesuits), lived here, and it was the Indian state with the largest Christian population. But the Goan people to me looked just like the Hindus, and although they spoke a different language it sounded just as foreign and strange to me.

In 1969 a guy called Eight-Fingered Eddy had found this pristine beach and settled there with his Asian girlfriend, and invited anyone who wanted to come. In no time a few dozen hippies had turned into a few hundred, and now this tropical paradise with its gorgeous beaches and perfect climate had a happening scene. Concerts on the beach and later what came to be known as the Goan sound originated here. The early hippies – like Eight-Fingered Eddy, Joe Bananas and other Americans and European – flocked to Goa for its beaches and freedom. They loved that the Goan people were a lot less prudish than Indians in general. At least the Goans tolerated these strange white foreigners with their long-haired men, tie-dyed clothes and bare-breasted women.

MEMOIRS OF A HIPPIE GIRL IN INDIA

I was a bit too young to make it to the Woodstock music festival in 1969, but I made it to Goa in '72 and it was the next-best thing. It had a spirit of sharing and acceptance, free love and freedom of expression. As a group we had no boundaries, no shame; our mantra was "anything goes." So, naturally, nudity, gender-bending and other eccentricities were welcome without judgment. I was one of those bare-breasted ladies, wearing only a sarong and a silver snake belt around my hips while dancing on the beach in total abandon like a Bacchanalian lady tripping on LSD. Although I was initially shy, I soon got used to being half-naked. Everyone there did it. Besides, I had a great pair of boobs and no reason to hide them.

I remember passing a handsome couple on the beach. He had the longest hair I'd ever seen on a man, and wore black Khol (cosmetic) on his eyes like Indian men I'd seen on movie posters. He looked French or maybe Italian; I couldn't quite guess. He had intense brown eyes and the Khol accents really brought them out against his olive skin. Shortly thereafter, Keith Richards and later Johnny Depp copied the black Khol-accented eye "look." This beautiful hippie didn't say much but

Anjuna Beach gang with Richard (of the Sunshine Brothers) second from left.

right away I detected a French accent. He was with a beautiful, blonde Danish lass named Mona. They were both totally nude and totally casual about it. They must have been pretty stoned, because they didn't say much, but their smiles were broad, bright and welcoming. No need for conversation here; they were just beaming good energy. It was that kind of high, a place where words were unnecessary.

As in many ex-pat communities, the small and intimate hippie community in Goa gave people nicknames, identifying their country of origin or other peculiarity. So there were names like Mushroom Dan and American Alice, German Joe and English Janet, the Earthman, New York Dave and Mescaline Bob. There was British Bill and Australian Andy, Goa Gil and Randy Crazyhorse, Krishna Dave, Eight-Fingered Eddy, Mental, Chillum Charlie, Kirtan Katy and Sunshine Sue. Everone knew everyone there, and it was a peaceful tribe indeed. Everyone in Goa also knew Joe Bananas, so with his referral we were welcomed with open arms. Joe had a shop in Calangute where he sold a few specialty items to the foreigners. Joe was a good connection and helpful, because he could receive and send mail, come up with fake documents, and get some good smoke, foreign cigarettes and even chocolate.

Joe told us to look for "the Heart House," which was easily recognized by the giant heart on its roof. We found

COUTESY OF CAITANYA MAHA PRABHU (MENTAL)

Mental with dotara in Anjuna Beach circa 1972.

the house but no one was there, and so we followed a dirt path through the jungle following the shoreline and soon found ourselves heading into the marketplace. As we approached the market we ran into a handsome American couple. They saw us coming from the direction of the heart house and

The famous Heart House, site of the first Goa party.

as they were sure we spoke English, they asked, "are you guys just coming from C and J's place?" When we said yes, the woman said C and J had gone to Amsterdam for a while. She introduced herself as Rene, a Canadian from British Columbia, while Tony was an American of Italian origin from Philadelphia. "Come back to our house. We've just been shopping and would love to have you share some food with us."

As they prepared the food I learned that they were fruitarians. I had never heard of this before. "What the heck is a fruitarian?" I asked. Chopping away at some carrots and onions she barely looked up as she politely advised me that "we eat mostly fruit. It's not that complicated. We eat a lot of fresh fruit, which is quite abundant here. And of course, we eat nuts and some vegetables. Mostly raw." I was shocked. "You mean you can live on that?" I asked. She paused, knife in the air, tilted her head and smiled at me as she gave a little wiggle. "Apparently so."

I have to say she looked gorgeous. She continued, "You guys are lucky because we have one day of the week when we eat cooked food and that is today. That's why we were in the market place buying root vegetables and rice." Rene began preparing a mini-feast with rice, lentils, nuts and raisins. It sounded pretty sparse to me, but when I ate it I thought I'd never eaten so well.

Both Tony and Rene were slender and looked vibrantly healthy. She had the most amazing white teeth I'd ever seen, and the most beautiful smile. She could have done toothpaste ads. Being health nuts wasn't so nutty after all, it appeared. I told myself that one day I would investigate this fruitarian concept. I watched in fascination as Rene prepared the meal. Lentils had soaked all morning, and she began to chop an onion and grind spices with a mortar and pestle. She moved with the slow, deliberate motion of a monk doing his daily washing with total focus on the task at hand. They had a tape deck playing Cat Stevens, which seemed out of place for this setting. Without electricity in the house, the tape deck was powered by a car battery. That's how things were.

We passed a wonderful tropical afternoon together, and I was impressed with their simple lifestyle and the peace of mind they seemed to have found. They looked to be very much in love. Tony and Rene had been in India for nearly a year, and seemed familiar with the culture. Rene asked me what I had seen of Goa. "Not much, I'm afraid. We've only been here two days."

"You definitely have to see some of the temples around here," Tony said. "This place has some of the most amazing architecture. A real mix of Portuguese, Mediterranean and Indian. You should see the Basilica of Bom Jesus nearby– it's really a trip, and about 400 years old. And then there's the Mahalakshmi Temple in Panji ... you've got to see it. It's like an acid trip, all glitter and distorted reality."

Sadhu Tom (of the Sunshine brothers)

Tony was constantly filling up the *chillum* pipe with hash and offering tokes. We spent the afternoon listening to tropical birds and Rene gently strumming on the *tamboura* (sitar-like instrument with only four strings). She sang some chants in Sanskrit, and pretty soon Tony was singing too. "Om Nama Shiva" was the chant, and I picked it up pretty quickly. I was singing harmony and Tony said that was pretty cool.

Later in the afternoon I was

craving some sweets, and Rene suggested we could walk to the market to buy dried fruit and see the local culture. While in the marketplace, Donny pointed to a poor woman bent over double with a crippling disease and only a cane and her aching, craned neck to lift her head to see. Donny laughed and said, "Ha, ha. Look at that penny-pincher. That's what happens when you spend a lifetime looking for pennies on the floor."

Flower girls in typical hippie fashion, Goa 1972.

GOAN DOMINIQUE

He laughed again, but Rene and Tony gave him a dirty look. "More likely crippled from a lifetime of working in the rice paddies for slave wages," Rene corrected him. Donny went red-faced and shut up.

We couldn't spend too long in the market because we had to return before dark. Because there was no electricity in this part of the world, you tried to get things done before dark or relied on moonlight and the stars and an occasional gas light to light your way back.

The marketplace didn't have much to offer: a few local fruits and vegetables and some cooking oil, some grains and spices and nuts. We came upon a stall selling dried fruits and nuts. I had never seen large dates, and asked about them in sign language. The vendor, a sweet lady in a pink cotton saree and wearing a crucifix, offered to let me taste one. Just as I was about to choose a date, a giant cockroach crawled out of the batch. I was terrified – the cockroach nearly touched me. And it appeared out of nowhere; its body was the same size, color and shape as the dates. How could I know the damn thing would move? When she saw how frightened I was, the vendor picked up the cockroach

Farewell to Goa .... Om Nama Shiva

with her bare fingers, its legs wiggling. Then she waved it in my face and threw it away. She and all the other vendors laughed hysterically at my silly fear of a little insect.

Our stay in Goa was quite brief, as Donny always knew that he could never really be a part of the scene there and I got the sense that he felt out of his element. Besides he had orchestrated this trip mostly for me because I wanted to be on a beach. Now we'd seen the beach and Donny wanted to split. Although I would have stayed for months, I think the whole lifestyle was a little too primitive for him, too much like camping, he said. Donny was calling the shots and he was anxious to get back to Bombay, where some money would surely be waiting for him and, he hoped, a few ready false-bottomed suitcases.

CHAPTER 5

Accusations and Allegations

WHEN WE GOT BACK TO BOMBAY, it was bad news for Donny. As soon as we arrived he went straight to American Express to see if there was any mail and, more important, any money. No money had come, but a collection of angry letters and telegrams had arrived from his partners back in Toronto. They hadn't received their hash and were pretty upset.

"Look at this bullshit," Donny said. He threw the pile of letters on the bed and lit a cigarette. "What's going on?" I asked. "They're accusing me of a rip-off, that's what's going on." I felt bad for Donny. I knew he had sent the hash because I had helped him pack it. Something was seriously wrong. What if Customs had intercepted the goods?

"Why don't you call J.P. and explain?" I suggested. Donny looked at me condescendingly and said, "You know what a nightmare it is trying to make a long-distance call from India." That was true. In those days of fairly primitive technology, overseas calls had to be directed into what was called a trunk call. The Indian operator had to pre-book an open line with the international operator, so you usually had to wait twenty-four hours for an overseas connection. Then you were lucky if the person you were calling was home – no one had answering machines then.

"Anyway, I can't very well discuss business on the phone," Donny said while pacing and smoking furiously.

We went to the Taj Mahal Hotel for our usual breakfast. Sitting a few tables over from us was an enormously fat and obviously wealthy man smoking a cigar. His bejeweled fat fingers were holding the cigar as he gazed at me with undisguised lust. Donny said, "Look at that guy over there. He can't take his eyes off you."

The Gateway to India faces the water, with the Taj Mahal Hotel right behind.

"Yeah, I know."

"Whatdya think? He must pretty rich, to be staying here at the Taj. Look at the massive gold chains around his neck ... I say he must be loaded. Maybe he's somebody famous ... maybe Mr. Tata himself."

Tata was a wealthy Persian Bombay family that owned just about everything. The Tata name was on billboards everywhere; they had built the Taj Mahal Hotel.

"Yeah, well, so what?" "Well ... you know these Indians – they really go nuts for white women. I'll bet a guy like that would pay a pretty price for a girl like you."

"Donny, I can't believe what you are saying!"

"Oh, just kidding," he said and gave me a kiss.

Still, he went on and on about the guy. I was getting upset with this talk and wanted to leave. The next day the man was there again, and Donny started the same conversation. He kept reminding me that we were "really strapped for cash now," as he had been counting on funds coming from Toronto. He kept pointing out I was costing him money and wasn't contributing anything. For a whole week he made my life miserable with suggestions about "Mr. Tata."

"Donny, please lay off. You know I'm not that type of girl. Whatever it is you think I can do ... I just don't dig your insinuation."

He laughed and said, "You know you wouldn't have to *do* anything. I mean just tease the guy a little ... work your charm. I'm sure you could get something out of him." I gave him an angry look. "C'mon, I'm just joking." He tried to calm me with his smiling eyes. Still, under his breath he said, "some girls would see an opportunity here. Man, I wish I was a chick."

After a week of fuming and stewing and worrying over the false accusations from his partners back home, and of unsuccessfully trying to pressure me into prostitution, Donny decided he would have to fly back to Toronto and straighten things out in person. Secretly I was glad he would be leaving. I was starting to not like him any more.

Having a valid return ticket, Donny decided to fly back right away. He said, "Look, sweetheart, I'm gonna have to leave you alone here for a while. This is the only way I can straighten things out. But Bruce will look after you while I'm gone."

A CHANCE TO ESCAPE

The minute we left the airport Bruce tried to seduce me. I was disgusted. I thought, "Some friend you are!" But at least now I had a chance to get my passport and some cash, because I knew Bruce was pretty dumb, in fact dumb enough to be tricked by a simple ruse. Since I wouldn't sleep with him, Bruce started pressuring me to do a dope run. He needed a mule to carry some hash to Canada.

Bruce had come to India on a scam, and was getting antsy. Having worked the requisite eight weeks, he had obtained unemployment insurance benefits in Canada and was having a friend sign his claim statements and deposit the funds in his account. Although it wasn't much money by Canadian standards, he could live quite well in India. But Bruce didn't want to stay in India and needed more money. Besides, he knew the UI benefits – his only source of income now – wouldn't last forever.

Unlike Donny, Bruce had no partners or financial backers. I knew he was disappointed in the mail scams he was doing, as they were labor-intensive and not very profitable. One could only move small quantities (up to an ounce) by mail, and it was risky. Often mail got lost, as had happened to Donny. Bruce was frustrated because he really hated India and had no desire to hobnob with the hippies on the scene. He had big plans to go to Mexico, but the only way to make them happen was to make some quick cash. All the real hashish operators shipped kilos, and the most common method was false-bottom suitcases via a "mule." A young, innocent-looking girl always made a great mule.

I pretended to go along with Bruce's idea, to win his trust in order to get my passport. I told him I would do it. Bruce was all excited and I could see his greedy eyes calculating the profits. I scanned my brain for ideas on how to escape. I couldn't really be a smuggler, so how the hell was I going to get out of this? I could book my flight out, pretend to take a loaded suitcase and then "accidentally" leave it at the airport, couldn't I? Did I dare? But where would I go? I had to get away from these creeps, and Donny said he'd be back in a few weeks. Should I do it? Did I have enough time?

DIPTY'S JUICE BAR

The next day I got up early and decided to explore the neighborhood a little. It felt good to be free of Donny. I hadn't been out much on my own yet, but felt as long as I didn't stray too far I could find my way back to the hotel. And so I landed at Dipty's juice bar. It was on the main drag just up the street from the Taj Mahal Hotel. The place was nothing special, just a hole in the wall with seating for about eight people. What was nice about this joint was that lot of hippies hung out there and over the last year or two had donated a tape deck and some hip music. At the time in Bombay, all you usually heard was Indian film music on the radio. But Dipty's had Eric Clapton, Hendrix, the Doors, the Stones, Van Morrison and Sly and the Family Stone. It was neat to hear some of our tribal music while siting in a Bombay juice bar with other hippies like myself.

Naturally it was crowded. There were two long wooden tables covered with torn, yellowed old linoleum and with bench-like seats. A nice-looking gentle hippie with somewhat effeminate manners and all dressed in silk smiled up at me and gestured for me to sit next to him. "This seat's not taken," he said in English.

Then he brightened up. "Hey, don't I know you? We met in Goa a few weeks ago, no? You're the girl from Calangute with some creepy guy ... Ronny, Danny?" I said "Donny," and sat down. He smelled delightfully of sandalwood oil, a scent I immediately fell in love with. He had a tattoo on his right hand between the thumb and forefinger. It was the Om symbol, I soon found out. "My name's Richard ... and you are?" "Ann," I said. He tilted his head like a curious dog. "Oh yeah, Canadian, right?" and smiled broadly. I noticed he had beautiful white straight teeth and a lovely mouth. I nodded.

"So what can I get you here? They make the most amazing mango *lassi* here. That's what I'm having."

"What's a lassi?" I wondered. He smiled a little condescendingly as if to say, "You poor dear, you haven't been here very long, have you?" Well, it was true.

"A lassi, my dear, is ... next to chai, India's second national drink. It is basically a yogurt drink but can be had sweet or sour. It is super healthy and tasty too. I suggest the mango lassi as it is mango season now." I nodded in agreement and soon he ordered my drink in the local language, which I later learned was not Hindi but Marathi. He seemed to know enough of the language to confidently order, and he seemed to know the owner. Richard was apparently not a novice to India.

I looked outside to watch an amusing scene: a monkey dressed in a little jacket and cap was chained to a tree, doing tricks for his owner

Street in the Muslim quarter; notice the scarcity of women.

and for change. Where else would one watch a monkey in a bellboy cap chained to an ancient banyan tree while smelling coconut oil, hash and curry, and drinking a mango lassi?

I felt enormously attracted to Richard, which made me a bit uncomfortable in his presence. He had a chain of wooden beads around his neck, long fingernails and wore an earring and lots of jewelry. Was he gay? I wasn't sure. By now I had seen lots of hippies dressed this way who were not. I had to find out.

Richard, it turns out, was not gay as evidenced by his keen interest in me. He was from California, originally from Santa Cruz, although he had spent time in the 'Frisco Bay area. Naturally, he was a surfer.

As we drank our lassis I noticed on the wall above me a somewhat tattered, gilt-framed picture of Krishna. The Hindu deity was in his flute-playing pose, charming a group of beautiful young women. In a moment of awkward silence I looked up at the picture and swear I saw Lord Krishna wink at me. Astonishing. I looked again, and again there was a twinkle in his eye – it sure looked like he winked at me. Or was it just the way the light hit the gilt on Krishna's crown, an optical illusion? Still, I was becoming intrigued by this childlike, androgynous, blue-bodied god I saw everywhere. Maybe it was because he looked somewhat human ... he didn't have multiple arms.

Richard shifted to adjust his lunghi. I noticed he wasn't wearing any underwear as I got an unsolicited peek. He had nice firm, tanned brown thighs, evidence of a surfer's body, and he wasn't overly hairy. I liked this. I later learned that it was not unusual for Indians, who mostly wore lunghis, to forego underwear. (Calvin Klein hadn't made it to India yet.)

Richard casually asked, "So, where's Donny?" I said, "Oh, he had to go away for a few weeks on business." Richard digested this information quickly and I could see him relax more when he asked how I liked the mango lassi. We were listening to the fabulous original song "Layla" by Derek and the Dominos, and a gentle breeze was blowing off the Arabian Sea that morning. The tablecloth was crawling with flies attracted to spilled pineapple juice. I saw a cockroach run up the wall and no one took notice, least of all Richard. I'd been in India for only a month and was still getting used to this very different culture and the casual acceptance of human dirt and nature's filth.

THE SUNSHINE BROTHERS

Richard said, "To be honest I didn't like your boyfriend Donny all that much. What are you doin' with him, anyway?" I didn't really have an answer and just shrugged.

"D'ya wanna go and smoke a chillum at my pad? I'm just across the street at the Rex-Stiffles." "Sure," I said and slurped up my lassi. I pulled out money to pay but Richard said it was taken care of. So I put my rupee note into the monkey's tin cup, to the delight of its owner.

The Rex-Stiffles Hotel had no lift (elevator) and no air conditioning – only the very modern and expensive hotels had them. By the time we walked up to the second floor, I felt sweaty with the humidity.

Richard waved me into his room. A simple, sun-lit room with a ceiling fan, two beds and a ton of books and musical instruments. Another beautiful, long-haired blonde, half-naked man was sitting on the edge of a bed, strumming a guitar and chanting in a strange language. Sanskrit? He was so absorbed that he barely noticed us when we walked in, and kept playing and singing. Then he greeted Richard and asked, "Who is this lovely lady?" Wow, he called me a Lady.

Richard introduced me to his friend Tom, and then the two began talking about mutual friends in Goa and who was doing what and who was coming for their big party in Anjuna at Christmas. They often referred to each other and some other friends as "Sunshine Brothers." I didn't understand why: maybe because they were from California? Or some kind of cult or tribe of acidheads? I didn't care. I felt intuitively drawn to these guys. In fact, I liked them a lot. They were so peaceful and easy going, totally laid back. They smoked a lot of hash, but you could tell they weren't junkies. They looked healthy.

I didn't understand everything they were saying, for they were both spiritual seekers and well read, it seemed, quoting scriptures like the *Vedas*. I was indeed curious, and impressed. They spoke in terms of consciousness and "self inquiry," the "absoluteness of the universe" and the "non-existence of being." I thought these guys must be real intellectuals. How could anyone travel and have so many books?

I began to get a sense of what it means to be "in the moment." Whether it was the hash or just from being in India, it seems these guys had achieved a state of inner peace. They had no trouble letting go and going with the flow. I asked them what drug they were on, and they both answered, "love, baby, love!" I was not a little taken aback.

Richard explained, "The Brotherhood of Eternal Love – that's our tribe and the drug is 'love man.' You know, like love for Shiva and love for the Guru and love for Jesus and love for all of creation and all of humanity. We love everyone we can. We especially love Kali, the bitch goddess, the quintessential mother-slut being who holds all the power of love and compassion in her heart. She is wide open, yet she's a fierce warrior goddess 'cause she cuts through all the illusion, all the bullshit."

Tom piped in, "Yeah, we just love to loooove, man. I'm in love with the whole of Brahma's creation and all the dramas and games. It's all an illusion, man, but it is also so real." Pausing to adjust his lunghi he leaned back and smiled. "It's all about love. Everything else is illusion, man." He lit up another chillum and closed his eyes. "Bom, Bom Bolay," he said, and exhaled a thick cloud of smoke. "We go through these relationships and dances with other people just to learn how to increase our love. Our universal, all-encompassing, unconditional love." The smile on his face was really like the sun breaking through clouds.

Now I was in a different world. Between numerous chillums offered to Shiva and just sitting there in silence, stoned and listening to these two sweet guys spewing their philosophy and their stream-of-consciousness-like poetry, I felt utterly safe and incredibly peaceful. They were both patient with me as a novice, and took turns explaining their philosophy and belief systems. Of course it included Krishna's love and his divine cohort, Radha. They talked of the Divine Couple. I thought that was so romantic: the Divine Couple. What did it mean? They also included the love of Shakti, "sensual love." And spoke of the Mother in reverent terms.

Soon they became silent, and we shared an easy, comfortable silence. Tom began to read to me from one of his books, written half in Sanskrit and half in English, which had large colorful, glossy pictures of mythological battles between demi-gods and multi-headed monsters with great chariots and balls of fire burning in the sky. I didn't really understand or care too much for this strange Hindu religion. The glossy pictures intrigued me, but it was hard to follow the mythology. Still, I listened politely and thought to myself, "Gee, I wouldn't mind having either one of these guys for my boyfriend." With all this talk of love I felt I could surely love both these guys.

The *Veda* stories were confusing and convoluted, and these half-gods and demons had no meaning to me. Noticing my lack of interest,

Tom stopped reading and said, "You don't need to know all this right now. And by the way, you have very cosmic eyes, really cosmic eyes. Doesn't she, brother?" While Richard nodded, Tom asked, "Would you like to smoke another chillum? Let's bring out the Nepalese fingers, bro', and get our friend here really stoned."

Then Richard said: "maybe the lady is thirsty. "Would you care for something to drink? Fresca, chai or another lassi?" It seemed these guys were willing to procure whatever my heart desired, and I felt like a princess to have these two guys so eager to please me. "I'm okay for now, but I wouldn't mind if you'd play a song." Tom picked up the guitar and began to play a lovely melody in open tuning. He held it like a sitar and played mostly the bottom four strings. Meanwhile, Richard picked up the text and read silently to himself, occasionally pausing to reflect. I thought to myself, "If only I could always be with people like this." Richard put down the book after a while and sang along with Tom. It was a haunting Indian raga.

I listened for a time, and then sat up abruptly. "You know, I really hate Donny." They both looked surprised at my sudden outburst. They could see I was like a little child just bursting to pour my heart out. My burden was so great I couldn't keep it in any more. Richard's face was showing real concern. "Why don't you just leave him?" he asked.

Then out came my whole story. The guys were outraged that Donny would try to pimp his own girlfriend. They seemed to understand how miserable and stressed out I was. And now they hated Donny even more. They were really empathetic and seemed awfully concerned, pumping me with questions. And then they declared that I simply had to leave "the bastard."

But if I was going to leave Donny, I would need some money. They asked if my folks could send me something, and I said, "No, I left on bad terms." It would be of no use to ask them for help now.

Besides, my mother had begged me not to go to India, as she was sure I'd get into trouble. My folks being smug, self-righteous types and total cheapskates, they would never permit their daughter to "take advantage" of them like this, begging for money when they had expressly warned me not to go to India. I couldn't imagine asking them – that would be to admit failure and that they were right. I'd be disgraced and they would never let me forget it. Even if they could help me, they simply would not, right now. Their philosophy was, "If you don't listen to us, then you'll have to learn the hard way."

Now the guys were scrambling for ideas. How could I get some money? The situation looked hopeless. I had no resources except 2,000 rupees ($200), which Donny had calculated should last me exactly two weeks. The boys looked at each other, and the glint in their eyes flashed instant telepathy as they both suddenly came to the same idea.

Richard asked me straight out: "Do you think you could do a run?" By now I was familiar with the term, because practically every foreigner I knew in Bombay was running hash one way or another. This was the second time I'd been asked in the last two days, and I had to think. Gosh, could I really do it? I didn't answer immediately. To encourage me, Richard said, "Hey, wouldn't you like to see Sweden? Meet some really cool people, hang out and party with some of our brothers and get totally stoned, and come back with a pocket full of cash?" Tom piped in "yeah, then you can tell Donny to go fuck himself."

I had to admit the thought tempted me. How could I do it? Richard said it was easy. A girl he'd sent two weeks earlier had just returned; it was a hassle-free run. Their people had devised a safe and proven route. They'd sent a couple of mules a month on these trips, and they had all been successful. It was very low risk, he explained, because they had worked out a route where customs procedures were minimal. They would take care of the arrangements; all I had to do was act cool. Tom added, "There's always a demand for good hash in Europe, and our partners are long-time trusted friends, our brothers." These sunshine people would take care of everything at the other end and show me a good time too! It would be quick and easy, and I'd be back in two weeks with $2,000 (US) of my own. I thought, "My God, two thousand bucks! I could live comfortably for a pretty long time in India on that. Then I could do whatever I wanted. Travel where I'd like ..."

I agreed to do it. And I was pretty sure I *could* do it. I was always a good actress. And I had already carried a stash of black-market money through a few borders ... how could carrying contraband cannabis be different? I was so grateful to my two new friends for helping me and caring so much about my situation I kind of fell in love with them both that day. I was so happy now that I had a solution. As we discussed plans to make things happen, Tom laid down some LSD. We all dropped the acid and talked a bit more, while Tom played some more guitar and I thought I was in heaven.

Then Tom left to do some errands, and Richard and I started to make love. It just happened. We got really quiet, and then he leaned toward me and gently put his hand under my chin and lifted my face to his. He looked deeply into my eyes and then we were kissing. Soon we were in the throes of wild passion on this hot tropical afternoon in Bombay ... while I began to trip on the LSD. The air pushed about by a ceiling fan brought fragrances of pineapples and mangoes and gardenia and roses just outside our window. Tropical flower scents mixed with street smells wafted through the warm air, but permeating all this was the heavenly fragrance of sandalwood oil and Richard's sweet summer sweat.

Wrapped in a lover's embrace – Richard had his arms around me and my legs were around his hips – I suddenly felt another pair of hands on my buttocks. How could that be? I knew I was tripping, but was I now making love with one of those four-armed deities? Could this be Shiva teasing me?

I realized quickly that this was not the case when Tom's voice insinuated itself into our breathing as he asked, "Is this okay, bro?" and Richard said, "It's up to her, man." I was so into the moment I could only moan in agreement. Tom's hands were caressing, practically worshipping my buttocks. He was gentle and didn't intrude in any other way. While Richard and I made love, Tom was masturbating. When he tried to get more intimate I stopped him, and he understood. So there I was like a goddess, worshipped by these two handsome male lovers and stoned out of my tree. It was more than sensual passion that day; I'm not sure what, but it sure didn't feel dirty or demeaning.

After we finished making love, we all collapsed in a heap of humid, exhausted human flesh and lay there for a while in the hot tropical breeze with flies buzzing. I moved to get up and Tom said, "Hey sister, where you going?" I said I'd like to wash up.

Richard said, "There's no shower here and no hot water. But if you like, we can order up some hot water." On cue, Tom left and came back a few minutes later with hot water in a bucket. He started to wash me gently with a warm, soapy cloth, and again I felt like I was in heaven. As my LSD buzz got more and more intense, I noticed that as he dripped warm water onto my body it took on the appearance of golden honey. Yes, I was hallucinating. Tom took on the appearance of Krishna, with his skin turning blue in the shade of the room. Richard gave me a long, lingering, loving kiss while Tom washed my thighs and private parts. Then Richard said, "Isn't this heaven? Right now ... isn't this bliss?"

I said, "yeah, this is bliss but I have to piss, so please let me up." I found a latrine down the hall, the usual keyhole-in-the-ground toilet with a little tap beside it and a metal bucket for washing. I was getting used to this "Indian toilet," learning to squat to do my business and to wash with the bucket using only my left hand. Under the unwritten code of hygiene in most of Asia, one uses only the left hand for cleaning after toilet, and never uses this hand for food or to touch others.

When I came back to the room Richard was smoking a *biddhi*. He offered me one, but I never did develop a taste for this cigar-like cigarette. Tom was gone. Richard and I spent another hour or so talking, and then I left for my hotel. I was the happiest girl in the world: I had a solution to my problem with Donny and I'd made two new, wonderful friends. That night I slept like a baby and dreamed I was making love with Krishna.

CHAPTER 6

A Dope Run to Europe

PREPARING FOR MY FIRST DOPE RUN was stressful, so I smoked a great big chillum of hash to relax. I said an incantation to Shiva – "Bom Bom Bolay, Hare Hare Mahadev, Om Nama Shivaya" – a custom I had recently adopted. I liked the idea of invoking the blessings of a god of cannabis. A knock at the door interrupted my sweet repose. It was Bruce, the nuisance. He said, "I heard that you're planning to do a run for someone else now, so what happened to our deal?" Hands on his hips in an accusatory stance, he added, "I thought you were doing a run for me."

Bruce hadn't come up with the money for a plane ticket or even a destination. Still, he was miffed to learn that I was going ahead with someone who had more concrete plans and the ability to make them happen. But Bruce always saw opportunity. "Hey, why not make it a two-in-one? You could take my suitcase up to Sweden, and I'll make sure you have the bread to book another flight to Canada."

Once he was onto this idea, he couldn't stop pushing it. His calculating mind was working overtime. He practically begged me to carry a suitcase for him too, but wanted me to do it without letting the other guys know. I didn't realize it then, but this way Bruce the cheapskate could save the cost of financing this run, especially my transportation and accommodation. He would be conveniently riding on the backs of the brothers.

"I've already arranged the hash, and I can have the suitcase ready in two days. I'll tell them to put a rush on it. I'll go out right now and talk to the guy. Maybe he can even have it ready for tomorrow. C'mon man, I really need you to do this for me."

His incessant whining was annoying, and he always made me feel guilty because I wouldn't have sex with him. "It really wouldn't be much more trouble to carry just one more suitcase, would it? Besides, it would mean more money for you!"

I honestly didn't care about the extra money, but seeing how pathetic and desperate he looked I began to feel sorry for him. My resolve was weakening. Besides, I needed to keep up the facade of doing a run for him to get my passport, and this was the perfect cover. But I needed time to think and strategize. I really didn't want to deceive my new friends the Sunshine Brothers, who were so good to me. Bruce was relentless, but I didn't feel like dealing with him and wanted to get rid of him, so I said I'd let him know in the morning.

He stood in the doorway, hesitating to leave, and gave me a sly look. "I sure hope so ... because I got a telegram from Donny today. And he's gonna call tomorrow. He's gonna wanna know how you're doin'."

The way he said it gave me the sense that he could sabotage my plans and tell Donny everything. The bastard. Blackmailing me? I had no choice but to play ball with this creep now. But I still had the option of leaving his suitcase at the airport; I could still fuck him over. And it would serve him right. I just didn't want him to tell Donny that I was doing a dope run for someone else. Donny would catch the first flight back to India if he knew. I said, "Okay, okay, I'll do it. Now would you please split?"

Two days later, on my way to the airport, I kept telling myself how stupid it was to take up Bruce's offer. Now things were much more complicated than originally planned. I had two completely mismatched suitcases and would have to pay overweight baggage fees at the airport. It would mean a bribe. Besides this, Bruce wanted me to go on to Canada with his suitcase, because the price of hash there was double that in Europe. This meant I'd be traveling more than double the distance and going through more customs, and committing all my time to travel. I wouldn't be able to hang out and party with the folks in Stockholm. Why the hell did I let him talk me into this? I cursed my own weakness.

The taxi dropped me off at the airport and I intended to leave his cheap Indian-made suitcase behind, but I simply couldn't. Each time I tried to leave the bag, someone would pick it up and carry it for me, saying, "You forgot your bag, *memsahib*." Fucking Indians, so eager to please ... how the hell does a foreign lady leave a suitcase behind in a crowded airport where everyone watches your every move, even in the bathroom? So I ended up with this stupid suitcase I couldn't lose.

TROUBLE IN TEL AVIV

Leaving Bombay, I was surprised how easily I got through the baggage check. They didn't even charge me for extra baggage. Later I discovered why: One of my bags had simply not been tagged.

At a stopover in Tel Aviv, where we had to change planes, the pilot made an urgent announcement just as we were leaving. "We have an unidentified suitcase here ... a black Samsonite suitcase." At first I did not respond to this announcement. Richard's suitcase was a Samsonite, but I was sure it was dark brown. The pilot repeated the message, and asked if the owner would please come and claim it. People looked around at one another. After two hours of waiting at the airport, everyone was anxious to take off. No one else claimed it.

Another urgent announcement: "Will the owner of a black Samsonite suitcase please come and claim it?" Suddenly I realized with horror that it could be the suitcase Richard had given me. Damn – was it black or dark brown? If it had been Bruce's suitcase, I would have just left it. Just my luck it had to be the good suitcase. Intuition told me that the Indians at the baggage check in Bombay typically fucked up and forgot to tag the second suitcase. I was annoyed. Now I was being a racist and I knew it. But sometimes they were just so incompetent ... why was that?

Worse, I was terrified. What if it was a trick? What if they'd found the hash and this was a ploy to identify the owner of the suitcase and arrest the smuggler? God, could it be a trick? I had no way of knowing. Again, I was terrified, undecided and nervous.

The pilot called out a third time. People seemed agitated in their seats and looked around them anxiously. I felt I had to take a chance and quickly raised my hand. "I ... I think it might be mine." To everyone's great relief I was quickly driven back to the terminal by a friendly Israeli official, When I saw the suitcase I said "you know I just bought this suitcase and I'm not even sure it's mine."

"Why don't you open it and see?" he suggested. I opened it and gazed long and hard at the contents. The Israeli pressed on. "So? It is yours?" Obviously puzzled by my nervousness, he gave me an odd look, which I misinterpreted. I wondered if he knew, but now I could stall no more. I had to answer. Something told me to just say "yes," and when I did the driver said "Good! Then we can get on." The drive from the security area to the plane was interminably long, but fortunately I was the beneficiary of divine intervention.

Beside my plane on the tarmac stood a large Sabena jet pockmarked with hundreds of bullet holes. I asked my host what it was doing there. He looked at me in surprise and said, "Haven't you heard? This plane was hijacked just last week and held under guard by heavily armed Palestinian terrorists for two days while full of innocent hostages. It was a nightmare for them, I'm sure."

I played dumb. "Really? Tell me more."

"You didn't know? But it's been all over the news. Anyway, the heroic Israeli army liberated them." To deflect attention from the suitcase and my strange behavior, I pretended deep interest, leaning towards him and begging for details. It worked. He spoke rapidly and excitedly in thickly accented English, spewing spittle as he excitedly recounted the historic hijacking and rescue.

"When did this happen?" I asked to keep him talking. "They liberated the hostages only two days ago. They have to study the plane – that's why it's still sitting there." Oh, he was proud to be able to tell the tale. He'd actually been there and seen it all. I thanked God that this guy didn't suspect anything. He babbled on till we reached the plane, and even shook my hand as we parted. He wished me luck in my travels. I entered the plane tentatively. Everyone stared at me, some clearly resenting being delayed. Profoundly embarrassed, I slunk into my seat and wished I could disappear. Soon we were in the sky again.

My trip, however, was not blessed with good karma.

During a three-hour stopover in Rome, I waited patiently, had a drink in a bar and avoided conversation. I bought some glossy fashion magazines and amused myself gazing at the outrageous Italian fashions adorning beautiful women in splendid settings. Two gentlemen approached me. Extremely well dressed and groomed, handsome and polite, very Italian, they asked me if I would be sitting there for long. I answered, "about an hour or so," and one of them replied, "Good! Would you do us the kindness of watching over our baggage while we have a drink?" Dazzled by these charmers, how could I say no?

This was in the days before warnings against such things in airports. They thanked me profusely and left with a gentlemanly bow.

The men returned an hour and a half later with an enormous bouquet of roses and a box of expensive Italian chocolates, offered with another gracious bow. Then each of these gents kissed my hand and thanked me again. "It is an honor to have such a beautiful lady protect our meager belongings. You are too kind." I was overwhelmed. I stared after them. Oh, those Italians ... they certainly had style.

Dreaming on after these two charming guys, I delved into the chocolates and continued to read my magazines. Fashionable Italians were into some pretty avant-garde stuff; I guess they always have been. But this was 1972, and they had already married erotica and art. I tried to translate the Italian, as I knew some French and had a facility for languages. But mostly I was engrossed by the glossy photos of gorgeous men and women fabulously dressed in dramatic settings.

I wasn't paying attention to the time when suddenly I heard a voice announce: "Last call, last call! Alitalia flight 103 to Brussels." My plane. Oh, my God, it was my plane. I grabbed my bags and began to run frantically. It was a long way down the hall to my gate. I ran and ran, huffing and puffing and waving to an Alitalia official, shouting "Wait for me, wait for me." The stewardesses saw me coming and yelled, "Hurry, hurry, everyone's on board ... the plane is leaving. Didn't you hear your name being paged? Oh, hurry, hurry. Please!"

I ran so fast that my chest hurt and I had a stitch in my side. Huffing and puffing and out of breath, I was whisked onto the plane. The engines were running already. I was in a state of panic and must have appeared disheveled and confused. Once again I felt thoroughly embarrassed as passengers regarded me with curious, annoyed and even hostile looks. I collapsed into my seat swearing to myself: "What an idiot! How did I lose track of the time?" What would I have done if I missed the plane? I didn't speak Italian and had never bought a plane ticket. I'd never really been alone in a foreign country before, and it would have been a disaster.

In Brussels I was supposed to transfer to a train for the rest of the journey to Stockholm. I had been given instructions to follow a specific route and time schedule. Brussels was a beautiful city, and I was sorry I wouldn't get to see much of it. I had a two-hour wait and had been advised not to leave the station because one could easily get lost. After a brief stroll just outside the Gare Centrale de Bruxelles, I returned to the station and stood on the platform observing the hustle and bustle of life moving in and out of the city.

I had plenty of time but nothing else to do, so I sat down and took in the lively noises and sights of Belgians going about their daily activity. I liked to see how people dressed differently from back home. Belgians consisted of all races, starting with the Flemish and the French. There were also tall Congolese (Zaireans) from the former Belgian Congo. I was struck by the beauty of a tall, elegantly dressed black lady whom I overheard speaking impeccable French. What a cosmopolitan city.

Many trains came and went, and the movement of the crowd was constant. I am a people watcher and I was practically hypnotized by the sounds, smells and sights. I watched in fascination as a young couple entwined in a loving embrace. They were both so young and vibrant, and extremely in love, I could tell. I was intrigued by the passion these two unabashedly exhibited in the train station – it was like a Harlequin Romance right before my eyes. Yeah, sometimes I used to read that kind of trash.

All I could think of was that it must be nice to be so much in love. I watched them kissing passionately and openly caressing each other, oblivious to the rest of the world. I sighed and daydreamed about Richard and me. "Oh, yes my darling, as soon as this is over we'll be together again and travel all over the world together!" And then heard myself hoping: "Please wait for me, Richard, Please!"

Thus wrapped up in my dreamy little world, I missed my train. Worse, I got on the wrong train. I ended up on a commuter train because I wasn't very proficient in French at the time and again wasn't clued into the announcements. By the time I discovered that this was not the train to Stockholm, I was already a good few kilometers down the track. Some kind Belgians helped me and reassured me that I could get off at the next stop and go back to Central Station. This was little reassurance, for I had been specifically told to take the night train to Stockholm to ensure minimum customs procedures. Because many transborder workers traveled by night train, I was told, the polite European customs officers didn't like to disturb passengers in their sleep and so would do a minimal inspection; a quick look at the passport and that's it. Now I felt panicky. I'd missed the night train. What would I do?

I got a local train back to the main station and found the station-master. Hopelessly, nervously, I began pleading my case, trying my best to speak French but crying and nearly hysterical. I explained to the man that I had to get the 8:00 p.m. train because my aunt was meeting me in Copenhagen and we were to board the first ferry to Stockholm in the morning. I told him that I had no way of reaching my aunt (she had no phone) and I simply had to be there in the morning. With my broken French it took him some time to understand the problem, but the stationmaster calmed me down with a simple solution. Another train was departing at 9:00 that arrived even earlier than my scheduled train, for it was an express. Although these were usually reserved for European commuters, he put a special stamp on my passport. Unknown to me this stamp basically eliminated all customs procedures. I finally made it safely to Stockholm, Sweden.

STOCKHOLM

In Stockholm, however, more trouble was waiting. An international environmental convention, the first ever, was taking place here and all the hotels were full. I couldn't get a room anywhere. Furthermore, my contact hadn't received the telegram notifying him of my arrival, and he was out of town for the weekend. I phoned repeatedly with no answer. Finally someone on the party line answered and said Joe was out of town. I would be stuck the whole weekend in Stockholm loaded down with 20 kilos of hash and not knowing a soul. In the midst of some bloody convention, too. What would I do?

I wandered the streets lugging my overweight suitcases until I found a relatively cheap room on the fifth floor of a pension, an old house with steep stairs. The woman running the pension had the no-nonsense look of a serious matron. The rules were simple: "In by 10:00 p.m. and no gentleman visitors." I didn't want to attract attention so I went to another hotel to place a long distance call to Bombay. Thank God, Richard was there and answered. I explained what was happening, and he said to just hang in there and gave me another number to call. He said to just keep trying to reach Joe.

The next day I managed to reach someone who would give a message to Joe and have him get back to me. I gave him my telephone and room number at the pension, and we eventually connected. Joe and his wife, Janet, were quite surprised at my arrival in Sweden; they were not expecting another delivery so soon. But they had finally gotten the telegram from Richard, so they knew what was up. They came to get me at the pension, took me in as a guest in their home and treated me royally. They offered me every comfort from a sauna to a hammock, fed me and smoked me up, and soon I was comfortable and totally relaxed. I instantly liked these people. They seemed so worldly and had great stories to tell. And they were so kind to me. I felt like I'd made some new friends.

Joe and Janet had been in India for some years, and were doing regular dope runs to Europe and apparently making a lot of money. They were living quite well in Stockholm, though only temporarily, for they had bought a house in Goa. "Have you been to Goa?" Joe asked. "Yeah, but I didn't spend much time there I'm afraid. My boyfriend didn't like it."

Janet said, "What's not to like about Goa?" and I explained that Donny couldn't get used to the 'primitive lifestyle' and was attached to his creature comforts. Janet said, "You really should come and spend Christmas in Goa. Last year we had a big party at Anjuna Beach and there were over 100 people. We had all kinds of drugs, and people came from all over. This year will be an even bigger party. We've got musicians and artists from all over. Naturally there will be lots of drugs and a huge cookout. We're planning the biggest party ever, and it's sure to be a blast." I thanked them for the offer and said I'd be there for sure.

After some friendly talk they asked to see the hash. Naturally they wanted to inspect the goods before committing to anything; another shipment so soon after the previous one might not be easy to off-load. However, if the hash was the same excellent quality as before, they'd have no problem getting rid of it. After opening Richard's suitcase, we proceeded to the next one. When my hosts saw the battered Indian suitcase that Bruce had given me, they became alarmed. It was of no particular brand name and bursting at the seams, for it was of flimsy construction with no proper framework and had been overstuffed with hash. It looked very suspect.

My new friends could not believe that some jerk expected me to take this suitcase to Canada. They urged me not to do it. "Ann, believe me, you won't even get out of Stockholm with that suitcase." I had to admit it looked pretty bad. "But what will I do?" I asked. "I can't very well bring it back to Bombay." "Why don't you let us take care of both suitcases? Then you won't have to go to Canada," said Joe. Perfect solution. I wasn't about to get busted for Bruce's stupid scam.

The hash sold fairly quickly and we spent several days changing and arranging money. Janet took me sightseeing while we visited banks to change the Swedish currency into American dollars. At that time you could not change more than $2,000 without arousing suspicion. We had to convert the equivalent of $20,000, so we ended up going to ten different banks in three days. This was tedious, but we spiced up the chore with shopping, lunch, visiting friends and smoking chillums, and I actually saw quite a bit of this charming city.

Soon I was headed back to Bombay, mission completed, with a suitcase full of money and a heart full of pride. I'd managed to unload 20 kilos of prime Afghani hash without a hitch. Now I was carrying twenty thousand US dollars in cash, more money than I had seen in my entire life. Of course it was not my money, and I would dutifully hand it over to the Sunshine Brothers and Bruce, and take my share. But I was sure that Richard and I would end up together, and so it would all work out well. I looked forward to spending Christmas in Goa with Richard and Joe and Janet and all the hippies. I also knew that I was in love with Richard. We had had an amazing connection, and in my foolish young girl's heart I was certain that this time it was real love.

ABANDONED

But when I got back to Bombay, Richard was cold and quite distant. He paid me $2,000, thanked me and sort of patted me on the head. "Good job, kid. Now you're free."

Free? I was devastated. He took his money and left me. He was scheduled to travel the following day to Kabul to meet his estranged lover, Françoise. By the way he spoke of her and the misty look in his eyes, I could tell this was a special lady and that he was hopelessly in love with her. Immediately I was insanely jealous of this woman I didn't know. Why do the French women always get these guys? My Richard ran off to Afghanistan and left me shattered in Bombay.

Deeply hurt and rejected, I didn't really want the money or the freedom he offered. It was Richard I wanted (or somebody like Richard). Tom was long gone, headed off to New Delhi, so he was not an option. I guess mostly I wanted, really just needed, someone to hang out with. Desperately trying to find my place, I wandered the streets alone again. Always the outsider and never fitting in – all I wanted was to belong somewhere.

There I was, a scared eighteen-year-old kid in India totally out of her element and needing security more than anything. How I longed to be accepted, to be cool, to be worthy of Richard's attention. With Richard and Tom gone, there was really no one left in town for me.

I did have Bruce, the nuisance, to deal with. He was hopping mad that I hadn't gone to Canada with his hash, because now he had only half as much money as he'd expected. Oh, was he upset. He even asked me to forego my share of the money (geez, I took all the risk!), but I steadfastly refused. Besides, he'd agreed to pay me only $1,000 while Richard had paid me $2,000 for carrying the same amount. I would not give in, but he moaned and whined and kept at me for days, which was annoying.

Worse, Donny returned and learned of my trip. He kept saying: "Jesus, if I'd a-known you were gonna do a dope run, you coulda done it for me." But he regarded me with newfound respect because he hadn't thought I had the guts to do a run. Still, it was a hollow victory, and I sulked. Richard was gone, Tom was gone, Joe and Janet were far away in Sweden, and here I was stuck in Bombay with these jerks. The rainy season was coming and all the cool people had left for sunnier destinations. Most people were headed north to the Himalayas or way south to Madras or Kerala, which had a different climate. So I ended up hanging out with Paul, a recent friend of Donny and my last resort. He was a fellow Canadian from Vancouver, and he and I had spent a bit of time together before I left for Sweden.

Paul was a good-looking man, intelligent and friendly but a little arrogant; he found me "somewhat amusing," he once told me.

Street beggar

Memoirs of a Hippie Girl in India

I had no illusions: he tolerated me because I had a great body and he couldn't wait to get into my pants. Although I knew this, I never slept with him. I tolerated him because he had a tape deck and some great music – we both loved Neil Young and John Mayall. He told some good stories, and I was a good listener. Besides, like me, he was a *chillum baba* (hash smoker).

But now even Paul was leaving. He was going to England to meet up with his mother, and would later travel to Munich to meet with Joe and Janet, who had a home there as well as in Stockholm and Goa. A whole gang would be in Munich for the Olympics that summer, and there would be a wild after-party. They knew all the media people and there would be lots of drugs, live music and cool people. I wondered if Richard would make his way there, with his French femme fatale. But I was not invited.

I was devastated. Great that I had my own money and could do what I wanted, but where would I go? Who could I hang out with? I couldn't (or wouldn't) go back to Canada. My return ticket had expired, and going home was tantamount to defeat. I had to prove something even if it was just to myself: that I could and would survive. I just had to hook up with the right people. That evening Paul was busy with some last-minute business and I went to Baghdaddy's Café. I knew a lot of local hippies hung out there. Maybe I'd meet someone interesting and catch a ride to wherever they were going. But the only people there were junkies. Now I was desperate.

Bombay Post Office

Beggars without legs surround the entrance of the huge edifice
Louder--the immobile pleading voices frantic
Some dash--through walking on their hands
Others crawl the weight of useless legs
All invoke the mercy of men
Eyes full of hunger and wonder

In the courtyard on the stairs
Deformed cripples with legs that function
Offer services
To "breakpath" thru the milling swarming mass
Guides thru the bureaucratic labyrinth

Asking the price "one rupee...
Nothing to the rest of humanity"

The foreigner must go
From floor to floor
To post the letter
While behind cages workers perform simple tasks
Motions automatic
In gigantic books piled high
Stamping or writing numbers or signing
Turning trees into paper
Another cycle of Bombay breath and death.

— *poem by Jerry Biesler, author of*
The Bandit of Kabul *(used by permission)*

Paul, my last friend, left Bombay the following day to meet up with his cool friends in Munich. I had nothing else to do, so I accompanied him to the airport. Donny came along for the ride. Although we had fought and then sort of made up, I made it clear that I was not his girlfriend any more. He was surprised at my stance, but more or less okay with it. I still needed to keep him close to me ... as they say, "Keep the enemy close to thy breast." We had decided we could be mature and civil with each other. We could at least escort a common friend to the airport together. Donny was quite impressed because I'd had the guts to do a dope run by myself, and it was a success. I knew he was still hoping I'd do a run for him. I may have intentionally led him to believe this was still possible, to keep him on his toes.

At the airport Paul was a bit concerned because he had a little pet, something like a mink, in a cage. He'd made all the proper arrangements ahead of time, so it got through customs with ease. Donny asked me if I wanted to hang around and watch the plane take off. It was a balmy tropical night and the stars were beautiful, so I agreed. "It will be cooler on the observation deck." As it turned out, staying at the airport was a big mistake.

Paul got into big trouble at customs, but it had nothing to do with his pet. Donny and I walked up to the outdoor deck and hung around to watch the plane take off. But we never saw it. Instead we saw two police officers approaching us with a very worried-looking Paul in tow. When they asked, "Do you know this man?" we said nothing but looked terrified. We were then told, "You're all under arrest for conspiracy to smuggle."

I nearly fainted on the spot. Seeing Paul, I knew this was serious. It turned out that Paul was on a blacklist of suspected smugglers at every airport in India. He had no contraband on him (he wouldn't be so foolish as to carry anything himself), but a mule he had sent a week earlier to Europe was arrested in Delhi and the girl had apparently talked.

Fuck! Guilty by association! The police inspected our passports and then escorted the three of us to our hotel rooms and conducted a search. Paul's vacated room at the Sea Palace Hotel revealed nothing, of course. I was surprised they even bothered to check it. But my room was another story. It was embarrassing to have all these officers in my room, for I'd just washed a week's worth of underwear and the room was full of panties, bras and other personal things strung on improvised clotheslines. Three policemen and two female officers accompanied me to my room. They were typically polite Indians, trying to avoid looking at my intimate things. But it was obvious these men were also embarrassed and the women full of envy, for luxuries like lingerie were not available to Indian women then.

They searched my writing desk and found a few ounces of hash and some chillums and other smoking paraphernalia. This did not really concern the police and I wasn't too worried, since smoking hash in India was generally tolerated. But then they stumbled upon a rubber stamp with the name "Jasmine's School of Dance" and a Bombay address and phone number. Then a stamp pad, a rolling pin, and many envelopes. Two envelopes were already stuffed with cards and addressed, to be mailed the next day. Torn open, the envelopes each revealed a thinly rolled 20-gram piece of hash. The police gave me accusatory looks – it was obvious that I was running a little mail operation, sending hash to friends in Toronto. The rolling pin was used to roll the soft Bombay hash paper-thin so it would fit nicely into an envelope. One of the officers playing the joker picked up the rolling pin to mime a woman rolling *chapatis* (flatbread). He said, "So, you like to make chapatis?" and all the cops had a good laugh. Their lightened mood helped me relax a bit, for I knew that in India a few ounces of hash was really no big deal.

But then we were escorted to Donny's hotel a few blocks away. There the police uncovered a suitcase with nine kilos of hashish – and I knew we were really in trouble. We were charged with smuggling, conspiracy to smuggle, possession of an illegal drug, exportation of an illegal substance and possession of undeclared currency. Everything was confiscated, and the three of us were told that we were "in very serious trouble indeed." The two lady officers were commissioned to take the illegal goods to the police station, while three male officers remained behind to further question us.

The officers understood these foreign hippies quite well. Although it was not easy to overlook the overt racism of many hippies, which even I found embarrassing at times, the police managed to politely ignore it. The officers could easily sense that these two young smart alecks did not like *Desis* (Indians), but now they had the upper hand and could teach these kids a lesson. So they did something quite unusual. Instead of being angry with us criminal Canadians, they decided to "educate" us. They said they wanted to give us a taste of real Indian culture. They asked us a few more questions, made sure we knew we were in serious trouble, and then took us to a fine Indian restaurant. What better way to introduce one to Indian culture than by eating? Furthermore, in India one cannot conduct business on an empty stomach.

The officers asked us if we knew any Indian artists, writers, or thinkers like ... Rabindranath Tagore? Mohandas Gandhi, Jawaharlal Nehru? Did we know V.S. Naipal? What about some of India's famous scientists, like the physicist Satyendra Nath Bose? Did we know that India is a very progressive country? That great social reformers like Anna Hazare and Dhondo Keshave Karve tried to eliminate the caste system and give rights to the untouchables? Had we heard good classical musicians? Not just Ravi Shankar, but other great Indian artists like Annapurna Devi, Ustad Ali Akbar Khan and Zakir Hussain? We hadn't, of course.

The dinner was delicious and our arresting officers were polite hosts, making sure our every desire was fulfilled. We sat for two hours enjoying the Indian culture. The officers even paid for our dinner. It was an obvious hint for a bribe, and such hints were dropped subtly throughout the meal as they told the three of us about the history, culture, richness and diversity of India. But, stupidly, not one of us got it. Donny and Paul accepted their hospitality as if this was normal, just the way things were done here. I, of course, was a newcomer and didn't have a clue.

Silly, gullible, naive Canadians, we couldn't understand the culture of bribery. Though a little puzzled at their generosity, we thoroughly enjoyed the meal and then were promptly taken to jail. It all seemed like a dream. Only afterwards did I realize the whole show was for a bribe, and we would certainly not have been sitting in jail if only we had been a little more aware of Indian culture. I was especially mad at Donny and Paul, who had been in India a lot longer than I had. Surely, they should have known better. In any case it was too late to be moaning over that, as I was now sitting in Arthur Road – Bombay's main jail.

CHAPTER 7

Jailed in Bombay

BEFORE I WENT TO SLEEP EACH NIGHT I had a little ritual: I put aside a portion of my food in the furthest corner of my jail cell so a certain rat would eat it and not bother me in my sleep. One night I had woken up to the horror of this gigantic rodent nibbling in my hair. In spite of my bloodcurdling scream, no one came to my aid; I had to fend for myself. Not easy, considering my sheltered former life. Terrified of the rat, I had no choice but to make it my friend, or at least an indifferent acquaintance.

I sat down on the hard floor on my pathetic little mat (which offered no comfort, for it was infested with fleas) and began to sob. "Why is this happening to me?" I wailed. I had been in India less than two months and now I was in jail. But of course I knew precisely why, and told myself it was because I did that "stupid dope run to Sweden."

I was thinking about that trip. It had been successful and a lot of fun, and I had returned to Bombay with my mission accomplished. No, the dope run was not exactly the problem. I was pretty sure that a local character nicknamed Junkie James had betrayed me. It was pretty dumb to have told him about my travel plans to Sweden; he surely figured out what I was up to. And he could have passed on that information for money. But what could I do? I needed his help then, as I didn't know my way around Bombay or even how to find the things I needed for the trip.

Junkie James had the distinction of being Bombay's oldest hippie resident. He'd been there so long that he spoke fluent Hindi and even some of the local dialect, Marathi. And he knew where to get anything. It was too late now to lament that I hadn't given him a proper bribe.

I was learning about how things really worked in India, including its known but unseen system of bribery. Maybe this was my wake-up call. But what good could it do me now, sitting in a jail cell not knowing when or even if I would get out? I had barely arrived in India and now found myself locked in a Bombay prison. "Talk about bad luck!" I thought glumly. Watching an enormous insect scurrying across the floor with a faint glimmer of sun streaming through the barred opening, I remembered how freaked out my mom was when I told her I was going to India. "Ann, please don't go," she had said. "I just know you'll get mixed up with the wrong kind of people, drug smugglers and people like that and you'll probably end up in jail." How did my frantic mom so accurately predict this? Was she psychic?

Feeling lonely and forlorn, all I could think about was my parents and my family and how much I missed them. After bragging to everyone back home about my upcoming travel adventures, now I was a scared little girl sitting in a jail cell in Bombay. I felt like such a fool. I knew my folks would be devastated if they knew, and I wanted to protect them from finding out. At least for now. But how could I be sure they wouldn't find out?

A Canadian diplomat, Mr. Patterson, had come to see me after being referred by the British High Commission. I specifically asked Mr. Patterson not to contact my parents, but he'd insisted that it was the best thing to do – and in fact the *only* thing he could do for me. I pleaded with him not to contact them, at least for now. Could I trust him? He seemed a nice enough guy and genuinely concerned.

I also asked Mr. Patterson if I could get some decent food and English reading material, and he arranged that. So instead of watery thin slop for breakfast, every day I got a boiled egg, warm milk, coarse bread and a banana. That was pretty good. By virtue of being a foreigner I even got cigarettes, which came in handy for trading. Mr. Patterson came through for me on that, and so I felt I had to trust him. I continued writing cheery postcards of lies to my folks. I told them I was happy and loving India, and described places I'd never visited, getting information from a fancy Indian magazine, the *Weekly Post*, and other glossy English-language magazines that I now had. I had to put up a facade and hope that my parents would believe it, at least until I could get out of this situation. But I had no clue as to how I could get out.

My first few weeks were spent in the central jail known as Arthur

Road Prison. That was the worst part of my incarceration, because there was only one holding cell for women and we were all crammed in together. I was the only foreign female in the prison and thus quite a novelty. To be fair, my jailers (all male) were not really bad guys. Sometimes they would let me out of my cell to smoke a biddhi in the hall or have some chai with them, and they'd ask me to teach them English. I remember laughing at seeing one of the officers wearing a belt buckle with the insignia "007". Indians were fascinated with James Bond movies, which had found their way to India. Based on movie billboards, they seemed to worship the dashing macho hero, whom many of their male movie stars emulated. So it was no stretch that a simple guard or beat cop would wear such a trinket. (Although their uniforms were standard issue, they provided their own belts and other accessories.)

At other times different guards were in charge, and I wasn't let out of my cell. Then I would witness some poor unfortunate guy being dragged off to the "discipline chamber." Even through a closed door I could hear screams from the floggings and canings. It was pretty hard to sleep those nights, hearing a man being savagely beaten just down the hall. As far as I know, they didn't beat any women. And the warden at this central prison seemed hard and serious, but with me he always smiled. Still, I didn't get any special treatment.

My jail cell had mostly homeless women, beggars and petty thieves, and it got pretty crowded. It was nearly impossible to sleep, and when I did I was robbed of another precious item. Within two weeks I lost my toothbrush, my hairbrush, my towel, even my underwear. Then I was left with literally the clothes on my back, which I slept in, of course.

THE CONVENT PRISON

Luckily, I was eventually moved to a long-term facility. I forget its name, but it was outside the city so the air was a lot cleaner and I could go outdoors. It had tropical forest all around and colorful songbirds in the air. In fact it seemed more like a retreat or a convent than a prison in some ways, as it had gardens and we were allowed to roam outside rather than being always confined to our cells.

My daily life in the new prison included congregating with the Indian women in their perpetual squatting position for the daily delousing. Several women would sit around one woman or a child's head and pick at lice and nits, squeezing the lice with their fingers and destroying the hard nit shells by pressing them between two thumb-nails until they popped. The women were expert and quick at finding the nits and popping them.

After several hours of nitpicking, which I learned to do quite well, we'd move on to other activities. The ladies would gather in the bath-house for their daily bath. Here all hell broke out the first time I en-tered. I was already a sensation because I was the only white woman in the prison, and for some ladies the first white woman they'd been this close to. But more shocking than my pale skin and foreign look was the total lack of shame and modesty I exhibited as I stood stark naked in the bathhouse. At first I didn't understand why the women were chat-tering and pointing at me and giggling. But as my eyes gained focus in the steam, I realized that every single woman had kept her panties on and in some cases even her bloomers. Soon it became apparent to me that in their rather prudish society, women never showed themselves naked even amongst other women, even in the bathhouse!

Despite this modesty they were otherwise comfortable washing one another's bodies or touching another woman's breast. I noticed there were no mirrors in the entire facility. Although this was a prison and one might not expect such a luxury here, I later discovered that no public bathhouse had a mirror. It was an interesting facet of their culture, as in the West any women's washroom, health club, spa or bathhouse would consider a mirror standard equipment.

Yet the women here didn't seem to need a mirror. Possibly they were simply not as vain as Western women, who constantly check themselves in the mirror. Instead, these women became mirrors to one another. I watched as they washed and combed and groomed others' hair, applying scented oils to make it gleaming and fragrant.

They offered me oil for my hair. I inspected the bottle. "Brahmi Amla Hair Oil. Good for the Brain," it boasted. I had seen this slogan on billboards around town. This outrageous claim always made me laugh because I knew the product was little more than coconut oil. I smeared it all over my hair, and found I rather enjoyed the heavy jasmine scent. I also found it strange but oddly logical that the women washed their private parts under their garments, conveniently washing their pant-ies at the same time. They would later, in private, remove the wet garments and put on dry ones.

Another daily ritual was the routine cleaning of the cells. We usually had an inspection by a subordinate, but occasionally by the prison warden himself, Mr. Chouderry. He was a quite a character. A short and slight man with unfortunately crooked teeth and excessive nose hair, he wore his uniform and oversized hat with great pride, marching around the prison as if he was running an army camp. He did not hide his distaste for the 'dirty women' – the slum dwellers, prostitutes and lower castes under his charge. Although he was somewhat intrigued by me, the foreigner, he treated me no differently than the other women.

After inspection we usually had free time and spent afternoons in the gardens. Sometimes a bunch of ladies were set to gather henna leaves, which grew abundantly there. I watched in fascination as they ground the henna leaves on a large flat stone, pounding the leaves with a rock and adding a few drops of water now and then. Soon the green pulp turned brownish-orange, and when it reached a particular color and consistency they began applying the henna to the palms of their hands and the soles of their feet, turning them bright orange. I could not believe that they considered this beautiful, for the contrast of bright orange feet with their dark skin was too abrupt and mostly just emphasized their poor calloused feet, and their cracked, work-worn hands. But it was colorful and they liked it.

Sometimes the women painted beautiful, elaborate designs on the backs of their hands, which took hours since for a tool they used the finest sliver of wood that could be fashioned. It was like the *Mehndi* done for weddings. But in prison the ladies did it for amusement; it was their art. I kept staring at the women's feet. Gosh, they looked rough. I'd never seen feet like that before: toes quite widespread, flat feet, and calloused heels cracked with deep, dirt-filled crevices now stained bright orange. "So this is what comes of a lifetime of walking barefoot," I thought. Most of the inmates were poor, and like most of the poor in India they had never owned a pair of shoes. It humbled me to realize that simply by growing up in Toronto I had worn shoes all my life. I looked at my own pampered feet and saw that they were pretty.

Another thing I noticed was how agile and graceful the Indian women were – these lovely women whom I, in my Western arrogance, had first thought unsophisticated. Their beauty lay in their natural gracefulness: partly genetic, partly a result of a lifestyle that demanded nothing less. From walking tall with heavy loads on their heads almost surpassing their own body weight. From giving birth alone in a field, and then slinging the baby onto their back and going straight to work in the rice paddies. No post-natal pampering here. They had strong legs from so much walking and sitting in the squatting position, the most natural position to humankind. They did not lose their sense of natural posture to the artificial constructions we call furniture.

I also saw great beauty in their physical structure. Most of the women were petite, yet voluptuous, with small waists and large breasts and hips, strong powerful limbs and backs. Considering their natural beauty, grace and charm, I questioned my own background as a Western woman and saw that it was altogether too prissy. Preoccupied with hair, pedicures, makeup, clothes – all the accoutrements of external beauty – I seemed to lack this natural inner beauty. How different I was. It struck me that I really was the oddity.

The women clamored about me daily; I was a big hit with my co-prisoners. We could not speak one another's language, but soon – with a lot of sign language and the aid of Kamla, the happy, fat prostitute with a vocabulary of about 20 English words – I was able to communicate with my fellow inmates. They were curious about me and asked a lot of questions.

"Where is she from?" they demanded of Kamla. "Where are her children? Where is her family?" "She has no children?" So many questions for poor Kamla to translate. It took forever, with sign language and broken English, but we all laughed together. "What is her name?" "How old is she?" "Is she rich?" A shy little woman asked, "Can we touch her hair?" Another wanted to know, "Is she married?" "What is it like in her country?" "How does she like India?" "Why is she in jail?"

THE GIRL FROM MADRAS

After answering these questions I began to learn some of their stories. Some were quite tragic. A sixteen-year-old girl from Madras (now called Chennai), a real beauty (and a mother of two already!) recounted her story as her baby suckled at her breasts. I found it odd, but quite compassionate, that in our long-term facility, children under five years old stayed with their mothers. At five, other family members would take them so they wouldn't spend their whole lives in jail.

This young Madrasi girl had killed her husband. It seemed he was some kind of pervert or just plain cruel; she stalked him one night and stabbed him to death with a kitchen knife, and now was in jail for murder. She said she was happier without him, even though she had to spend her life in jail. She thought that was okay.

I couldn't believe that this girl (younger than me), who looked the picture of goodness and innocence, could cold-bloodedly murder her husband. But I had to consider that marriages in India are arranged by the parents, and women have basically no rights. I asked myself what I would do if I was stuck with a perverted or cruel husband. In India a woman was supposed to accept her lot in life. Divorce was unheard of, escape impossible and an unmarried or separated woman was an "old maid" destined to a life of begging. Her situation was hopeless. I tried to imagine myself like that, but concluded that I could never kill somebody. I'd probably become a beggar.

There were many intriguing stories. Kamla, the prostitute, was in jail because she was caught smuggling gold. Several women were apparently in the gold racket; as with everything else in India, there was a black market for gold. Some of the women were merely homeless and had nowhere else to go as the monsoon season was upon us.

There were quite a few elderly beggar ladies. One was in for smuggling rice! Smuggling *rice*? How could a rice-producing country have a black market for rice? I learned that the best rice, the fragrant basmati, was in short supply and mostly reserved for export. Only a few corrupt officials could afford to eat India's best. Others stole it from loading docks or warehouses and sold it at inflated prices. There were always rich Indians ready to pay for the rare basmati. Besides, eating well was a status symbol.

It seemed that anything could be had on the black market in India. In my first week in Bombay, I quickly learned about the black market for changing money. There were two systems: banks paid seven rupees for a dollar and the black market paid eleven, sometimes twelve. Changing on the black market would almost double my money. Besides, like stealing towels in hotels, almost everybody did it. There was always a demand for American currency in India, and anyone trying to leave needed foreign currency. Believe me, many people wanted to leave.

Still, it was not easy for even a moderately rich Indian to go abroad.

The usual formula consisted of the whole family rallying around one bright, promising son, sending him off to England or America to be educated. Then he would find work and send money home. At the same time he would try to get the necessary papers to bring over his entire family. I could see that life worked on a whole different level in India. It seemed that bribery, corruption and crime was an accepted way of life, and people learned to work with it.

Monsoon rains drench a typical urban building in India.

THE PRISON WARDEN

The second week of my incarceration in the new prison facility found me sweeping out my cell in preparation for the weekly inspection by Mr. Chouderry, the prison warden. A former military man, he came in his usual khaki uniform (decorated of course), and even wore white gloves. I found his demeanor quite comical, with his oversized hat and massively inflated ego. He always carried a handy weapon, a brass-tipped wooden baton hanging on a chain at his wrist called a *lathi* – which he didn't hesitate to use. He had no qualms about beating someone who stepped out of line.

He was full of himself and liked to terrorize people with every gesture, but I realized that without his hat and impressive uniform he would be greatly diminished. Underneath it all, I could see an ordinary, simple Indian man who looked more like a peasant than an aristocrat. But he was tough and powerful and ran the prison like a military camp, in a no-nonsense, disciplined manner, marching with an entourage of sycophants desperately trying to anticipate his whims. Everyone seemed in morbid fear of him – but I was not. I saw a relatively insignificant man who, deep in his consciousness, felt inferior. Though he wore the uniform and spoke the clipped English of the British, he simultaneously despised and admired the colonizers.

The first time he came to inspect my cell, he freaked out. He gave me absolute hell and a long lecture in rapid-fire English, shouting until the veins in his neck fairly popped. His screaming terrified everyone around him. "What is the meaning of this?" he demanded. All I had done was turn my sleeping mat perpendicular to the wall (a decorative touch), but he insisted that I put it back in its former position alongside the wall. Gesticulating with his arms he asked, "why do you disturb the order of your room? Do you think you are somebody *special* just because you are not Indian? Why must you foreigners always be so contrary?" Then he stood stiffly, removing and re-inserting his baton under his right arm and tapping his foot impatiently as he waited for me to obey.

Everyone looked on in apprehension. Humiliated, I moved slowly, begrudgingly obeying him – until I couldn't stand it any more. I stood up angrily, hands on my hips, and defiantly shouted as loudly as I could. "Sir: I put my mat this way to keep the rats away from me, if you really want to know. I woke up to find a bloody rat nibbling at my hair.

I screamed and no one came. This place is full of cockroaches and the food in here is absolutely disgusting. I'm sick every day." Obviously not used to having people challenge him, he seemed a little stunned by my sudden outburst and did not react for some moments, though his eyes grew wider and wider.

I continued. "I can't sleep for the fleas in my mat and the toilet is backed up. I need medical attention – do you hear me? I think I'm pregnant!" A few of his entourage gasped. Then I started to cry. Without answering me, he turned his back and left. I had no idea if he was going to acknowledge my request or simply ignore me and let me rot in prison. But later I was politely advised that a doctor made the rounds on the first of every month and he would see me here next Monday.

I went back to performing my daily ritual of writing lies to my parents. I was pretty fortunate to have magazines and books in English. I read an article with detailed pictures about some ancient caves in Bombay. It looked amazing, so I decided to "visit the caves" and began to write of my false adventures to my parents and friends. Also, dreaming about actually being a tourist and seeing some of India kept me distracted for a while. I wrote my folks and friends about what a great time I was having, how much I was learning and how I missed everyone back home and loved them, and so on. I put down the postcard and chewed on my pen, gazing out at the gloomy monsoon rain. I rolled up my clothes to make a pillow and began to read.

In prison I read voraciously, even things I didn't understand or had no interest in, such as Indian cricket matches and movie reviews. I read everything I could get my hands on that was in English, and often read out of sheer boredom. I had a glossy English-language magazine with pictures, like an Indian version of *LIFE* magazine. In no time I was introduced to Indian culture, its literature and arts, poets and scholars. I read of the turbulent Indian politics, and the continued tension and recent war with Pakistan and its devastating creation of homeless refugees. I learned about India's fabulous film industry (before it became known as Bollywood) and knew the faces of the hottest actors: Dilip Kumar, Rajesh Hamal and Shashi Kapoor. I read accounts of crooks in Bombay who'd set up a network of 200 kidnapped orphaned children to beg in the streets and pulled in 50,000 rupees a month.

I read to keep my mind off the aching cramps in my belly. I read to keep my mind off the lice. I read to remind myself that I was still functioning, because when I didn't read all I could do was cry. I cried and cried until I thought I had no more tears. Then I would sleep a while, awake and start reading again. There wasn't much else to do. I read excerpts from Rabindranath Tagore's poetry and Mohandas Gandhi's teachings, and the teachings of Krishnamurti and books of philosophy. Tired of culture, I turned to the spiritual teachings of Bhagwan Shree Rajneesh, Paramahansa Yogananda, and Baba Ram Dass. These spiritual books were a special delight, not just because of the stimulation but because they became my companions and represented great human kindness.

Unknown baba.

Kindness also came in the form of two lovely Rajneesh devotees, Tony and Rene, hippies from western Canada whom I had met at Anjuna Beach in Goa. When they came to Bombay and learned of my misfortune, they took pity. They visited me in jail nearly every day and brought most of the books and magazines I had – with thoughtful, cleverly hidden gifts inside: money, incense, a peacock feather, and often little encouraging notes. They were truly a godsend. I was eternally grateful to this couple, since I hardly knew them, felt awkward in their kindness and didn't quite know how to show appreciation.

I remember the first time I got a note. "To a beautiful and brave lady, the cosmic reincarnation of Durga: Your courage inspires us." I thought it was a mistake and meant for someone else (Durga was a Hindu goddess), and tried to give it back to Rene; it hadn't occurred to me that the note was meant for me.

One book that really impressed me was *Autobiography of a Yogi* by Paramahansa Yogananda. I read about the life of yogis, the austerities that many yogis endured and their amazing feats. They could levitate, go for months without eating, stop their heartbeat, and practically defy death! Naturally I was curious. There was a story about a naked yogi who refused to clothe himself despite outrage in his village, so he was put in jail. In spite of a sturdy cell and a 24-hour watch, he escaped every night and was found in the morning sitting totally naked in the lotus position meditating on the rooftop. He did not try to get away; he merely wanted to demonstrate that all physical barriers and restrictions were an illusion. They could never keep him locked up; like Houdini he always escaped. What a trick!

A thought struck me: are all physical barriers an illusion? I remembered trying astral traveling back in Toronto. If I could get out of my body with astral travel, then could I also become invisible, dematerialize? Escape? So I set to learning the yogi trick. I fasted till my tongue turned pink, did yoga breathing for half an hour each day, said the Lord's Prayer for good measure, and stood on my head. I was pretty good at headstands and could do it for a while. I tried hard to focus my mind's eye on the image of freedom. But each time I opened my eyes I was only standing on my head in jail.

Still I read on, slowly absorbing new and unfamiliar concepts, and soon enough I got their meaning. It occurred to me that maybe something beyond my control was directing my destiny. Fate or the universe or God had brought me to India ... but why? Just to have me land in jail? To have me sit here a victim of circumstance and in the dark about my future? The pressing question that was always on my mind was, "Will I ever get out?" At times I thought I'd have to spend the rest of my life in this jail. I'd wail and cry in my misery, like a child without a mother. It was painful.

Again I decided to try the yogi trick, closing my eyes and concentrating hard on visualizing myself on the roof of the jailhouse. But it didn't work. I tried and tried for hours each day for several days, but each time my physical body refused to move. It was hopeless; I didn't have the mind-power to do such tricks.

I began to sense that I needed a teacher, maybe a guru. I'd heard many fellow travelers talk about how their guru had "called them to India," and everybody seemed to have a guru these days. I'd heard people say they were Sai Baba or Neem Karoli Baba devotees, or Mahara-ji premies. Or, like Tony and Rene, those who called themselves Neo-Sannyasins, the saffron-robed devotees of Bhagwan Shree Rajneesh. Tony and Rene often talked of how much the guru had taught them about love and compassion. They certainly demonstrated compassion to me.

Yep, I decided I probably needed a guru. But how should I pick one? The gurus I knew of had pretty much the same philosophy. Certain ones were known for special characteristics, but in the end I figured they were all the same. I always liked the fatherly-looking ones with great locks of long gray hair and beards that, to silly me, symbolized wisdom. I imagined that a guru like a wise father would stroke his beard, gaze into my eyes and give me right guidance and good counsel. Of course I was foolishly only looking at their physical characteristics. But I realized that there were many false gurus among them. India seemed to have an ascetic on every corner: fortune-tellers and visionaries as well as some authentic teachers. The skinny, bald-headed guys standing on one leg for six months were a little too strange for me.

I later discovered that there are many different kinds of yogis, and different kinds of yoga too. As I became more familiar with the names and talents of at least a dozen popular gurus in India, I faced the tough decision of picking the right one.

Then it occurred to me that maybe it was not up to me to choose a guru, but up to the guru to choose me. In fact, maybe I already had a guru who hadn't revealed himself yet. This thought gave me some comfort, and I began to read the writings of Rajneesh, Meher Baba and Papa Ram Dass (an older Hindu man unrelated to Baba Ram Dass), Sri Ramakrishna, Sri Aurobindo and many other teachers. My bible was the seminal *Be Here Now* by Baba Ram Dass, the former Harvard professor known as Richard Alpert. These teachers talked about death as rebirth, about former lives and karma. They talked about overcoming ego, about good moral behavior, about right thinking and about the alchemy of spirit.

Baba Ram Dass, author of
Be Here Now.

I felt I kind of knew what they were talking about. In fact I felt I was going through a serious kind of personal alchemy – a transformation of spirit – right now, in jail. Imprisoned, trapped and disempowered, I felt challenged to confront all my ideas of who I was, and to reconsider all my constructs of reality, which I'd never questioned before. Now the safety of my familiar home, mom and dad were gone. I was far away from my friends in Scarborough, and missed them terribly. I was all alone and in a prison halfway across the world, wasting away.

And I was sick. On top of that, I hadn't had my period in two months and was sure that I was pregnant. Worse, I didn't even know if it was by Donny or Richard. Feeling abandoned, frightened and alone, I spent many hours of the day just crying my heart out. Sometimes I cried so much I had no tears left. I could also read no more, as my eyes were sore, red and swollen.

Sometimes I lay for hours staring at the ceiling, watching an insect and trying to block out the irritation of commercial Indian music on a scratchy and tinny radio. I don't know why that music irritated me so ... it seemed like the women sang in a kind of Minnie Mouse cartoon voice, and these overly orchestrated popular songs attacked me in staccato, wearing on my nerves. So I learned to block out certain things.

I also prayed a lot, earnestly and sincerely, begging God to get me out of this and promising to be good ever after. This went on for weeks and God didn't answer; my hopes were shattered. I was reduced to a pitiful, weeping, lost child, and despised myself even more. I was angry with myself and kept saying, "I'm so stupid. How could I get myself into this mess?" On and on with self-blame and torment, the questions and non-answers and all the uncertainties that had left me shattered. Really broken.

But miraculously, out of the broken shell something new began to emerge. I was barely aware of it, but the test of endurance I was undergoing proved to be a vital and necessary step for my survival in general. And necessary for my spiritual evolution as well. I didn't understand this then, but discovered it much later. Meanwhile, things were going to get worse.

THE SLOW WHEELS OF JUSTICE

Many Indians told me proudly that India followed the British justice system and that my rights were the same as in Canada. But I found their justice system painfully slow. Our case came up for a preliminary hearing after two weeks, but the judge was too busy to look at it and dismissed us. This was frustrating because we didn't even know what charges we were facing. Every two weeks we'd go to court, and then I would see Paul and Donny. It was a relief to talk with someone who spoke English. But these visits were brief and gave me small comfort because little was accomplished in court and the obvious camaraderie and private conversations between Donny and Paul made me feel left out and envious. They had each other for companionship, which made my loneliness all the more bleak.

After the second court appearance, when the charges were finally laid, Donny and Paul managed to get a lawyer, Mr. Prakash. He said our case didn't look good and was non-committal concerning the big question: "When the fuck do we get out of jail!" At this point I feared I was going to die in jail.

Lately I hadn't slept at all and was rapidly losing weight. My dysentery was so bad that some nights I lay in my bed moaning and groaning, doubled over in pain, rolling over and clutching my poor cramped belly. I had never known such acute pain and discomfort. If you've ever had a serious attack of dysentery or a gall bladder attack, you probably know what I mean. It comes out all water. I must have been dehydrated as well, because I never drank the tap water and bottled water wasn't available in those days. So I virtually lived on Coca-Cola and Fresca, which I could buy with the money Tony and Rene gave me. But I got sicker and sicker. Worse, nobody came when I screamed. I was rolling in pain on the floor, begging for relief, screaming for help. But nobody came; nobody cared. God, where are you now? Could things possibly be worse?

The next Monday the doctor did come. I begged him to give me something for the terrible cramps, and he said I had chronic dysentery and prescribed something. Then I told him I thought I was pregnant. He ordered someone to bring some medicine, gave me a bitter concoction to drink and told me not to worry, that I would have my period in three days. I asked, "What if my period doesn't come in three days?" He answered, quite matter-of-factly, "Then you are definitely pregnant!"

This was not what I wanted to hear. He asked if I'd had a cholera shot, and I answered yes. He then dismissed me and went about giving the inmates vaccinations, causing the young children to scream at the stinging needles.

Three days went by and I did not get my period. I woke up the fourth day devastated, certain that I was pregnant. Something in my good Toronto upbringing convinced me that being pregnant was worse than the other curse: being in jail. "But why compare? I am both pregnant and in jail." I began to weep and weep in despair. I had never felt so lost and confused and forgotten. Soon I was crying convulsively and wailing. No one came. I now demanded of God: "Can't You hear me? Why won't You help me?"

My chronic dysentery brought me running to the toilet frequently, and there I squatted once again, clutching my belly and continuing to sob. I felt so sick and forlorn that all I wanted was to die. I remembered Jesus' words on the cross – "Why hast Thou forsaken me?" – and spoke them out loud with great passion. I said them again and again, practically screaming at God while squatting on the Indian toilet. I didn't care any more if anyone heard me. I cried out several times. "Why? Why? Why, Lord, hast Thou forsaken me? What did I do to deserve this? O Lord, please don't abandon me. Please, please help me."

When I finished emptying my bowels and began to pour the bucket of water to flush, I saw a bright red stain gleaming on the porcelain. I was stunned. Could it be true? Yes! I was menstruating! Hallelujah, there is a God after all!

Ecstatically happy that day, I wanted to celebrate so I shared some of my precious cigarettes with Kamla the prostitute. In return Kamla shared her dinner of curried brains, which a thoughtful friend had brought to the jail. The Indian prison system allows family members to bring home-cooked food to the inmates. Many inmates had someone bring their food, and as far as I know the food was never inspected. Kamla had a friend who brought her lovely meals made by his mother. It always amazed me that the "lunch wallah" knew which *tiffin* (lunch) tins belonged to which family, because they all looked exactly alike. They were aluminum dishes with tops that stacked atop one another in graduating sizes. One contained rice, another curry, another chapatis.

That day Kamla offered me some of her lunch. When I discovered through sign language that we were eating brains, I was repulsed.

I simply was not used to eating organ meats. Still it was real food and it sure smelled good. And I was perpetually hungry. I ate some, and it was truly delicious. Kamla laughed and laughed. I don't know how she could be such a happy person considering her tragic life. But I really enjoyed her company. We became best friends in jail. By virtue of her smattering of English and her hefty build, Kamla became my official interpreter and protector. She was motherly and generous with hugs.

KAMLA THE PROSTITUTE

Kamla's story was quite interesting. Although she'd worked in Bombay brothels most of her life, Kamla told me she came from the state of Gujarat, a beautiful place about 200 miles north of Bombay. When she spoke of her home village, her eyes were misty and she smiled, showing several gold teeth. She told me that as a child of 10, she and her older brother, Patil, were brought to Bombay with several other children to work in textile mills. This was common in those days, for many families had too many children to feed and enormous debts. They often sent their children to work in the large industrial centers, hoping one day to reunite after their children's labors had paid off their debts. But this rarely happened, for the owner of these child laborers kept them perpetually in debt.

After her brother, already in poor health, died a couple of years later due to the unhealthy working conditions, Kamla was kept as a slave worker to help pay for her brother's funeral. The employer was a cruel man who never paid his child employees or gave them a day off. When Kamla reached puberty the man began to molest her. She ran away and soon became a captive prostitute in the famous Bombay Cages, where enslaved girls were displayed like animals in a zoo. Unknown to most tourists, this was no gimmick. These girls actually were confined to and pretty much lived in these cages, let out only to consort with their clients and for bathing.

Luckily, Kamla found a sympathetic client; an Indian businessman of some note who purchased her freedom. She spoke of him with the greatest reverence as "Uncle," and considered him the kindest man in the world. He gave her freedom and the status of working for herself. He gave her an apartment and brought her wealthy clients. He took only a small cut and gave her extravagant presents. Several years of the good life took their toll, however, and Kamla gained considerable weight until she no longer possessed her once stunning figure. She still had a few faithful clients, but Uncle died and she was forced to supplement her income by smuggling gold. She was only thirty-five, but looked a lot older.

I was deeply touched by Kamla's story, although I found it hard to digest. I thought child labor had been abolished in the previous century. I later learned that although this was so in Europe and the America, in India in the 1970s indentured servitude and child labor were still widely practiced. Though many parents were told their offspring were being "borrowed" to pay off their debt, they intuitively expected to never again see their children. The cost of keeping such a servant was greater than what he/she earned, hence a continuous loop of increasing debt. What a horrible thing for a parent to face: with too many mouths to feed, you have to sell a child. Which one do you pick? Why?

I considered myself lucky to have had any kind of a childhood. What I formerly thought of as a somewhat underprivileged early life suddenly seemed pampered. This observation brightened me up for some minutes, but then I realized that my past was no comfort now. Kamla claimed she had psychic powers, so I asked her the obvious question: "Do you think there is some chance that soon I can leave? Go out from jail?" Kamla thought long and hard before answering. She seemed to be processing my request. Then she pulled on her earlobes, rolled her eyes upward and said, "Bhagwan, Bhagwan!" God only knows. I was clearly disappointed. Seeing my forlorn face she offered, "Maybe with baksheesh?"

Yes! Of course – maybe with baksheesh (money, a bribe). Why hadn't I thought of this? Suddenly I had hope again – maybe I could buy my way out. How much would it cost? I did have a stash of money, though it was "undeclared" and obviously derived from crime. How could I access my money now that the police had confiscated it? Did they have the right to keep it, or was there some way to get it back? It was *my* money and they couldn't really prove where it came from. I would ask my lawyer.

Kamla left me alone with my thoughts. Surely there had to be a way to buy my way out of jail; this country positively thrived on bribery. But how would I negotiate my way through the complex hierarchy of bribing? How many people would I have to bribe? Did I have enough money?

It was pouring rain again, the incessant monsoon rain that continued day and night for weeks on end. I was getting tired of the rain. Soon I began to write, "I remember a time when the sun did shine, my life was mine, and all was fine." It was a pathetic attempt at Zen poetry. But I was feeling thoughtful and melancholic, for I had just smoked a big fat joint. I had managed to purchase some hash from a sympathetic guard with the money that my compassionate Canadian friends slipped to me in their gifts. I spent all my money ... hadn't even thought of saving it to be able to bribe my way out of jail. How dumb! Of course, that's why my friends put it there in the first place. Now I mentally scolded myself. How stupid, how dumb. The gift money was nearly gone, so I had to figure out a way to get back the money that the police had confiscated.

Unknown to me at the time, my very being was transforming, and metamorphosis always implies a shedding or letting go of one form to shape into another. It was painful, yet there wasn't a darn thing I could do about it. As a result of having lost control over practically every aspect of my life and being reduced to nothing, I began to surrender. They say surrender is sweet. But I did not want to surrender. Certainly not to being in jail forever. No! I would not surrender. But I could surrender in spirit and trust that God had better plans for me. I vacillated between surrender and rebellion.

And so the battle continued. You can't imagine the hellish internal conflict. At one point it seemed that every aspect of my self-definition was shattered, my whole take on reality completely vague. I no longer knew who I was. In fact I even had a new name. The women in jail couldn't get used to my foreign name of only one syllable and renamed me Gita, which is Sanskrit for "song." They'd heard me softly singing once and often asked me to sing Elvis Presley. Elvis Presley? He was the only foreign singer they knew. What did I know of Elvis? I was a hippie girl who sang folk songs of Judy Collins and Leonard Cohen.

But I no longer sang. I no longer felt I was that innocent girl. In fact, I no longer associated with my past. Life in the suburbs of Scarborough seemed so far away, an illusion. Here I had to deal with my present self, a sorry girl indeed. I wanted and needed my mother. But mom was far away in Canada completely unaware of my dilemma, and the closest friend I had was Kamla. Kamla was a great comfort but she was scheduled for release soon, and the anticipated loss of her depressed me even more.

Sometimes it took all my willpower to force myself to keep going. Rather than wallow in sadness, I read. I read about several female saints: Mother Krishnabai, Mirabai the Sufi saint, Sarada Devi and Shri Aurobindo's devotee, known simply as "The Mother". I learned through reading that the Hindu religion really honors the mother. The archetypal mother is embodied in many forms and images, but her ultimate quality is compassion. I found that so cool. I thought that if I prayed to the Mother-God-Being I might be able to invoke some sympathy and help my cause. So I prayed again ... with all my heart, for hours. "O Great Mother of compassion, if I have ever done anything good in my life at all, anything to please you, then please help me now. Mother, Mother, help me get out of here."

Read and pray. Meditate. Read and pray. Walk in the garden. Eat, sleep, read and pray. In a way, this time in jail was like a retreat.

COURTESY OF EDWARD FANABERIA

I was sequestered in the company of only women, and in fairly comfortable though sparse living quarters. The gardens were marvelous, though; the birds were a godsend whose songs and chatter reminded me of a paradise I never knew. Could this be what it was like in the original garden? The Garden of Eden? I picked up another book and began to read: the *Kama Sutra*, the yoga of sensual love. I was introduced to the idea of Shakti as the embodiment of the divine feminine,

The Mother and Sree Aurobindo in the 1970s.

and the Hindu goddess Saraswati equivalent to the voluptuous Roman goddess Venus. Then I learned about Kali, the ferocious black goddess who ate live raw men, and had no Western equivalent.

It was rather confusing. I thought the Hindus had a strange approach to sex. In these modern times they were prudish and sexually repressed in many ways (no kissing or public expression of intimacy), yet their ancient temples depicted massive orgies of explicit sexuality in a variety of impossible positions. Many gurus taught strict abstinence from sex; the path of Yoga in general taught austerities and self-restraint. Yet Bhagwan Shree Rajneesh and some other gurus promoted *Tantric* sex, saying it was a way to "awaken the *kundalini*, the sensual energy that can carry you to the spiritual realm." That made a lot of sense. I remembered my crazy afternoon with Richard and Tom, when I had definitely experienced something high, something beyond sex. But I had thought that was a love connection and the sex just a vehicle.

I drifted back to that experience and remembered fondly how cool these guys were. I wondered where they were now, and why they hadn't come to my rescue. Surely they must have heard that I was in jail. Word got around fast in Bombay's ex-pat community; it was a small community and everybody knew everybody. The last I'd heard from Tony and Rene was that Richard was in Kabul. I didn't know what happened to Tom. Anyway, it was Richard that I thought of most. "If only I could be with you now, my beautiful Richard," I lamented. Then I scolded myself that "everything would have been fine and I'd be in your arms right now if only I hadn't trusted Junkie James."

Already two months had gone by. Two months of incarceration and it seemed like forever. Kamla left and I had no one else to talk to. Although I had picked up some Hindi words and sign language and managed to make some new friends in jail, there were still too many lonely hours when I cried myself to exhaustion. If anybody heard me, nobody cared. I carried on with the boring routine of nitpicking, making henna, cleaning my cell, and of course reading for hours on end.

The rat no longer came to visit me at night; I supposed it had found better food elsewhere. My dysentery had just about cleared up. Things were looking up. A telegram from Mr. Prakash, my lawyer, said he thought he might be able to arrange something. But while I had desperately clung to hope for two months already, progress was interminably slow and I was being worn down. God, how long would it take?

Somewhere nearby a radio played pop songs from the latest films. How could I block out the noise? I couldn't bear to think of where I was, so I threw myself into reading everything in English I could get my hands on. Luckily my books and magazines were never stolen, as they were of no particular interest to my mostly illiterate cellmates and no one could read English anyway.

Earlier I had picked up a square book, *Be Here Now*, that my friends Tony and Rene had left. I flipped through it out of boredom without intending to read, but certain passages immediately captivated me. Suddenly I was totally engrossed. With only a high school education, I had not yet been introduced to higher subjects like philosophy and metaphysics. Some of the vocabulary was a bit sophisticated for me, but I was able to get the basic message and was becoming familiar with esoteric terms. The guru featured in this book was a lovely-looking, bald and fat little man whose eyes radiated childlike innocence and laughter. His only possession in life was his blanket, but in the photos he always looked joyful. His devotees, both Indian and Western (including Ram Dass, the author of the book), believed he was a saint and considered it an honor just to be in his presence. Little did I realize I would later meet this wonderful master, Neem Karoli Baba, and obtain his blessings before he died.

I also did a lot of thinking in jail. Too much thinking, maybe. As a child I wasn't allowed to think much. Not really. I was taught that kids are not entitled to an opinion, and must obey adults without question. Probably for the first time in my life – perversely, only because I was in jail – I now had the freedom to think. Through my reading and meditations I began to realize that all the physical world we live in is just an illusion, including even me – my personhood, my body, my mind, my personality. This was an intriguing discovery.

Soon I was reflecting on the deeper side of life. It occurred to me that an inherent part of the human condition might just be that all human beings are merely specks in God's great universe, and that the only significant thing to do in life is to reconnect with the soul's higher purpose and eventually go back to our source and to become one with God. I guess this was the beginning of my lifelong yoga training.

MY YOGA TRAINING

I began to realize that no matter what the external circumstances, with the right mindset one could still attain some inner peace. It didn't really matter if I was sitting in jail or in a palace. I began to adopt a detached outlook on life, and managed to develop an inner peace or at least a kind of surrender. I figured that God had helped me with my near-pregnancy, and surely He would come through for me again. I figured that God was probably testing me, and that I would actually get through this too. Deep down I had a firm faith.

I found a way to calm myself to some extent with meditation, and managed to find trust that allowed me some inner peace. But this state lasted only so long. Then I'd see a giant cockroach landing on my dress and freak out again. Usually I was fine for an hour or two after meditation, but slowly the demon of doubtful thoughts took over and I was a mess all over again. I couldn't believe I could cry that many tears ... it seemed as if I'd cried buckets and buckets – no, oceans – of tears.

I discovered other interesting survival techniques in jail. For instance, how to bathe using buckets of water and squatting Indian-style, and how to dry myself without a towel. (I'd shimmy like a dog and use the flat end of my palm as a squeegee to whip the water off my body. Of course in a warm climate I dried quickly anyway.) I also learned how to brush my hair with only my fingers, spreading them stiffly like a pick. And how to brush my teeth without a toothbrush. The Indian ladies had this black powder that you would put in the palm of your hand and dampen. Then with your pointer finger you would smudge the paste onto your teeth and rub vigorously and then rinse. It really worked well and I found for the rest of my time in India that this was the only way I could brush my teeth as they had no such things as a toothbrush.

As I adapted to the simpler Indian ways, I soon became a beloved member of this community of imprisoned women. They showed me some dances they would do for festivals like Ganesh Chaturthi. They also taught me songs in Hindi, and I picked up the language quickly. I finally let the ladies henna my hair and then my fingernails – instead of staining my entire palms red, which I found unattractive. My hair looked great with a reddish sheen, but getting my fingernails done was a mistake. My fingernails were stained orange for six months after that, and if you didn't know it was henna they looked like the tobacco-stained nails of a heavy smoker. I just hated it, but had to wait for the nails to grow out.

Every day I got warm milk for breakfast. I hated warm milk, but dared not complain, so I gave it to the mothers with babies. They all took turns and never fought over it. Pretty soon I was accepted as one of the clan, and I no longer felt like such an oddity. Although I enjoyed my status with these women, I longed to speak English with someone. I missed Kamla very much, and of course it seemed unfair that Donny and Paul had each other while I had nobody.

I thought back to the time when I was at Arthur Road Prison and my kind Canadian friends, Tony and Rene, came to visit twice or three times a week. They were so sweet and concerned about me. They brought me healthy carrot juice, mango lassis, samosas, incense, some sweets and always books. Lots and lots of books. Mostly spiritual books with little gifts inside: a peacock feather, incense and always cash. Oh how nice it was to look forward to their visits.

But after I was transferred to the new prison without warning they just stopped coming. I was so disappointed. I figured they were probably drawing heat by visiting me often and may have become "persons of interest" to the police. Most likely they had to leave town. In any case I never forgot them and their consistent kindness, and promised myself that one day I would find and repay them. Without them I wouldn't have had books to pass the time with, or the healthy food they brought, or the nice messages and cigarettes. If not for them, I'd probably have gone crazy. I'd been pretty lucky so far.

THE LION GODDESS

After several weeks at the new facility a new woman was brought in. She was young, probably about eighteen years old, and astonishingly beautiful. This woman had the form of a goddess, but the character of a raging lioness. I don't know what her crime was, but she was hysterical and they dragged her in kicking and screaming. They locked her in a single cell just across from mine and I could see her pacing and panting and panicking. She was positively wild. She didn't stop screaming and cursing and ranting and raving. She threw her head about so that her beautiful tresses were like the wild mane of a lion. I could see that she was not much older than me, but certainly deranged.

I had never before seen such a beautiful creature, nor one so savage. I was entranced and found myself staring at her, wanting to reach out and comfort her. But what could I do? I could only watch in fascination and speculate about her. Was she a prostitute? I kept looking at the girl's voluptuous figure, which could not be tamed even with her modest saree. She was very light-skinned with massive black hair that was unkempt and out of character for Indian women, who nearly always coiffed their hair. I liked this rebellious aspect of her right away.

The girl looked like she just didn't care. Her saree was torn and half coming off, her hair a tangled mess, and she was dirty and probably a little bruised from having tussled with her captors ... but still she was radiantly beautiful. I wondered at my own reaction. I felt aroused just looking at this beauty. It was almost sexual. Oh my God ... it was sexual! I realized with horror how fascinated I was, and asked myself, "Am I becoming a lesbian?"

This thought disturbed me greatly, for a part of me was still conditioned by my very proper upbringing in 1960s Toronto, where lesbians were considered a perversion, an unnatural and unhealthy deviation from the norm. But wow, this girl was hot, and suddenly I didn't know any more. All I could think of was how turned on I was, and if a woman like me could get this turned on looking at this girl, how much more would a man? I tried calling out to her, but the lioness/goddess was so preoccupied with her own hysteria she didn't even notice me. The next day she was gone, and I never did find out who she was or what happened to her.

BACK TO COURT

Finally I was going to court again. This would be my fifth appearance in ten weeks and I hoped desperately for progress. Longing for some familiar faces and the chance to talk to someone, I even got excited at the prospect of seeing Donny and Paul. And I had to see if I was still attracted to men; my latent lesbianism was getting to me. Of course I hadn't had sex for quite a while but, oddly, I didn't really miss it. I just wanted company.

To go to court it was important to be polite, clean and properly groomed. The women fussed over my appearance, blackening my eyes with Khol and braiding my hair. One woman (miraculously) produced a comb. I was groomed Indian-fashion and wrapped in a saree lent by a kind inmate, and went off to court with everyone wishing me luck. I met Donny and Paul in the main building and gave them each a hug, but when I embraced Paul I think I lingered a little longer. I enjoyed feeling my body against his and feeling his heart beat faster for the excitement. Even though he was a bit thinner, I still found him attractive and thought that one day we might become lovers.

We huddled in the van with the other inmates. I was the only woman, and all the men ogled me. I hated this and felt uncomfortable, so I began chatting with Paul and Donny. Then Paul said nonchalantly, "Have you ever noticed how the really stupid Indians even look stupid?" I was stunned. "What's that supposed to mean?"

He said, "Look at the shape of their skulls. You can always tell a stupid Indian by the shape of his head." He pointed to several men around him, grinning and implying that these men were obviously stupid because of their features or the shape of their head. I hated this racist talk. Donny agreed with Paul, and the two of them continued to make similar disparaging remarks and stupid jokes about Indians – right in front of the Indian prisoners. Now I was furious and ashamed of being in their company. What if one of these supposedly "stupid" Indians could understand English? In any case, they probably understood the intent ... they weren't as stupid as my friends imagined. Suddenly I really didn't like Paul any more. And Donny, well, Donny I already hated. But I was stuck with these two jerks. They were the only company I had, and circumstances had tied my fate to theirs.

Nothing was accomplished in court that day, so I faced at least another two weeks of jail. These weeks passed uneventfully, and on my next court appearance things started to look more promising. Our lawyer said that if we would plead guilty to all the charges he was sure he could get us off with just a fine, though probably quite a stiff fine. We were ecstatic. A fine? Who cares how much it cost? As smugglers, we had so much more money than they could even imagine.

We pled guilty and the judge was stern. Oh, he gave us such a lecture. He made a point of telling us that India is not a lawless society. People cannot just come here and profit from criminal activities. He assured us that India followed the same British justice system as Canada: laws are laws and the punishments are the same. He reminded us of what a grave offense we had committed, and said he hoped our time already served had given us pause to think and perhaps to redeem ourselves. He went on at length about the great achievements of Indian society, the wonderful justice system that aims to be fair to all. Looking hard at Donny and Paul, he reminded us that smuggling contraband goods was, regrettably, a serious affair. (This would mean a substantial bribe.) He said he would accept our guilty plea, think things over and pronounce judgment at our next appearance.

Next appearance? What, another two weeks? God, why can't he decide today? Why does everything have to take so fucking long here? Okay, okay, India has a great justice system ... it just moves at a snail's pace. I spent the next two weeks in anguish and uncertainty. What would be our punishment? Might we really get off with a just a fine? At least now there was a little hope, and I clung tenaciously to the faint hope that soon I might be free.

Donny and Paul were frantic, yelling at our lawyer, Mr. Prakash, to find out what was going on. I too was devastated and mad with anxiety. But there was nothing we could do. The wheels of justice sometimes grind to a halt and you're stuck.

Two weeks later the big day came, and the judge reiterated our crimes, accepted our guilt and handed down our fines; it was over in minutes. He fined Donny and Paul each 5,000 rupees (about $500 US) for "masterminding the scheme," and me only 2,000 rupees ($200) as an accomplice. The judge felt that I was more or less an innocent girl who had been duped by my two friends. Payment of the fines would be arranged with our lawyer and then, astoundingly, after three months of jail we would be free at last! It was almost too good to be true.

Bombay police hat like the prison warden's.

The next day I found myself waiting in Mr. Chouderry's office as he arranged for my personal effects and got a taxi for me. I was glad to see that there were still a few hundred rupees amongst my things. Due to the terrible heat and the fact that the electricity was out again, it was like a steam bath. Typically, the office had only a fan, as air conditioning was practically unheard of in those days, but now the fan was still. So Mr. Chouderry took off his hat. I'd never seen him without his impressive hat, and was struck by how diminished he appeared without it. He continued his paperwork ignoring me.

Then he was called out of the office just as a taxi arrived for me, and I saw an opportunity to steal his hat. Which I did. Don't ask me why or how I had the nerve to do something so stupid just as I was being released from jail, but I really wanted his hat as a trophy, and in minutes I would be whisked away into the unknown masses of Bombay. It delighted me to no end to think of his confusion and puzzlement when he discovered his hat was gone. I kept the hat for months, and eventually left it with some other belongings at New Delhi's YMCA. For all I know it might still be there.

CHAPTER 8

Freedom

AS IT HAPPENED, THE DAY I GOT OUT OF JAIL – August 15, 1972 – was Independence Day, the twenty-fifth anniversary of India's independence from British colonial rule. After three months of jail, I was free and India was celebrating its freedom. There was noise and music, as people danced and paraded in the street joyously, ecstatically. The monsoon was long over and summer was in the air. The air was fragrant with tropical flowers like plumeria, lilies, jasmine and frangipani, and the breath of renewal, hope and freedom. I wondered if it was a coincidence that the whole country was celebrating with me, or was divine intervention at play? Was God trying to tell me something, or just playing tricks on me? O Lord, you have such a sense of humor sometimes.

As I went into the street in search of food, I was swept up in a sea of bodies, dancing and shouting and making such a ruckus I felt like I was hallucinating. I'd never seen such an enormous crowd of people. There was so much happiness all around me, and so much activity and music and noise, indeed it was a bit overwhelming. And although I was a part of it, I still felt strangely removed from it all. Maybe I was still in shock at being free.

It felt really good to be finally free. Then I thought, "What *is* freedom?" I realized, disappointed, that even with my freedom I was still alone. While thrust about in the sea of ecstatic dancing bodies in this city of millions, I knew I did not belong here. I danced a little, for my own joy. I should have been celebrating with some of my people, but where were they? Clearly, I was still imprisoned in my loneliness. No one to talk to, no one to share my joy with. I thought, "Why am I still so lonely?" and started to cry. Oh God, how lonely I felt for my people, my spiritual family, my tribe … whoever and wherever they were.

Donny and Paul had quickly dismissed me. Almost as soon as we got out of jail and booked hotels, they said they wanted to take showers and go out. In particular they wanted to get some hookers and head off to the opium dens. I was supposed to understand this "guy thing" and that they couldn't invite me along. So once again I felt abandoned. Even though they were such jerks, I still wished they were with me. It was so unfair that they had had each other throughout the three months of jail while I was alone, and now, on our first night out, they didn't even invite me along to eat.

Depressed as hell, I felt like getting high and wanted some hash, but was too scared to go downtown alone. So I went over to Baghdaddy's Cafe, which was in the neighborhood. A lot hippies hung out there because of its good, home-cooked and cheap food. The owner, a Persian and a progressive, did not despise the hippies as many upper-class Indians did. If people were hungry and had no money, he fed them anyway. He did have one rule, though: no shooting heroin in his joint.

I wasn't crazy about the place because it was a bit too funky and dirty-looking, but I knew I'd meet someone there who spoke English. Sure enough, I ran into a British girl named Nancy who got friendly. In no time she bummed some money from me for a bite to eat and a fix. After we ate, Nancy took me along to her favorite 'pharmacist,' bought heroin and offered me some. I said, "No thanks, but I wouldn't mind if we could get some hash." She then took me to smoke some chillums to a supposedly big drug dealer who had the best hash.

When we got to the dealer's, my friend shot herself full of heroin while I politely drank chai and smoked. When our host stepped out of the room for a minute, Nancy leaned over and whispered, "Be very cool. K. is a really tough guy … he's a former mercenary."

"Mercenary? What's that?" I asked. Nancy replied, "A hit man, you fool, somebody who bloody kills people for money." My eyes widened in fear and shock; I was not a little stunned. From then on I made a point of being respectful when K. was in the room, and remained quiet and deeply pensive. I could hardly believe what she told me about this charming, educated and well-groomed man, who looked like some straight older tourists in Bombay. A hit man! I was a bit alarmed that he could be so laid back, knowing that his reputation preceded him.

While he was relaxed, I felt quite agitated and after a while made a feeble excuse to leave and went back to my hotel. I was back at the Sea Palace Hotel, where I'd stayed before jail, as I had liked its clean beds. Oh, for a real mattress, clean, white, crisp sheets, a pillow! What a change from the flea-infested mat I had curled up on for three months. But despite the incredible comfort of a warm shower and clean beds, I was frightened, miserable and alone again. And just as I had every night for the last three months in jail, I cried myself to sleep.

The next day I woke up delightfully refreshed. Still marveling at my freedom, I decided to celebrate a little on my own and didn't invite Donny and Paul. "Screw them!" I thought. After an indulgent breakfast and a chillum or two, I went to the Buckley Court Hotel to inquire about my kind friends Tony and Rene, who had so suddenly disappeared. The hotel clerk told me they'd left for Amsterdam some time ago. "How long ago, please?" He checked the records and said, "Six weeks ago, memsahib." So the police were onto them after all, I thought to myself. And probably because of me. At least I knew they were safe, and resolved that one day I would see them again and repay their kindness.

Standing behind me, a large, animated white lady speaking Hindi to a child had overheard my inquiries. She was American yet dressed in a saree, which she struggled with incessantly. "Excuse me? I heard you mention Tony and Rene. These are some dear friends of mine. Perhaps we should talk?" She paused. "But not here. Let's go out for a walk. Would you join me for some tea?"

Her name was Shoshonna. A blissfully happy, overweight, Jewish lady from New York, she was traveling the guru circuit in India. I explained my interest in Tony and Rene, and when I told her my prison story, Shoshonna became motherly and concerned. "What are you going to do now?" she asked. "I really don't know yet. I guess I'll have to go to Delhi at some point to retrieve my money from the Ministry of Finance ... at least that's what my lawyer tells me. I might go with him and his wife. They want to visit some family there soon."

Shoshonna could see I had no friends in town, and I think her motherly nature decided on the spot to take me under her wing. She said she was supposed to leave for Nainital to see her guru in two days, and asked, "Do you know Mahara-ji?" I answered, "You mean Neem Karoli Baba, of *Be Here Now*? Of course I do!"

Shoshonna boasted proudly, "He is *my* guru!" Then she looked deep into my eyes and said, "It is definitely karmic that we met. I'm sure Mahara-ji arranged this for some reason. He's so good at arranging things." Then she rolled her eyes upward. "Oh guru," she cried, "you always manage these cosmic connections."

She told me she would go to a special meeting of all the *chelas* (devotees) in Nainital, which was Neem Karoli Baba's principal residence although he had another ashram in Vrindavan. "But you will stay here in Bombay and rest. I will put you up with my Indian family."

"You have an Indian family? Wow!" I was incredulous. "We kind of adopted each other, actually. Matajee will not mind. You will adore her. She is the Divine Mother incarnate. She is pure Bhakti. She'll take care of you."

SHIVAJI PARK

And so it was arranged. The whole family welcomed me warmly into their middle-class home and lifestyle in a modest suburb near Shivaji Park in the north end of Bombay. The mother, whom Shoshonna called Matajee, welcomed me like a long-lost daughter and naturally thought that I was too skinny and wanted to fatten me up. The two teenage sisters were soon fussing over me and dressing me up in their best sarees and jewelry.

But the family was of modest means. I soon found out that several years earlier, the family patron had died of a heart attack at only forty-six years old. Matajee never got over the loss of her husband. She was a devout woman and I could hear her early morning prayers and chanting, which comforted me in an odd way. An older son was studying in England, so it fell to the younger son, Rajiv, to become the family's sole supporter. Through Rajiv I learned their tragic story.

Long ago, their ancestors had been quite wealthy. They belonged to the Rajput clan and owned a tiny kingdom in northern Rajasthan, but when the British came in the eighteenth century they apparently lost their land. Since then the family had lived in "reduced circumstances," as my friend put it. "As if that wasn't bad enough," he went on, "there were also some family jewels that might have sustained us" but had mysteriously disappeared. A long-gone servant was suspected of the grand theft, but he was never found. Rajiv's father, like his father before him, struggled a lifetime fighting British and Indian bureaucracy to retrieve his title to the land, but died in vain. Rajiv was convinced that his mission in life was to continue the search for ancestral ties and to reclaim his family's former wealth. However, his search was continuously stonewalled and meanwhile he had to make a living.

And so he took up dealing drugs. This he did mostly for his mom, whom he genuinely loved and pitied. She never complained; but she was always ill and hardly ever went out. Rajiv knew why: in Indian society at that time a woman was basically worthless without a husband, and poor Matajee did not want her kinfolk to pity her. Rajiv felt that if he could revive his father's dream, she would have a part of him back and at least some of the physical comfort she deserved.

He also did it for himself, because he was offended that his elder brother, Sundeep, was the lucky one chosen to study abroad while he was left with the burden of supporting the family. Rajiv was humble enough to accept his fate, however, and at the same time proud enough to want to do his best and impress everybody. Especially Sundeep. If his older brother could be the brains of the family, then Rajiv would be the power. Also, he wanted his sisters to marry well, to foreigners. He wanted to give them the opportunity to get out of India. He was determined to get only the best for his family. "What better way," he asked himself, "than to sell hashish to the rich American hippies?"

He and his cousin Ravendra, who spoke some English, had befriended a couple of foreigners in Colaba. They convinced the hippies that they could get a much better price for the hash they were buying. Rajiv was lying through his teeth and wasn't sure how he was going to do it, but he was innovative. He was a true hustler, a man obviously driven by passion – fed by his conviction that he must strive to retrieve what was rightfully his. The problem was that he tried a bit too hard. His eagerness to be cool, to be "Western," came across as affected and distasteful to the easy-going hippies. Besides, they knew that, try as he might, poor Rajiv could never lose his essential "Indian-ness." No matter what they professed, many of the hippies were still a little elitist: Indians were just not hip.

Rajiv welcomed me into his home most gallantly as the host and official head of the family. He gave me a tour of the house and offered me assistance from the servants and use of all the facilities. He apologized because the family had a humble abode and only two servants, which in India meant they were at the low end of the middle class. Rajiv was embarrassed because he couldn't offer me a private servant. He introduced me to Babu, a skinny, toothless little man of indeterminate age, and Chandra, a girl of about fifteen. "Chandra will look after all your personal needs," he told me.

"Rajiv, I don't get it ... how can you afford servants if you're living in 'reduced circumstances'?" "Oh, we don't pay them," he said. "We just feed them. And give them a safe place to sleep. But don't worry: They are completely loyal and will do whatever you ask." I learned that Babu slept on the front door stoop like a dog guarding the house, and Chandra slept in the kitchen. And so I was introduced to a middle-class Indian household.

On my first day there I was delighted to discover how middle-class Indians bathe. Chandra knocked on my door and led me to a concrete stall with a single tap about knee-high from the ground and a drain in the floor. I guessed this was the bathing room. There was a little wooden stool covered by a clean towel, and several buckets of steaming hot water. I was invited to undress discreetly in a corner of the room curtained off for the purpose. When I stepped out, Chandra gestured for me to sit on the stool. It occurred to me that she had probably been up for over an hour just to supervise the boiling of the water. Even the suburbs of Bombay had no such luxury as hot water, so I knew the water would be heated on their pathetic little stove, a propane burner in the kitchen.

Then Chandra hauled buckets nearly full to the brim with four liters of boiling water each and – two at a time – brought them into the bath chamber without spilling a drop. She had a large empty tub in which to blend the hot water with cool tap water to the right temperature. Then, with a plastic vessel about the size of a one-liter milk jug she dipped and scooped up enough water to shower me from above. Soon she was washing me with a lather she made from an overly perfumed Indian soap called Lux.

Chandra showed no shame in washing me all over, and I could see that she was used to this, but she did giggle when she washed my private parts. So did I. I later discovered that Chandra was new to the household and had not met Shoshonna. I also found out that she had never before washed a white woman. She was curious about my nipples, though I didn't understand what she was saying. She pointed to my breast and then to hers, and back and forth again, giggling – but I didn't get it. Then she reached a hand into her saree top and pulled out her breast and showed me her nipple. It was purple/black against her dark brown skin. Then she reached out and touched my nipple and giggled. I later learned from the sisters that Chandra was amazed that my nipples were pink.

It felt odd and a bit discomfiting, at first, to have someone wash me from head to toe. But it also felt luxurious, and when I finally surrendered I discovered that I enjoyed this Indian way of bathing. I felt so babied, so pampered. For me it was doubly delicious as a change from my previous three months of self-bathing, self-nurturing and self-pitying. I felt mothered, loved and nurtured for the first time in a long time. A part of me wanted to stay forever with this delightful family.

Having replaced a servant who left a week before to care for her dying mother, Chandra was still learning her way around the household. She was beautiful, demure and strong-limbed. Her tasks were to cook, clean, launder clothes, and offer any services to the females in the house. The men would have Babu bathe them, in much the same manner. After this delightful introduction to the middle-class style of bathing and feeling so welcomed by the servants, the sisters and Matajee, I felt terribly indebted but didn't know how to repay them. They treated me like royalty.

RAJIV'S SPECIAL WELCOME

Soon Rajiv decided to give me a special welcome. On my third night in the house, I woke up to find that he had crawled into bed with me. I began to scream, and he quickly put his hand over my mouth. But it was too late; Babu had heard and came to investigate. Rajiv immediately apologized and begged me to "not tell," and I was too stunned to say anything when the curious servant arrived.

Rajiv explained in rapid Hindi something like, "the young lady had seen a rat," that he had heroically rushed in to help but "forgot to turn on the light" and "inadvertently frightened her." Or some such bullshit. He was pretty quick with a story, I noticed, but I didn't think the servant bought it. Still, a servant knows his place, and he knew enough to be gone. Now alone, Rajiv and I began to bicker in barely controlled angry whispers.

"What the hell do you think you're doing?" I asked angrily. He shushed me and said, "I'm so sorry … I thought it was my bed." "You don't know where your own bedroom is?" I asked incredulously. "I'm really sorry … I didn't mean to scare you   just please don't tell anybody. I am so ashamed of myself. Please, Ann, don't tell anyone." He continued apologizing and begging me not to mention the incident, even promising me money and several grams of hashish. I didn't care about the bribe and said, "Get out and just forget about it, okay? Just don't let this happen again."

But he did not leave. Instead, he sat glumly and began to tell me his whole tragic story. He started to cry. I couldn't believe it. Unlike back home, where kids are sexually active in their teens, in modern, sexually repressed India, a man is often still a virgin at the age of twenty-two. Rajiv sobbed, holding his head in his hands like a beaten man. "I don't know how to tell you this, but I just feel so … so powerless. I hate my family, I hate the responsibility. I want to leave India. All I need is a nice girl like you to make it possible. I could make lots of money with a beautiful girl beside me."

"What's your problem, man?" I countered. "You're a nice-looking guy … why don't you get yourself a nice Indian girl?" I was genuinely concerned.

"Indian girls are too square, and all they care about is marrying a rich and powerful man. I like you hippie girls … you are so free and not so materialistic." He hung his head like a beaten dog and I tried to understand his plight, but I hardly knew what to say.

Barely looking at me out of the corner of his eye and still sobbing, he went on. "I never told you, but I went to Toronto last year. I was there in your very own beautiful city. It was my first time leaving India, even my first time on a plane. When I got to Toronto all the girls were dressed so sexy and they seemed really interested in me. They were even kissing me and teasing me and asking me why I didn't wear a turban and stuff. I mean they were really forward. But I couldn't do it, you know, I just couldn't do it." And he began sobbing again.

I could easily imagine that Rajiv – a handsome and exotic-looking guy, with lots of money and driving a nice car – would have Toronto girls hitting on him. But there he was: terrified of the sex act, afraid they might find out he was a virgin, fearing he might not be able to perform or whatever the virgin male dilemma is. And complicated by a cultural difference: he stuttered in English and said all the wrong things. Poor Rajiv was so horny and frustrated. Now I was supposed to understand him, as if this explained why he came into my room.

My first thought was to wonder why he was telling me all this. Is he expecting me to do something about his problem? I said, "I'm sorry you're having such a rough time, but I just got out of jail and I really need some rest." Again he apologized profusely and begged me not to tell anyone. What was he so afraid of, I wondered. I promised not to mention it and kept my promise. The next day I found a hundred-rupee note and a *tola* (large chunk) of hashish on my bedside table. He never bothered me again, and I was grateful for that.

FESTIVAL OF THE ELEPHANT GOD

Staying in the suburbs for several days showed me a different side of Bombay. Everywhere I looked, people were building outdoor structures and painting clay or plaster-of-paris statues in anticipation of some event. I asked Surya, the younger sister, what was going on. She said, "It is Ganesh Chaturthi, a national festival we make every year. It is for Ganesha. You know Ganesha, yes?" I answered, "the son of Shiva. He has an elephant head and brings good luck, right?"

"Oh yes, very good. So you know. We are making the clay statues for ten days and on the eleventh day we bring the images to the water and submerge them."

This was a popular festival in many parts of India, particularly in Maharashtra, the state Bombay is in. During Ganesh Chaturthi, communities gather to make the largest and most impressive Ganesha statue they can contrive. Some statues are up to 30 feet high. In communities near Shivaji Park, local families fashioned Ganeshas and all the neighborhood kids were involved. Throughout this time sweets were prepared and offered to Ganesha, and then offered to family and guests. Chandra and Matajee spent each morning cooking special foods and making a divine sweetmeat called *modak*, which was made with rice flour, *jaggery* (a kind of raw sugar) and coconut.

Traditionally, on the eleventh day the whole neighborhood gathered their household deities and parade all the Ganesha statues down to the water, in this case Mahim Bay at Shivaji Park. I was invited to participate in this intriguing ceremony. That day the sisters, pumped with excitement, woke me up early. They laid out their best outfits for the parade. Matajee was singing all morning, a special chant for Ganesh. Even Rajiv, usually blasé about his culture and heritage, got excited.

After breakfast and morning chores, we left the house to gather at the flower-festooned Pandal, the structure housing a giant Ganesha. The neighborhood Ganesha was 20 feet tall, a pretty big thing to lug around. A priest dressed in red arrived, and performed a lengthy invocation and convoluted ritual for the statue. I was told that he was symbolically "breathing life" into it.

After the priest's blessing and offerings of coconut, jaggery, sweetmeats, blades of grass and red flowers, the giant statue was covered in a red sandalwood paste. The priest chanted more Vedic hymns ... long and monotonous to my ears. Then several men came with ropes and strapped the statue securely onto its specially designed cart and wheeled it out into the street. The crowd went crazy as we dragged the 20-foot statue along. It was a little wobbly at first and at one point I thought it would topple over, but with precision teamwork and lots of shouting they got it secured eventually. Luckily we didn't have to go far with it.

We walked, skipped, danced and sang all the way to the water, where I saw an enormous crowd: vendors selling sweets, bands playing, trumpeters, dancers on stilts and all kinds of entertainment. It was like a carnival. Surya took my hand as we skipped like little schoolgirls and chanted. "Jai Ganesh, Jai Ganesh, Jai Ganesha, Deva Mata Terry Pond Teryy Pitta Mahadeva." I still remember that chant after all these years.

Meanwhile a priest chanted Vedic scriptures and people clanged cymbals and tooted horns. There wasn't a single vehicle in sight; the crowd took over the streets. It was crazy. Some police officers were there, presumably to control the crowds, but with a crowd that size there was no such thing as crowd control.

When we got to the water's edge the statues were submerged, turning the water red and green and yellow from the dyes. I wondered if this was polluting the water. I also found it rather sad, because the statues were beautiful works of art. They were mostly made of clay or plaster of paris, so would eventually dissolve in the water. I asked Surya, "Why, after all these days of preparation, do you put the beauti-

Ganesh Chaturthi festival circa 1972.

ful statues in the water just to have them melt into nothing?" Her mom, curious about everything I said, nudged Surya's arm. Surya turned to translate the question, and a little dialogue in Hindi ensued. Then Surya said, "We are sending the Lord off to his abode in Kailash [a sacred mountain in the Himalayas]. When he goes, he takes with him all the misfortunes and bad luck of his devotees."

This festival was more than a local folk festival to honor the elephant god. It was also a political event, and in recent times had taken on a secular tone. In 1893 Lokmanya Tilak, a pundit, Indian freedom fighter and social reformer, transformed the annual domestic ceremony into a large, well-organized public event. Tilak saw the wide appeal of the deity Ganesha as the "god for everybody," and the festival as a way to bridge the gap between Brahmins (the highest caste) and other castes. He wanted to unify Indians of all castes and communities to generate national fervor against British colonial rule. Today the festival has evolved into a national festival, bigger than ever and featuring major concerts, art exhibits, theater, local bands and celebrities, and corporate sponsors. Some businesses make their most of their profits during this one event – like Christmas in the West.

THE FIRST GURU

Shoshonna was gone to see her guru, but soon I had new friends. Although I liked Rajiv's sisters, I found them a bit too square. I preferred to hang out with the hyper Rajiv, because at least through him I met some cool people and could smoke my hash without embarrassment. In India ladies don't smoke, and certainly not the "filthy hashish those dirty hippies smoked." I didn't want to disappoint my host family with my embarrassing habit, although they probably knew I smoked with Rajiv.

I met a couple of guys from Toronto. Halfway around the world and I meet these Toronto boys. How cool! They too thought it was quite a coincidence; in those days few Canadians were on the Bombay scene. These guys had odd nicknames from Toronto: Mental and Curator. But then Mental had his name changed to Caitanya Maha Prabhu because he found a guru, was initiated and started wearing orange robes. Of the two, I preferred Mental (Caitanya), but he didn't seem too interested in me. (I suspected that he was gay – my first gay friend.) Curator was a nice guy and not bad-looking, but lacked some of Caitanya's charm and intellect; he was often quiet and dazed in a junkie stupor, while Caitanya was animated.

I met them at a cafe Rajiv took me to; the guys were potential customers for his drugs. It was an expensive Western-style cafe at the Oberoi, a fancy Bombay hotel frequented by foreigners and rich Indians. During our lunch I discovered that Caitanya was a newly initiated disciple of the controversial Acharya Shree Rajneesh. Curator hadn't taken the leap yet, but he sure was enamored of the rising new guru. Of course I was quite familiar with this Shree Rajneesh, since my friends Tony and Rene were devotees and had brought me many of his books and pictures in jail. I felt I already knew him from having seen his photos, in which he was fatherly looking and had kind, warm, smiling eyes. I liked Rajneesh and his somewhat unconventional approach to the ancient Hindu teachings.

When I mentioned to Caitanya and Curator that I had read several of his books, they said, "Why don't you come to the meditation with us tomorrow?" Every morning at 6 a.m. several Rajneesh devotees gathered on Chowpatty Beach to practice the "dynamic meditation" he had taught them. They would pick me up at 5 a.m.

But since the guys were staying at the Star of Asia Hotel, much closer to Chowpatty Beach than my hotel, I accepted their invitation to stay with them that night. "What a nice change" from the all-too-proper Indian girls and their brother the horny Rajiv, I thought. I liked that these guys did not come on to me, though I wasn't sure if it was the heroin or if they were practising Brahmacharya (celibacy). Of course I didn't sleep with either of them, just watching as they cranked themselves up with heroin and nodded out in a junkie stupor.

I amused myself looking over magazines and appraising Caitanya's artwork. He'd given me his sketchbook to check out and immediately I became absorbed. He was quite a good artist. He pointed out which ones were done under the influence of hash and which while on opium. I mostly liked his opium-inspired sketches, which were tight little universes of bustling interactivity of geometric form ... but apparently shapeless at the same time. Almost like fractals. Interesting.

The next morning, to my disbelief, we were awake before dawn and dashing off to Chowpatty Beach. As the sleepy citizens of Bombay came to life, dawn found a motley crew of about a dozen devotees gathered on the beach, all dressed in saffron except me and another newcomer.

"Dynamic" meditation is a ritual that tries to force an experience of ecstasy. You breathe intensely for a good ten minutes or so, and then begin to chant, dance, tremble and shake – working yourself up into a state of frenzy, which is interpreted as ecstasy. But even with intense breathing I couldn't drum up a state of ecstasy, so I faked it most of the time. I suspected that at least some of the others were doing the same; it looked like hyperventilating more than anything else. At one point I opened my eyes and glimpsed a young Indian man hiding behind the trees with a huge erection, openly masturbating while ogling the white women dancing like crazy intoxicated bacchanals. Other Indians simply stared in curiosity as the funny foreigners acted out their frenzy. I thought it was all a bit contrived and over the top.

Soon the devotees began to drop one by one, collapsing in a heap from exhaustion, I suppose. At this point one was supposed to experience "waves of ecstasy" coursing through one's body. I looked all around and decided that though I couldn't feel waves of ecstasy I had to lie down anyway. What else could I do? I'd feel like an idiot if I was the only one left standing. So I kind of fell (to make it look real) to the ground, and lay on the cold sand waiting for waves of ecstasy. But the only waves coursing over me were from the ocean.

"So how was it?" asked Caitanya. "Um, okay, I guess. I'm not sure I get it. I didn't really feel much." I answered honestly. Curator piped in, "It takes a little while for the energy to build. You'll see: after a few sessions you'll get it."

"Oh, I see." I didn't know what else to say. "Of course, it helps once you've been initiated by Acharya," Caitanya offered. "He'll open up the kundalini channels."

When we got back to the Star of Asia Hotel, we had an enormous breakfast and smoked a few chillums of hash. Afterwards we went to the American Express office to see if Caitanya had received any money (he hadn't). This was a daily ritual for most foreigners in the city, as many relied on AmEx to receive money, packages and letters from home.

Then we went shopping. In those days you could get beautiful silks for next to nothing. Caitanya had had a tailor design a multi-layered vest that had eighteen hidden pockets, and he was looking for some fabric to have a copy made. I was looking for some new sarees. I had been in India for four months now, and ever since the silver market mob scene I wore nothing but Indian-style clothing. I really enjoyed wearing a saree anyway. This delightful garment obliges one to walk in a different manner, in a more feminine way, I might say. Once I got used to it I really felt quite comfortable and walked more elegantly.

Rajiv's oldest sister, Devaki, gave me a lovely green organza saree, a magnificent gift. In ancient times, it was rumored, Indian craftsmen could spin and weave a cloth so fine, so sheer, that an entire six-meter saree could be folded into a single matchbox of about one inch square. I'm sure it was an exaggeration, but this delicate saree may have come close. It was a shade of green close to olive, enhanced with gold thread and embroidered in the Parsee (Persian) style. Devaki said it was a good color for me because it complemented my green eyes and light bronze skin. I chose to wear the underskirt a little low on the hips (my own modern adaptation) to reveal my navel through the veil of the transparent saree. It was a little daring for Indian society, but I enjoyed the sexiness. The two sisters approved and told me I could be a film star in India. At this I laughed, but later I did get to be in an Indian film. I had a non-speaking part as a harem girl in a silly movie and got close to Amitabh Bachchan, India's hottest male star at the time.

Shoshonna came back from her retreat. She was incredibly high, her eyes sparkling and her mood always happy. I could see that she was blown away from having seen her guru. I thought he must be really special to have such an effect on her. She kept hugging people and saying, "Everything is grace, the world is grace, it's all pure love" as though she was high on LSD. I thought it must be quite something to experience such a transformation just by sitting in the presence of a wrinkled, half-naked old man.

"Why does your guru have such a powerful effect on you?" I asked. Shoshonna smiled serenely and answered with dancing eyes. "Because he is the Supreme Being, in human form. Because he is so wise, so humble, so playful and joyful, so full of laughter. He is pure love."

"Can a guru make such a difference?" I wondered. She rolled her eyes in response. "Oh yes!"

"By the way," I asked, "what do you think of Acharya Shree Rajneesh?" She hesitated, choosing her words carefully. "Rajneesh? He is good for some people. I think he has some *siddhis* (powers), but I am totally in love with my guru. Why do you ask?"

"I've read a lot of his books, and his teachings seem to make sense. I tried the chaotic meditation a few times too, but it doesn't do much for me. Some devotees suggested I need his blessing. I'm thinking about going to see him," I said apprehensively. "Good!" Shoshonna exclaimed. "He will raise your kundalini."

HANGING GARDENS ASHRAM, BOMBAY

I found myself naked on the master's bed, lying on my belly face down while the guru's hand hovered over my buttocks. How did I end up in this ridiculous position? I was tormented by the thought that he might touch me. What kind of guru needs to see me naked, I wondered. Surely if Bhagwan Shree Rajneesh was all-powerful and all-seeing (Bhagwan means "God"), he could see through my clothes? Why did he ask me to undress?

His soothing voice kept telling me to relax. "In order to raise the kundalini, one must first overcome fear." "You must let go of your fear, Diksha, just let it go. I will not harm you, just trust, trust," he said in a soothing fatherly voice.

"Diksha!" I could hardly get used to my new name. How can I let go of fear when the one I fear is telling me to not fear? How do I know this guy isn't a pervert?

"But if he really is a guru, who am I to judge?" countered another voice. "What if he can read my mind and knows that I just called him a pervert? What if he's reading my mind right now? What if he decides to jump on me?"

I had been escorted to his private chambers by his private secretary, Ma Ananda Lakshma, who was obviously one of his most ardent admirers. She told me how lucky I was to be getting a private audience with the great master. I had worn my best green saree in deference to the Indian tradition. I entered his chamber gracefully but humbly, bowing before the master until I was fully prostrate before him. I knew this was the way to show reverence to a holy man in India. Then, absurdly, I found myself kissing his feet. He urged me to rise.

The moment I looked into his kind face I was struck by his radiant countenance. He was an utterly beautiful man. His eyes glowed with mischievous laughter, he had magnificent, long curly locks of black hair and a slightly graying beard to match. He was dressed in the cleanest (were they starched?) white robes I'd ever seen, and had an unusual but pleasant fragrance. He wore an expensive gold watch (which I thought odd, since gurus were not supposed to have possessions).

He said, "Come, come closer my child." As I snuggled closer to his lap he cupped my face in his hands, raised it up to him and asked, "What is your name?" I answered, "My name is Ann." The guru smiled. He was silent for some time, then slowly said, "Very nice name. Ann.

Yes, Ann, you are an angel. But why do you come here to see me?"

"I'm not sure. Really. I was having trouble with the chaotic meditation, and some chelas (devotees) said I should come to see you." He had incredibly soft hands that felt and even smelled like baby powder. I couldn't help but notice how gentle his touch was, both fatherly and loving. And oh, his eyes communicated such joy. "I have done the chaotic meditation for about a week, but nothing happens. I thought maybe with your blessings ..." I couldn't look him in the eyes any more. Suddenly I felt weak, powerless and completely in his presence.

Rajneesh asked me to stand up. "Turn around, child," he coaxed. "That is a verrry beyootiful saree you are wearing. And you are a verrry beyootiful girrl," he noted with approving eyes. "But," he continued, "the color is wrong. When you become Sannyasin you must wear saffron. It is the color of the renunciant."

He paused for a moment, then gazed deeply into my eyes. I felt intoxicated from the power of his gaze. What was it about his eyes? "Do you wish to become a Sannyasin?" he asked. I knew Sannyasin meant renunciant: one who gives up all of life's pleasures for the greater satisfaction of spiritual attainment, like becoming a monk.

I hesitated a moment as I wasn't really sure. Then his hypnotic gaze melted my resistance, and I knelt before him again and eagerly answered, "Oh, yes!"

The guru smiled, and it seemed like the sun breaking through an overly cloudy day. "I will call you Diksha. Ma Ananda Diksha. Diksha means Initiation. Ma Ananda Diksha is 'Initiation into Bliss'. He placed a string of prayer beads over my head, laid his baby-soft hands gently on my head and said, "I will initiate you into bliss. I am sure you are making the right decision. The path of the Sannyasin is not always easy, however. You must endure several

Acharya Shree Rajneesh
circa 1972.

tests." He paused a moment to look at me, to emphasize that I must pass certain tests. "Do you understand? He gazed lovingly and longingly at me and said, "You will take off your saree now."

What? I could not believe my ears. Take off the saree? He must be kidding. What should I do? I could not say no. This was an impossible situation. The great master had asked, or rather, *commanded* me. Perhaps this was one of the tests. I knew that one was not supposed to doubt or judge a guru. But what if he's just a dirty old man who wanted to see me naked? How could I know? Didn't I catch a teeny glint of desire in his fatherly gaze? Why did I always get these messages confused? I was tormented as these thoughts raced through my head. You're not supposed to doubt the guru, but I didn't budge. "Do not be afraid my child ... I will not hurt you," he said.

As if in a hypnotic state I began to remove my saree, intensely aware of his eyes. Obviously nervous, I asked gingerly, "My underthings as well?" "Oh, yes!" he responded. Now I was totally naked and sure that he was salivating and devouring me with his eyes. But it was too late. He had me in his power now, and I was hooked. My natural defenses did not kick in because I had a weird disassociation complex, an invisible disability that I discovered only much later.

I was at war with myself again. Perhaps he was not lustful; perhaps just my ego was thinking that. Perhaps I needed to learn to trust. Certainly his look communicated nothing but pure love. Most people would say go on instinct, but my instinct wasn't working. In spite of his obvious lust, I felt that he was sincere and in control, restrained and a gentleman. Believe it or not, I trusted that his love was really for my spiritual growth and that he would not hurt me. Maybe my kundalini was a bit low. Admittedly I was a little uptight sexually. I'd never really felt comfortable with sex, being so young and pretty new to it all.

The guru beckoned me to lie down on his bed. Odd that the only two pieces of furniture in his private chamber were his high-backed leather swivel chair and this enormous bed. Why had I not noticed this before? Like someone hypnotized, I moved toward the bed and obediently followed his instructions.

He asked me to lie on my tummy, and this I did without question. He placed his hand gently over my buttocks. I could sense his hand was there, although it seemed that he did not actually touch me. For the longest time he was silent, with his hand hovering over my backside.

Terrified, I wondered what he was doing. What if he wanted to screw me? He must be some kind of pervert. Why wasn't he doing anything? Why was he just standing there tormenting me?

The guru sensed my fear and was very gentle. But when he touched my spine and told me in soothing tones that he would raise my kundalini, I thought, "Kundalini, my foot! This guy's just tripping on having a naked girl in his bed." Immediately I felt guilty for having such thoughts and doubting his intent. His touch, I decided, communicated nothing sexual. He did not caress my buttocks or approach me in any way that could be construed as sexual. Maybe he really was trying to raise my kundalini. Maybe the guru was able to rise above nudity and sexual attraction.

"Please try to relax, Diksha," he coaxed. "You are very nervous. This makes it difficult to raise the kundalini." For a good ten minutes or so I lay like this, my thoughts racing back and forth between doubting and trusting him, and wondering what he was going to do next.

Finally he gave up on the kundalini business and asked me to turn onto my back. "Raise your knees and keep your eyes closed," he told me. "You must now imagine that you are making love with your lover. Just pretend that he is here with you in this room and you are making wild passionate love with him." This I simply could not do. First, I was not that experienced. And second, I was not an exhibitionist. I had been a virgin until the age of seventeen. Now at eighteen I had had little sexual experience. I was still quite shy, and it was beyond my capacity to imagine making love with someone while someone else was watching. Still, I wanted to please the guru and tried to imagine what he told me. He then asked me to "go through the motions," to physically enact making love, but I found this request absurd and embarrassing. I just could not do it.

After several minutes of coaxing me, the guru gave up. Rajneesh realized that I was just too uptight. He told me I could dress, and at this I breathed an enormous sigh of relief.

After I dressed he asked me to come by his chair. He offered me an egg-shaped polished stone object, which he told me was a "Shiva lingam." I knew from my reading that a lingam was a phallic object, a sacred fertility symbol. He cupped it in his two hands and rolled his eyes upward in ecstatic joy as if it were something truly precious, and told me I must learn to "love it." He kissed the egg, and exclaimed over and over again that I must "love it. Worship it!" He handed the stone lingam to me and told me that I must also practise the exercise on my bed. Twice a day I must practice imaginary lovemaking. And most of all, he told me, I must learn to love the penis. Confused, I thanked him weakly for the gift and left. I did not bow down or kiss his feet this time.

The whole experience had been disturbing and confusing. As I left his private chamber I encountered a young English girl, obviously a chela dressed in saffron. She asked me eagerly, "So, how was it? How was your meeting with Bhagwan?" I didn't know how to answer her. Had Rajneesh asked this girl, a pretty young thing, to undress too? I wondered if he treated all his female devotees this way, or only me. I was tempted to ask the girl, then thought better of it. I could see how her eyes had the glazed look of someone in love or maybe of a drug addict or religious fanatic. I didn't want to spoil her dream.

"Isn't Bhagwan wonderful?" the girl asked me. I said, "Yeah, wonderful," and walked out in disgust.

CHAPTER 9

To New Delhi

I TRIED THE "DYNAMIC MEDITATION" on Chowpatty Beach a few more times, mainly to be with my new friends. But after my unpleasant experience at the ashram I lost faith in the guru, and his meditation appeared to be equally a sham. Soon I stopped going.

One morning I got a call from my lawyer, Mr. Prakash, who had finally arranged a meeting with the finance authorities in New Delhi, India's capital. We would travel there by train, second class, the next Monday. I was delighted. I had been living mostly on charity, kindly arranged by Shoshonna, but now I would finally get my own money. When I was arrested the police had confiscated my undeclared foreign currency, $3,000 US, which was a small fortune in India at the time. My lawyer also had a keen interest in this trip, since he had not yet been paid and knew that depended on me getting access to my funds. Mr. Prakash thought at the same time he would take his wife to visit relatives.

I was excited to visit New Delhi. I had been in India for five months, but except for a little side trip to Goa and the dope run to Sweden had not traveled much, especially inside the country – I'd mainly seen Bombay and the inside of a prison. New Delhi would be fun. Plus it was close to Agra, site of the world-famous Taj Mahal. I understood it was one of the world's seven wonders and very much wanted to see it.

Mr. Prakash and his wife arranged the train booking to New Delhi, and became my hosts and tour guides for the trip. They also devised a social schedule. By now I understood that even with pre-arranged meetings, government schedules messed up things. We anticipated spending at least a week in Delhi, so we had plenty of time to sightsee. I saw the Red Fort in Old Delhi and visited magnificent marble palaces, including the Halls of Public and Private Audience and the Pearl Mosque. We saw Hindu temples, Moghul architecture, crowded aromatic bazaars and magnificent parks with exquisite gardens; royal tombs and ruins were everywhere.

My hosts put me up in a modest but clean hostel while they stayed with relatives. They took me out for Indian meals and cultural events: music and dance. We saw so many sights I got bored with ruins of temples and monuments. All this cultural and touristy stuff was distracting for a while, but my hosts were square and I longed for company of my own kind. Where were the hippies?

Out of loneliness I became a friendly nuisance at the local travellers' hostel, around the corner from my rooming house, where I saw a lot of hippies hanging out. Most of this hostel's residents were too laid back or stoned to respond to enthusiastic overtures of friendship. However, a French man staying there saw an opportunity and invited me for tea. Robert (which he pronounced "Robe Air") said he was anxious to practise his English, and suggested we go for chai to a nice shop around the corner. We were barely seated a few minutes, awkward in our language barrier, when I noticed a tall, slender, golden-haired white man enter the room with the presence of a sage.

A typical slum dwelling and dress of the 1970s.

SITAR SAM

This is how I met Sitar Sam, who would become my most significant lover and teacher in my young life. He was the one who taught me how to survive in India; the one who brought me deeper into the path of self-discovery. He started by rescuing me from the clutches of the unscrupulous Frenchman, who was a hustler trying to con me. Sitar Sam, an experienced world traveler and long-time resident of India, overheard some of our conversation and realized that I was gullible and believed the Frenchman's sob story.

Robert said he was from Suresnes, near Paris. "High been in H'India for six month now and high been ripped off ... dey took every ting. Dis place really bad, man. High got nut-ting left. Don't heven know how I gonn pay my room."

I offered, "Can't you arrange something with the landlord ... do a trade, maybe offer some work?" "Ha, dey don't need work haround ere. Indian work for slave wage, you know?" I didn't know. "What about borrowing just enough to send a telegram home and get someone to send you some bread?" Robert sighed deeply like a beaten-down man. "You don't hunderstand, do you? Ow long ave you been here?"

He ordered some chai (on credit, I suppose; he seemed to know the owner). Then he told me his landlady had already threatened to throw him out. His rent was two months overdue and she couldn't afford to keep him any longer, though her rooms were cheap and nearly always full. He would be forced to sleep on the street, but having no passport or other papers he would surely be picked up by the police. It seemed a hopeless situation and I felt sorry for him. I was just about to give him some money when Sitar Sam stepped in.

Later, Sam told me that he was outraged at the obvious con, and couldn't let a sweet, naive girl like me get taken. But he also confessed that he was very attracted to me and wanted to know more about me. The tall stranger introduced himself and asked if he could join us. The Frenchman gave him a dirty look, but I smiled a warm welcome. Without waiting for an answer, he sat down, zeroed in on me and said, "Didn't I see you in the American Express office yesterday?" "Yes, I was there about two o'clock," I told him.

Before long we were conversing rapidly in English and completely ignoring the Frenchman, who abruptly left. I liked the way this stranger looked. Long-haired, Semitic, obviously American (by his accent) and, as it turned out, from California. He had that laid-back California style. He was cute, with curly, sandy-brown locks and a full beard, a long straight nose and blue eyes. He looked like a cross between Jesus and John Lennon, two of my girlhood heroes. I found him interesting, intelligent and charming. He was gentle-mannered and quite soft-spoken; yet confident and self-assured when need be. As he'd just demonstrated.

Soon we left the restaurant and started walking toward Connaught Place, where he was staying and not far from where I was staying. My new friend proved quite engaging. "So you are Canadian. That's pretty cool. Don't meet too many on this trail. I'm not sure if you realize it, but that guy was really trying to hustle you." I felt a little embarrassed at the incident and also became instantly comfortable with him. He had no sleazy vibe at all.

"My name is Sitar Sam. Of course it's just a nickname, but I kind of like it – so that's what I'm called now." His real name, I later learned, was Samuel William Gainsburg, and he was indeed from California. Beverly Hills, to be exact.

"Sweetheart, I hope you don't mind, but I wanna go to AmEx and check on my mail." I knew this would take a while, as there were always line-ups at the American Express office. But I didn't mind, as I had nothing else to do. "After that we can go to Chandni Chowk, where I need to see a tailor, and we can do some shopping if you like. If you don't mind coming along on these little errands, that is. Then we can have lunch and go to my place afterwards for a chillum or two. Unless you've got other plans?"

"Chandni Chowk? What is it?" I asked.

"You really haven't seen much of Delhi yet, I see. Chandni Chowk is a bazaar in the old quarter, and it really has the feel of ancient India." I remembered a bazaar that seemed like something out of an Old Testament painting. "I was in the old city with the Prakashes and saw a smelly bazaar there," I said. "What's so special about it?"

"It's in the original city and the roads are pretty narrow – only pedestrian traffic and animals can get through. It's a trip to see ... kind of like a village in the middle of the city. And it's where all the best hash dens and chai shops are. I'll take you around to some interesting places in Old Delhi and down by the river ... not just the touristy stuff. By the way, have you been to the Jantar Mantar park?" he asked.

"I'm not sure," I said. "I saw some parks and gardens and stuff as we drove around."

"You have to see this park. It's a trip and a half. It's actually an observatory but a natural one. It's got astronomical structures and there's a huge sundial just like they used in ancient Egypt. If you saw it, you would have remembered this place. Anyway, we'll go for sure one of these days."

"Sure," I said – I was willing to go to the ends of the earth with him. So I accompanied my new friend for the day, and found him relaxed and easy to be with. We walked and talked up a storm as we wound through the busy streets leading to Connaught Place. He asked me a lot of questions and I was eager to learn more about him too. "How did you get the name Sitar Sam?" I asked.

He laughed as if he was used to this question. "When I first got to India I went nuts for the sitar. That was two years ago. I bought one right away, a real beauty with beautiful inlaid marble stuff, and I paid a lot for it. Then I tried learning to play the damn thing, and I tell you it's a complicated instrument. But I was determined, and I dragged it with me on bullock carts and trains and boats and camels, and even on my back at times. Sometimes I had to pay for another passenger just to bring it along with me. It became a bit of a joke with friends 'cuz I would leave anything behind but I always had to take my sitar. So for a whole year I dragged that sitar all over India and kept trying to learn how to play. It was a joke – too many damn strings. So I gave it up ... but by then everyone was used to seeing me with the sitar, and because my name is Sam the name Sitar Sam just stuck."

"Do you still have it?" I asked. "No ... not any more. I figured if I couldn't play it, it had no more value for me. So there was certainly no point in lugging it around India any more. But I still wanted to make it useful so I, well ... let's just say I found a creative way to use the sitar. I'll tell you about that some other time." He smiled mischievously.

"No! Come on, tell me no-oo-w pleeeease!" I whined like a child.

He laughed and said, half-jokingly, "You gotta promise not to tell anyone," and I nodded in agreement. "I stashed a bunch of hash in it and sent it off to America, and it got through. The proceeds kept me going for nearly a year in India," he said with a little pride.

"Wow! How did you send it?" "That my dear, shall remain a smuggler's secret forever sealed behind these lips."

Sitar Sam had been in India for two years and spoke passable Hindi. He had apparently arrived in New Delhi just a week before me after a forty-day retreat in the mountains near Rishikesh in northern India, where he had gone to see his master and underwent intense yoga training involving "austerities" and purification rituals.

"What do you mean by austerities?" I wondered.

"You have to endure several conditions of testing the body for endurance and to develop mind power. Like … let's say temperature conditions, for one thing. When you are a yogi in the mountains, you renounce all possessions and you basically have no clothes. All you have is a blanket, a metal pot for bathing and a beggar's bowl. You live in a cave and the only thing to keep you warm is a fire … the Dhouni. But this is a sacred fire and it has to be fed constantly. You're supposed to never let it go out."

"You mean you lived in a cave and ran around half naked up in the mountains with nothing but a blanket? What did you eat?"

"Not very much. Sometimes villagers brought me milk and rice. A yogi doesn't eat that much. Sometimes I found some berries. Or I would sprout some chickpeas and eat the sprouts. Mostly I just fasted."

"You fasted? For two months? Are you nuts?" I couldn't help myself and just blurted it out. But this to me was rather extreme.

He laughed again. "I know it sounds a little wacky and I don't expect you to understand. But let's just say you learn to overcome the needs of the body. The 'austerities' are to remind you of how little one actually needs to survive. When you are sitting still and practising presence and trying to just *be* … it doesn't burn up a whole lot of calories … you know what I mean?"

"I'm not sure I follow. What you're saying is that you don't actually feel the body that much. But how you can you stop from getting really cold and hungry? And don't you get bored with just sitting around and doing nothing all day?" He looked at me a bit condescendingly and said, "You'll understand one day."

Sitar Sam took me to a restaurant, and as he ordered our food I was impressed with his extensive knowledge of the local cuisine and language. I munched away on carrot *halva* (who would've thought you could make a sweet out of carrots?). There was such a variety of foods to discover – I didn't know there were that many different kinds of curry. I discovered coconut-based curries and milk-based and butter-based, with an infinite variety of spice combinations, some with more cumin and some with more cinnamon. And it was all vegetarian. Sitar Sam explained the virtues of being a vegetarian, and in no time I was a convert. At least ideologically. Considering that I was still adjusting to the spicy Indian cuisine and that I really did not like vegetables, it was a huge leap. But soon I came to love simple meals of dal and chapati (lentils and flatbread).

As we walked along the main drag I noticed a huge crowd gathered in front of a cinema. The movie just released was called *Hare Rama Hare Krishna.* Just as we were passing, some of the crowd shouted out, "Dirty hippies ... go home!" I asked Sitar Sam why they were so hostile. He told me that the movie portrayed hippies as a bad cultural influence on the youth of India. He knew the story as some of his friends acted in the film.

I told him I had been in an Indian movie recently, in Bombay. I played a non-speaking part as an extra. "What was the movie called?" Sitar Sam asked.

"Oh, I can't remember these Indian names. But I do remember that the star was Shashi Kapoor." Sitar Sam was impressed and said, "Wow, that must have been fun," to which I replied, "Not really. It was boring as all hell. You just hang around the set all day and wait for them to call you for the scene. I got to play a harem girl all done up in glittery

A typical Indian film shoot in the 1970s.

costume, and I waved palm fronds while Shashi Kapoor sat in a pool. That was about it. But they paid us forty rupees for the day, so I was pretty happy."

"Forty rupees … not bad. But weren't you interested in the movie or any of the stars?" he wondered. "Not really, I don't get Indian movies. And their stars are all pretty square if you ask me – they look like something from the '50s. Shashi Kapoor is not bad-looking, but he's not my type."

Sitar Sam said, "Indian movies are a strange cultural phenomena. I've been to a few. You're right of course. Most of the stories are pretty simple ones from the *Vedas*, or a really sappy soap opera, or a guns-and-robbers shoot-'em-up. The characters are pretty black and white. The evil guy always has a big handlebar mustache, and there's always someone who doesn't know his identity and eventually discovers he is someone he thought he wasn't. And so much corny singing and dancing. And always a wet saree scene. They're really a hoot to watch even if you don't understand the language.

"What's a wet saree scene?" I asked. Sitar Sam replied, "Indians are too modest to really show any skin or any kind of female sexuality in the movies. So they always have the leading lady fall into a river or a fountain, and then she has this wet saree, and it's pretty sexy. It's so funny and so lame." "That's hilarious," I said.

Suddenly we smelled something awful. Sitar Sam looked down and realized that someone had thrown some shit onto his shoes. A minute later a kid came out and offered to clean his shoes for two rupees. Sitar Sam got mad and started yelling at the kid in Hindi. The kid cleaned his shoes and Sam paid him. "Did he do that on purpose?" I asked. Sam said, "Yeah, it happens here sometimes. There's not much you can do about it. People are so desperately poor that they'll do anything to get a rupee from a wealthy foreigner."

"I'm amazed that you paid him. Isn't that just encouraging them?" Sitar Sam was already over the incident. He said, "Welcome to India. So tell me more about your gig at the film studio."

"The producers seemed to like me a lot. They used me in another movie as well, where I had to dress in a mini skirt. All the Indians were dressed Western-style and drinking martinis and stuff. I think it was called *Billy* or *Bobby* or something like that. The main thing is I got paid."

"Good for you. Let's go see a movie some time. But not this one – it makes the hippies look bad."

Sitar Sam stopped at a street vendor to buy some *biddhis*, small cigars that are basically a tobacco leaf wrapped and tied with a little string. He offered me one, and we lit it from a burning hemp rope the vendor had. Sitar Sam explained that even matches were a luxury so it was easier to light from a continuous burning wick.

"I wonder why the Indians are so into cinema," I said. "They really go nuts for these movies, don't they?" Sitar Sam replied, "That's because most of them don't have televisions In fact, most don't even have electricity, so how could they have a TV? But the cinema is only 50 paise (5 cents), so even the poorest street sweeper can afford to go. It's the only entertainment they have."

"Oh, I see," I said. "When I was staying at the YWCA in Bombay and they came around scouting for young girls for bit parts, they only wanted white girls. I remember there were two beautiful girls from Mysore – just gorgeous. But instead they picked me and a bunch of skinny junkies. The two girls were pretty pissed off. Why did they only want white women?"

Sitar Sam replied, "It's an unfortunate aspect of their culture and maybe something left over from the British dominance. Indians tend to go for female stars who are very light-skinned. In effect, they are prejudiced against their own people. It doesn't make a whole lot of sense to me either, as I've seen some of the most beautiful women in the world right here in India. Who cares if they are light- or dark-skinned? But there you go ... another enigma about this country.

Finally we got to Chandni Chowk. "Hey, I was here a few days ago with the Prakashes," I said, instantly recognizing the bazaar. "So this is the famous bazaar. Can we go to a hash den, please?"

Sam smiled and said, "I was going to surprise you, but you read my mind. There's one right around the corner." Sure enough, within minutes we were comfortably stretched out in the Eye of Shiva hash den. It wasn't much really, like someone's garage in decor. What I remember best was the brass spittoons near each smoking station, just like saloon spittoons in old Western movies. I knew right away what they were. Chronic hash smokers have a tendency to spit up phlegm, so spittoons were provided.

The hash den was dark and damp, and I didn't particularly like it. We were the only foreigners in the place. A couple of old men who smoked incessantly but barely talked looked up as we entered and took a mild interest in us for a few minutes, and then went back to their smoking ritual. The radio was playing the usual staticky Hindi music. It was very irritating, and so after two chillums we left.

I was eager for more of Sam's story. "So you're from California, eh? What was that like ... I mean growing up there?" There wasn't much to tell about his "boring life" in Beverly Hills, he assured me. "I was raised ... pretty comfortably. Me and a brother. My father was a professor of sociology at UCLA, my mom mostly a homemaker and an artist. I had a pretty average upbringing, I guess."

"What made you come to India?" I asked. "Ah ... the great question. What makes *anyone* come to India?" he laughed. "Seriously ... I'm sure it was my guru that called me here, like right through the ether, man. I had no idea I was coming to India until I was coming to India. You know what I mean? I also had no idea who he was until I got here, but I'm sure it was the invisible hand of destiny that brought me here. We have this past life connection, and guru-ji brought me here."

I pestered him with questions. "What about your time in the Himalayas? What was your teacher like? Did you meet any other teachers or gurus there? I hear that the Himalayas are full of holy men: yogis, swamis and sadhus."

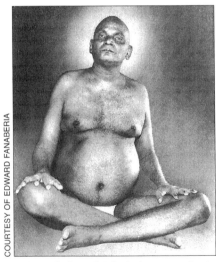

COURTESY OF EDWARD FANABERIA

Some babas drink their own urine!

He said he was sworn to secrecy on the identity of his teacher, so did not reveal it. And although I later learned his teacher's identity, I too have to honor that request. Sitar Sam explained some of the rituals he voluntarily endured to purify and prepare himself for long periods of meditation and sitting with his master. This retreat involved fasting and drinking only water for 40 days while maintaining a 24-hour vigil over a sacred fire, continuously chanting some sacred Sanskrit syllables and smearing ashes

Memoirs of a Hippie Girl in India

from the sacred fire all over his body. After the first ten days he began to drink his urine, and continued to do this until his urine was as clear as water.

"You drank your own piss?" I asked incredulously. "You're kidding, right?" He shook his head as if to say no. "Oh, my God, I can't believe you're telling me this. Doesn't it taste awful? And what's the point?"

"It's called Shivambu Kalpa, and it is a purification method. Basically your urine is nothing more than a distilled form of your blood. And your blood has a kind of DNA map of your whole system. So it tells you what you need and don't need. That's why doctors always examine your urine to look for signs of disease or the presence of toxins."

"But isn't it kind of like drinking poison? The reason we piss out is because we're supposed to get rid of it. Isn't our urine full of poison?"

"You're right. It is a method of elimination of toxins. But as you eliminate toxins you also eliminate a lot of good things: nutrients, minerals and stuff your gut hasn't totally absorbed. When you drink your urine you re-absorb these minerals and nutrients in a more potent way. But you can only do this after fasting for at least 10 days."

"Why?" I asked.

"Because your body has to be really pure to start with. So you do a ten-day fast and eliminate all the built-up toxins with laxative herbs and some yoga colonic cleansing, and then you start to feel really light and vigorous. It is really a different kind of high."

"But if you feel that good after fasting for ten days, why would you want to start drinking your urine?" I had to ask.

"Because this is a deeper kind of detoxification. It goes on a much deeper level. I wouldn't recommend it for everybody. But you know that Mahatma Gandhi and many other saints in India were proponents of Shivambu Kalpa. They call it urine therapy in the West."

"Holy shit, I never would've thought. But doesn't drinking your own body poison make you sick?"

"You keep saying 'poison', but you've got to remember that the body is already quite clean from ten days of fasting and drinking tons of pure water. So your pee is not that foul. You think it probably tastes awful, but it doesn't then. It doesn't even smell that bad. It just tastes like blood. If you've ever sucked your own blood from an insect bite or a wound, then you know the taste. It's really not that disagreeable.

"Anyway, you drink only your morning urine and then nothing but water for the rest of the day. By then the body is pretty pure. Even so, you might still feel a little bit sick the first day or two because now you are starting to absorb poisons into your body, and it takes intense mental and physical effort to transform them. But after a couple of days it just starts to happen naturally."

"What happens naturally?"

"The transmutation of poison into nourishment. I know it sounds weird but it works. You start to feel really good. By about the seventh day on Shivambu Kalpa, you're flying high. You can't even imagine eating food at that point. You feel so light and airy. Remember, you are drinking a lot of water as well. I also did some other practices, like sun-gazing and intense breathing exercises, to fortify my body. It's amazing how the body can practically live on light and water."

All the way to American Express and back to the hotel, Sitar Sam had me entranced with his stories. He had learned to walk barefoot in the snow and feel no cold. He learned to sleep in a lotus pose, and spent long periods standing in complex yoga postures. He undertook these austerities willingly enough, so it appeared to me that he was a serious yogi. I found it hard to believe some of the endurance tests he subjected himself to, but they didn't seem to have done him any harm. He was healthy-looking, lean with good muscle tone, nice clear eyes and golden radiant skin. How could I argue with that?

He had endless stories about his time in the Himalayas, and it was obvious that his recent forty-day retreat and the time with his teacher had been intense. He'd been silent for so long that now, back in society, he welcomed the chance to talk. I enjoyed his stories and was eager to learn, and it flattered his ego that I was an attentive listener. We were getting finely attuned to each other – and I began to feel like we were falling in love.

Sitar Sam said he was done with austerities for now. He had proved to himself that he could do them, and that was all he wanted. Would he do them again? Laughing, he said, "I don't think so. Not for quite a while, anyways."

Back in the city, seeing old friends and making new ones, Sitar Sam was in an upbeat mood. He wanted to indulge in some of the hedonistic pleasures he had been denying himself. He suggested we go to a disco. "A disco? I didn't know they had discos in India!"

"They don't, really. But here in Delhi, there's one at the Oberoi

Hotel. It's the only one I know of, and the music is pretty good. It's got mirrors everywhere, and the classic disco ball and all the glitzy decor. A bunch of people I know like to go dancing there." It sounded like fun. I couldn't believe I could go out dancing in India.

Sitar Sam pulled out some black hash formed into ropes, which I thought a bit unusual. He said they were "Nepalese fingers ... nice stuff." I played with a finger like it was Play-Doh or putty and savored the fragrance as it increased with the warmth of my hand. We smoked the stuff and it was really smooth, a wonderful high. We passed the afternoon together smoking, drinking tea and talking. This was at the Janpath Hotel just off of Connaught Place, where Sitar Sam was staying. We nuzzled together kissing and cuddling for a while, and then he started to read to me and I fell asleep.

MEETING KALI ON LSD

When I woke up Sitar Sam offered me some LSD. We took showers and got dressed. I had a beautiful new saree top made of burgundy velvet and a pair of harem pants in burgundy and gold silk. Normally one would cover one's midsection with a large shawl, but I thought, "forget the shawl" – I wanted to be sexy that night. Sitar Sam bought me a beautiful garland of jasmine flowers and helped place it in my hair. It was like a crown of white flowers and contrasted nicely with my chestnut-brown hair. We popped the acid and went off in a taxi to the disco.

Dancing that night, I soon began to hallucinate like crazy. I was feeling exhilarated, as the music had hypnotized me. I hadn't danced to my own tribal music since I left Toronto. We listened to the The Who, Sly and the Family Stone, Derek and the Dominoes, Fleetwood Mac, Santana, the Stones, Steely Dan and Van Morrison. It was amazing that they even had this music. The clientele was mainly foreign, but there weren't many of us. A few hip Indians (film star types) were interspersed, but with only about twenty people in all we had the club pretty much to ourselves.

A young Sikh in pants far too tight jumped onto the dance floor. He was dressed in Western fashion, in jeans and a tie-dyed tee shirt, but his ritual dagger and ever-present turban were quite evident. He was really wild. Was he on acid? He began to leap about and whirl like a dervish. He took off his shirt, and his brown skin was shiny and wet with sweat. His turban started to untangle, but instead of putting it back in place as a proper Sikh would, he began to untangle the mass of over two yards of material ... and his massive, long black hair spilled out. I could not believe how much hair he had under the turban, but I knew that Sikhs are forbidden to cut their hair. I also knew that Sikh-dom considered it almost a sin to remove the turban in public. I rather liked the idea that he was committing a sin and really letting go, and with everyone else there I applauded him. His hair was incredibly long (to his buttocks) and voluminous, with great locks of jet-black curls all shiny, no doubt from many applications of Brahmi Amla Hair Oil.

Soon he began rotating his head such that his hair began to move in a huge circle. The strobe light chopped his movements into split-second stop motion, and the more he danced the more intense was his presence. He was a Sikh gone wild. And the crowd went wild too. Everyone was applauding and shouting encouragement as he spun himself into a maddeningly obsessive, dervish whirl.

The Sikh was totally absorbed in the ecstasy of the dance. The music playing was The Who's "Baba O'Riley" with its captivating violin solo, the first time I'd heard it. I couldn't sit still, and began to dance in step with the Sikh. Soon three or four others were whirling to the intensifying music. The Sikh's dancing so perfectly matched the rhythm it was entrancing, while the solo and underlying rhythm had us all hypnotized. Although seemingly exotic, it was also somehow appropriate for the setting.

Soon I began to really hallucinate and I watched the whirly Sikh transform into a monster, a black demon with four arms and naked to the waist. At this point I couldn't tell if the Sikh/demon was male or female, but it seemed to have bloody fangs and a strange necklace of shrunken skulls. I couldn't make out if they were human. Its mouth dripped blood and the eyes bulged with anger. The transformed Sikh/demon looked ferocious, and I was frightened. I felt dizzy and some-what nauseous, and asked Sitar Sam if we could leave. He took me to a park and gently inquired if everything was all right.

"How's the acid ... are you tripping?" I answered, "Oh, yeah. I'm tripping. The stuff is amazing." Restored from the walk and the fresh air, I finally told him what I had seen. He said, "Great! You have met Kali!"

"Who?" I asked. "Kali, the Great Mother, the black goddess," Sitar Sam replied. "Oh yeah, the monster goddess that eats men or something," I remembered.

Sitar Sam laughed heartily at my casual brushoff. "This 'monster' goddess means you have been touched by Shiva. It is very significant, an encounter with Kali. Maybe you will become a Shaivite." He gave me an odd look as if to say, "Could you be one?"

We sat silently for a while on a bench in a park, and he began to prepare a chillum. I observed his technique. He unfurled a silk cloth containing his paraphernalia. Then took out his lovely carved chillum with the figure of Shiva on it. He blew into it hard a few times to clean it and prepared the special Safi cloth by sprinkling Ganges water (from a little container that he carried around) on it. The whole while he was chanting, which I assumed was blessing the vessel as well as the contents. I later learned that the word "Safi" had the same root as "Sufi," "Saf" referring to the coarse cloth Sufis wore in protest against the fine silks fashionable amongst the elite of their time. Sitar Sam gave the chillum a quick clean by passing a twisted cloth through the pipe to remove excess resin. Then he placed in the center of the little pipe a pebble, the "chillum stone," which he kept wrapped in a dirty grey cloth. He filled the improvised bowl with a half-and-half mixture of hash and tobacco that he'd rubbed together in the palm of his hand while chanting.

He looked so intense in this little ritual that I did not want to disturb him. Once the chillum was full, he placed the newly rinsed Safi cloth around the bottom of the pipe and, forming a kind of airless enclosure with his hands around the base, tested it for airtightness and prepared to light it. He invoked Shiva when lighting the chillum, raising it to his forehead. "Bom, Bom Bolé, Hare Hare Mahadev, Bom Shiva Shankar," he chanted and then inhaled a huge cloud of smoke.

By now I was familiar with the invocation, but I wanted to know more. "Why do we say 'Bom Shiva Shankar' when we light the chillum?" He paused for moment to reflect, to blow out a huge cloud of smoke and pass the pipe to me. Pausing to enjoy the buzz and thinking about my question, he leaned back and stared at me intensely. "For me? It is because I love Shiva. I offer everything to Shiva, especially the sacred herb."

"You mean he's sort of the god of hash?" I asked.

"Yeah, I guess you could say that. According to the *Vedas*, thousands and thousands of years ago Shiva roamed the planet as a human being. Shiva was a true yogi. Actually he was the original hippie, in the sense that he was a rebel and renounced the world and decided to journey to the other side. He was a soul searcher."

I was intrigued. "How do you mean he was a hippie? " I wondered.

"I'm saying he was a hippie because he was totally anti-establishment and didn't want anything to do with the material world at the time. So he split, and went to the jungle to find out the meaning of life. He gave up all his possessions and went totally naked. He sat on a tiger skin to keep warm. He never ate food; the scriptures say that he consumed only 'food for the soul: ganja and charas' (marijuana and hashish). He spent years and years and years just sitting there meditating on life. The Hindus call him the sky-clad one, meaning that he was naked. But what most people don't realize is that he was totally wise. Shiva is one of the wisest, most far-out creatures that ever touched the planet. I rate him with Jesus and the Buddha."

Indescribable bliss was evident in Sitar Sam's eyes. I could see that he was talking about one of his favorite subjects. "Go on, tell me more."

"Shiva is part of the great Hindu trinity of Brahma, Vishnu and Shiva, who represent Creation, Preservation and Destruction. It is said that Shiva is the God of destruction, but it isn't just destruction; it is destruction for the purpose of resurrection, and this is important. Ultimately, it is the destruction of illusion. Kali, the black goddess who visited you in the disco, is in fact a manifestation of Shiva; she represents the female side. But not like Parvati, who is his actual consort."

"I thought Shakti was Shiva's mate," I said. "Isn't she a sex goddess, like Venus or something?" Sitar Sam thought for a moment. "Actually, Shakti is not really a deity. Shakti is just sexual energy. People get that mixed up sometimes."

"So does Kali have Shakti. I mean she's so ugly; does she really have a sexual aspect?" Sitar Sam laughed at this. "You shouldn't say Kali is ugly. She won't like that and might strike you down with one of her swords. Or tie your severed skull to her necklace."

I wondered ... is this guy serious? I laughed and asked for more about Shiva. "He and Parvati were a couple, and together they produced Ganesha the elephant god." "What? They're the parents of the elephant god? That's too weird," I told him.

Sitar Sam prepared another chillum and I watched his slow, deliberate movements in the dark, with his hand lit by an elegant Victorian street lamp overhead. He was so casual about smoking in the park. I asked, "Aren't you a bit worried about smoking chillums in a public place?" He said, "I come here a lot and I know the security guard. I've given him lots of baksheesh, so he lets me be. Actually, he kind of protects me from muggers and thieves."

"So how does Kali fit in with Shiva and his consort? I mean, if Parvati is Shiva's wife or mate, doesn't she get jealous that Kali has such an influence on Shiva?"

"No not at all. Because Kali is Shiva, but in another form. You know the Hindu gods can morph and change genders. So Kali is the terrible female. But in order to become Shiva she must destroy all illusion, and that is why she is often pictured doing the dance of life on his dead body – she has effectively conquered death. Kali is the culmination of all the dark forces especially expressed in womanhood. She is like the witch, the bitch, the vicious female with the monstrous appetite for men's hearts. I love her!"

I had a hard time following all this. More than once I thought, "This Sitar Sam's a little wacky ... he drinks his own piss and is in love with a monster." But I didn't really care – he had me spellbound. I realized that I knew little about Hinduism, and this guy had actually read most of the *Vedas*. He must be a serious seeker, perhaps a guru in training if there was such a thing. He seemed knowledgeable about so many things. And oh, how those blue eyes kept penetrating me with beams of love. I felt wonderful, protected and secure in his presence.

We talked all night about Shiva, Hinduism, philosophy, India and life ... with him doing most of the talking and me asking questions and listening. The moon was full and I could smell the fragrance of nearby jasmine, the beautiful queen of the night. Then the most wonderful thing happened. Sitar Sam stopped talking. The silence was perfect. He put his arm around me and kissed me with devotion. My fate was sealed; I was going to be his that night.

We made passionate love later in his hotel room. Tripping on LSD, I felt like I was making love with the multi-armed Shiva himself. The next morning I awoke to the sound of Sitar Sam chanting softly in the early morning light as he strummed on a two-stringed *dotara*, a drone instrument. I showered and we went out for breakfast. He took me to an ordinary-looking restaurant where the food was extraordinarily good. I called Mr. Prakash and informed him that I would now be staying at the Janpath Hotel in Connaught Place, and gave him the phone number. Sitar Sam had convinced me to move from my hostel because it was full of square Indians – business people and the like – and they had pretty strict rules. I eagerly agreed. We spent several days together in lovers' bliss, and over the course of this time I met several of Sitar Sam's friends.

FISCAL FREEDOM

On my seventh day in Delhi I learned that I finally had an appointment with the official from the finance minister's office. Mr. Prakash coached me carefully on how to elicit sympathy. "You must be a supreme actress. You must explain to him that you are a college student and just got mixed up with the wrong people. And now you wish only to go home and be with your family. Tell him the truth, show him your expired airline ticket ... but make sure you cry. You have to cry. The tears will really help."

I did precisely this, and at the end of half an hour I had won the man's sympathy. He gave me a writ to retrieve my money, but on one condition: I'd have to accept it in rupees only and at the current exchange rate. This meant the bank rate of seven to one rather than the black market's ten to one. I'd lose about a third of my money but this seemed fair enough since technically the government could have kept all of it. So this left me two thousand dollars in rupees, enough to manage for a while. I was ecstatic. I called Sitar Sam as soon as it was over, and he too was happy for me.

"Now what are you going to do?" he asked. I said, "I'm not sure. I have to pay off my lawyer, and then I guess I'll go back to Bombay."

"Why not just stay here with me?" he asked. I fairly jumped at the invitation. Next I called Mr. Prakash to arrange to meet him. When I had paid the 500 rupees I owed and thanked him, I informed him that I'd decided to stay in Delhi. I left his company feeling like the happiest girl on Earth. Freedom!

With just under two thousand dollars, I felt I could do whatever I wanted. For Sitar Sam it couldn't have come at a better time, as his funds were getting low and he was feeling pressure to think up a scam to get some quick cash. But with my money we'd be okay for a few months at least.

We spent the next six glorious weeks together, during which we moved into the New Palace Hotel in Connaught Place. There a spontaneous commune had sprung up, and we were there from its inception. It was a reasonable hotel, ideally located and pretty cheap, so a lot of hippies ended up staying in it. Soon there were spontaneous nude body painting parties, poetry readings and musical jam sessions.

Once an Italian film crew come to the hotel to film Shanty, one of Sitar Sam's dearest friends. Shanty was a handsome Italian hippie who said he was a sadhu and had learned to levitate. There was a lot of anticipation and a lot of fuss getting the film crew hooked up with proper electrical outlets, etc. Poor Shanty couldn't actually do it that day, but he sure tried hard. He really did. Everyone was disappointed, but made excuses such as there being too many people and the technical energy of the cameras and lights interfering with his psychic space. The filmmakers had to settle for a philosophical interview, and then spontaneous chanting as someone pulled out a harmonium and someone else started drumming. (There were always enough musicians to create an instant jam session wherever I found myself.) So a wonderful jam session ensued and that was filmed instead. I never did see the film.

The New Palace Hotel was virtually taken over by hippies at that time, and it was just like a commune. Doors were left open, and people shared lovers as easily as clothes (without even asking, I noticed), and musicians – Western and Eastern – gathered for jam sessions that went on for hours. You could get lost in the trance of East-meets-West music. Lots of drugs were available; they were always free and nobody hassled anybody for money. If someone brought out acid, there would be enough for everyone. It just worked magically.

We often read Vedic scriptures or Sufi poetry or Tibetan *sutras* at these sessions, and then a discussion always ensued: philosophy, esoteric studies, belief systems or psychology. Each day there were different readings, or sometimes performances or happenings. Someone read from *The Hundred Thousand Songs of Milarepa* with beautiful musical accompaniment. Another time we heard from *Ramayana*. People discussed Gurdjieff and Sri Ramakrishna, Jung and Goethe, Gandhi and the Dalai Lama, Krishnamurti and Yogananda. Many people were enamored of the new sensation: a meditation teacher from

In my saree with a nose ring.

Burma named Goenka. Esoteric experiences were gingerly retold and altered perceptions discussed and shared.

Without any kind of real organization somehow there was always a feast to share. I don't know how things like that happened, but someone always made sure there was food for everyone, while others made sure that it got cooked and served. Nobody questioned who provided the meal; some devotees said, "in Krishna's grace, all just appears." According to many who understand the yoga of selfless devotion and karma yoga, that had the ring of truth.

In addition to teachings and transcendence were tales of treacherous travel. Most people had come overland and been through Iran, Afghanistan, Pakistan, etc., and they all had fascinating stories. But mostly people talked about their spiritual journeys and merits of their particular guru, or their style of meditation or their mantra. And no matter who your guru was, the catchword was "BLISS".

I melded into the commune life cautiously at first, mainly because artists, academics and scholars surrounded me, and I felt I didn't fit in. These people, these world travelers, sure were pursuing some interesting stuff. One guy was even there to study Sanskrit. Being the youngest there, I felt unsure of myself. The naive kid from Toronto, they must have thought. But though I might have come across as gullible, many people responded to my dumb questions with kindness and patience. They weren't snobs at all. Eventually I felt comfortable and got used to being there. These smart, well-traveled older hippies referred to me as "the kid," and soon enough I felt like one of the gang.

CONVERSATION WITH DATTA RAM

One of the guys staying at the New Palace Hotel was Datta Ram. Well, that was his Indian name. His real name was Gabriel and he was from Montreal. Datta Ram had just come down from Rishikesh, where he had some amazing encounters with sadhus and holy men.

One day he invited me for lunch. He was handsome, and even though I was with Sitar Sam I couldn't resist having lunch with this charming and educated man. Sitar Sam said Datta Ram had studied a lot of philosophy and came to India to find a purpose.

"Can we just stop at Amex first?" I asked. "I want to see if I got any mail. I've been waiting for some news from my family."

"No problem," he smiled. "It's right on the way anyway."

We walked around Connaught Place to the American Express office, which along with an English-language newspaper was our link to the outside world. En route to a hotel restaurant we strode in silence, but I noticed that he was checking me out. Datta Ram was a bit older than me and appeared wise. I was totally infatuated.

I had only heard him speak the day before when he arrived at the New Palace Hotel. But he spoke softly and with authority, and I noticed he really listened to his opponents. He was not the least bit confrontational, although someone had tried to engage him in a conflict. He handled it beautifully ... the way a great teacher would. The way I imagined Ram Dass would.

"Sitar Sam told me you've been in India for quite a while and that you've been on 'the path' for a long time. He told me you were an 'old soul' ... whatever that means."

Datta Ram laughed at this. "I doubt very much that I am an 'old soul' but I am flattered. I've been through a few interesting experiences, but I still feel very much like a novice."

We found our restaurant, spectacularly clean (for India) in a high-class hotel.

Datta Ram ordered for both of us. Like most travellers I met these days, he was a vegetarian. When you saw how meat was slaughtered, handled and stored in India, it was easy to switch. They didn't have proper refrigeration and you often saw a carcass of a goat or some other animal with a huge block of ice on it and a lot of flies swarming around. That's how meat was transported.

When Datta Ram told me that he'd ordered *saag paneer*, I protested. "I don't like spinach." He replied, "Too bad. Eat it anyway – it's good for you. You need the iron" and smiled a fatherly smile at me. I couldn't argue with him. When I tasted the spinach in this classic Indian dish that day, for the first time, I was very surprised. I really liked it.

Datta Ram pointed out gently, "You see how you resisted the idea of spinach and yet when circumstances forced you, you were able to taste it differently? And you liked it? This is a very powerful teaching for you."

We ate mostly in silence after that, as was the custom in India. I thought about what he told me. It was true; I had to learn to be more flexible in perceiving things, including my own likes and dislikes. The food was delicious, and though I had never liked vegetables I realized I was beginning to love Indian vegetarian food.

I had even learned the Indian technique of eating with my right hand. In jail I had been taught how to form rice and sauce into little balls and pop them into my mouth like the Indians. But this restaurant had silverware and cloth napkins and waiters in gloves. The whole shebang.

I was on my best behavior, as something about Datta Ram's demeanor made me think he was brought up with good manners. I felt a bit awkward with my own background and lack of sophistication, so I was trying my best to stay alert. I noticed that Datta Ram was another one of these rare hippies who never smoked. He just said he "didn't need it" and made no judgment about others (practically everybody) who were smoking around him.

Of course, I dared not smoke hash in public places like this, but I did light up a cigarette after our meal. Datta Ram said point blank, "why do you smoke right after such a delicious meal?" I said, "I dunno … it's just a habit, I guess. Does it bother you?"

"Honestly, yes," he said. "I am curious, though; I guess I always have been. As a non-smoker I am always curious about why people smoke immediately after a fine meal. Don't they enjoy the lingering taste of the food? I don't expect any concrete answers."

I put out my cigarette and stared at him. "Tell me about your trip to Pondicherry, please. I've heard so much about the Mother. You just spent time there, I heard. What was that like?"

"The Mother is a fascinating creature. She was totally devoted to

Shree Aurobindo, and served him for many years. But through her devotion she became enlightened herself. There's not much to tell, really; you have to meet her. When you are in her presence the whole room lights up."

"Wow, that sure sounds amazing. And

Datta Ram

what about Tat Wala Baba? Sitar Sam says he is the real deal. But you know how these yogis are; they can transform and appear and disappear just as quickly. What do you know about Tat Wala Baba?"

Datta Ram ordered our chai and sweets. The waiter came and cleared out dishes and brought us a dessert. "This is *gulab jamun*," Datta Ram told me. "Have you ever tried it? It's made with rosewater. The name gulab means rose. Try some – it's delicious."

After dessert we sat in conversation a little longer and I noticed only one cockroach the whole time we were there. We must have been there over an hour – a record for me. I was having a great time. And I was so engrossed in conversation with Datta Ram that I didn't even feel the need to smoke. What was it about this guy? He reminded me of a guru, but who? Yet he was so attractive I was practically having sex with him in my mind. I kept reminding myself that I was with my beautiful lover Sitar Sam and would always be true to him. So this was just flirting. And it felt okay.

Datta Ram seemed to enjoy my company and didn't mind my endless questions. He said he wanted to get some things in the market and invited me along. He seemed sure of his way around Delhi. I knew that Sitar Sam would be busy most of the day as he was preparing for an important friend from Amsterdam to arrive.

"I notice a lot of people are reading Gurdjieff at the commune," I said. "It seems like everyone is reading Gurdjieff or Ouspensky these days. I don't get it; what's with these Russian guys?"

"These Russian guys?" he laughed. "Oh you are so cute."

To New Delhi

"Seriously, who really is Gurdjieff ... is he some kind of guru?" Datta Ram laughed heartily at that but didn't respond.

I told him, "I've tried reading *All and Everything,* but I must admit that I don't understand anything of what he says. Then I tried Ouspensky's *In Search of the Miraculous.* I guess it's 'cuz I never studied much philosophy or anything."

"No, no, Diksha. Many people don't *get* Gurdjieff. I'm not even sure I do, to be honest. I think it takes years of study and a lot of self-inquiry and introspection. But forget all that. You don't need to know this stuff now."

When we got to the market, Datta Ram bargained like a pro. His command of Hindi was quite impressive. Next we went to a laundress where he picked up some clothes. I noticed he was a neat freak. His clothes were immaculate ... ironed even! I wondered how on earth he could have lived in a cave.

"Sitar Sam told me that you had lived in a cave once. What was that like?" "Yes, that was up in Rishikesh. There's really not much to tell. It's cold and pretty barren, and the ideal environment for serious introspection."

"I heard that Rishikesh is the holy city. What makes Rishikesh so special? How come all the sadhus, saints and Sufis go up there?"

Datta Ram: "I don't know, really, why Rishikesh is so special. Actually, it's not the only holy city. There's Allahabad, Benares, Vrindavan and Rishikesh, so India has four holy cities. All of them have sadhus."

"I'm really interested in yoga, but it's hard to know which path to take. It seems there are so many paths. Rajneesh preaches the path of sexual liberation and kundalini yoga, and Goenka teaches just sitting and meditating for ten hours a day. And then the Hare Krishnas are totally into the devotional thing ... Bhakti yoga with non-stop chanting.

"Sitar Sam just did a forty-day yoga retreat with his guru and told me a bit about his experiences. He had to practise a lot of austerities. Things like fasting, and walking barefoot on the snow, and not sleeping for days, and just sitting and meditating and smearing his body with ashes. I don't understand this business of austerities. Did you ever practise austerities?"

Datta Ram: "Smearing ashes? I think he was practising Naga Baba yoga. It's pretty out there, and obviously it demands sacrifices. Austerities have their place, certainly, in teaching discipline and how to overcome the weakness of the flesh. But at some point it becomes a bit like self-flagellation. I don't think it is necessary. Anyway, Gurdjieff says austerities are for idiots."

"Wow! That's pretty funny. But what does he mean?"

"What he means is that our every impulse is to find comfort and release from suffering. It's what drives us. Yet, some people go out of their way to inflict suffering on the self, thinking somehow this will bring them closer to God. Honestly, I don't think God wants us to hurt ourselves. Look what Ram Dass says: 'If suffering comes your way, accept it and try to use it for its lessons or for your growth. But don't go out of your way to look for suffering; don't inflict it upon yourself.' Anyway, that's my interpretation."

"Are we supposed to then just indulge all of our senses and go about like animals and live in ignorance? Bhaktivedanta (of the Hare Krishnas) says that most people spend their whole lives in total ignorance – just eating, sleeping, fucking and making war. I think the human condition is pretty pathetic. I am interested in becoming more self-aware, maybe a little more mindful. Maybe I will find a guru who can give me his *darshan* (blessings and guidance) and help me become more mindful."

"You don't really need a guru for that. The blessings are already there. The guidance comes from within. Remember what Krishnamurti said: You are your own guru. Stop searching 'out there.'"

"I know but for someone like me ... I don't really have enough self-discipline. I think I need a teacher."

Datta Ram continued. "Didn't you tell me earlier that you had just spent three months in jail in Bombay? Surely you experienced some 'austerities' there – you had to do without a lot of things. And naturally you developed tremendous discipline. I think it's remarkable that you are still intact, and that you don't seem to carry any anger about it. That's discipline."

"Well, it was kind of forced on me ... I didn't have much choice. I had to train myself to stay centered or I would've gone crazy. Meditation and prayer really helped a lot. And singing. I used to just sing to hear my own voice. I would sing to God every day then and I didn't care if any one thought I was nuts."

"So you see, even the bird in the cage still sings. That's beautiful. Personally, I wouldn't recommend austerities for you. You've had enough austerities here in India. I think three months in jail is enough austerities for you. Just enjoy yourself and have a good time in Simla. It's okay to travel and to be in love and to just have fun, too. It doesn't always have to be about a formal spiritual seeking. I know you will find your way."

When we got back to the hotel an informal jam session had sprung up. We both joined in the call-and-response chanting, and naturally I smoked too many chillums. The hash was always abundant and freely shared. No one ever asked you to pay for what you consumed. In the spirit of the commune those who had means shared with those who didn't. It all worked out somehow.

THE TAJ MAHAL ON LSD

During this time the New Palace Hotel gang arranged an excursion. Someone had come back from California with first-rate LSD, and as the full moon was approaching we decided to go to the Taj Mahal and drop acid there. Three taxis were hired for the day to take fourteen of us to Agra, about three hours' drive from Delhi. We contributed collectively to food and expenses, and were on our way.

I was ecstatic. The Taj Mahal! The most romantic tribute to love ever built! I knew the story well, as I had read about it in jail.

One of the most beautiful and costly tombs in the world, it was built by the Indian ruler Shah Jahan in memory of his wife, Mumtaz-i-Mahal, who tragically died in childbirth. He built it directly across the river from his own impressive red stone palace, but entirely in white marble and bedecked with real gemstones – primarily rubies and emeralds. An octagon with a magnificent dome 126 feet high and minarets at each intersection, it was graced by a long reflecting pool and lush gardens – and was often seen to glow in moonlight. It took twenty thousand workmen (many of whom died in the effort) and twenty-one years to build, but was a true masterpiece of architecture.

For the remainder of his life, the Shah isolated himself in a tower to view the building of the tomb and commune daily with his dead wife. Affairs of state were left to his ministers, while the king mourned in privacy. But things began to fall apart and soon his son, thinking his father had gone mad, imprisoned him in his tower. Shah Jahan mourned for twenty-one long years and then died only a few years after the tomb's completion. He died gazing at the monument to his beloved wife; they say he died of a broken heart.

Now I was on my way to visit this famous monument. I snuggled up to Sitar Sam as we drove through gorgeous countryside that featured birds such as parakeets, doves, even peacocks (in their natural habitat, I marveled). Women washed their clothes in the streams; children played games with stones; beasts of burden in the fields and people too carried enormous loads of grasses on their heads; a group of men tried to coax a stubborn donkey to pull the wheel that would draw water from a well. Women and children carried water in large jugs on their heads while others gathered dung for cooking fuel, and men sat around chewing *paan* (betel nut), drinking tea or smoking biddhis.

I had to go to the bathroom, and so we stopped at a village along the way. Our driver told us there were no washrooms until we got to Agra. I couldn't wait that long, and didn't really believe him anyway. So he stopped nowhere particular, in a little enclave of dwellings, and asked someone the stupidest question in rural India: "Is there a toilet where the lady can do her business?" The woman he asked looked first at him in puzzlement, then at me as if she'd never seen a foreigner before. She pointed off to her right with a sweep of her arm, and I followed. I couldn't believe it ... no bathroom or outhouse or anything like a toilet. The woman indicated that I was to go behind a shed, with no screen or privacy. I wondered how these people go to the bathroom. (Then and still today, millions of people have no toilets.)

Finally we arrived in Agra. The weather was perfect, not a cloud in the sky. Compared with Delhi, Agra was a small city with not many Western conveniences. One of India's oldest cities, it was known for gold, lace, delicately inlaid mosaics and, of course, the Taj Mahal. We decided to let the cab drivers go, and had a picnic along the Jumna River right next to the Taj. I could not take my eyes off it. "Is it true that it glows in moonlight?" I asked.

"Yes, it is – we'll see tonight," said Shanty. "That's why they had to cover the damn thing with a huge tarpaulin last year when they were at war with Pakistan. They were afraid the Pakistanis would bomb it. The Indian army had to construct a special tarpaulin big enough." How did he know stuff like this, about the tarpaulin?

After a simple lunch of rotis and lentils, we smoked a few chillums and rested in the shade of trees in the hot afternoon sun. Then we dropped the acid and went in groups of three and four to explore the gardens and grounds of the Taj Mahal. Sitar Sam and I went alone to circumnavigate the structure before entering the tomb, a ritual he did at all temples and tombs. As we walked silently, hand in hand, an Indian gentleman with a camera approached us and said, "Here! Smell this!" He handed us a gorgeous, fragrant oriental flower, took our picture and left.

Soon I began to feel effects from the acid. "How strange," I thought, "for a man like that, a perfect stranger, to come up to two foreigners like us and give us a flower." Sitar Sam smiled and said, "This kind of thing only happens in India. I really love this country; you know people here are so cool. Think about it ... where else in the world do they donate a whole beach to a bunch of nude hippies?"

"You mean Goa?" "Exactly!" he beamed. "You don't think a whole scene like that just happens and Indira [the prime minister] doesn't know about it? She's the mother of the country. Of course she knows, but she's so beautiful ... she just lets it happen." I only half heard him, and absently said, "Wow!" But my mind was wandering to another time as I inspected a beautiful piece of ivory latticework that looked like lace and marveled at the thought of thousands of craftsmen carving stonework by hand with primitive tools and methods, yet creating such exquisite geometric perfection.

We entered the tomb of Mumtaz-i-Mahal and instantly went silent, befitting its sacredness, I suppose. Two or three other people were also gazing at the sarcophagus, silently or speaking in very hushed whispers. When they left, Sitar Sam whispered, "The acoustics in here are incredible. This is where Paul Horn recorded an album last year." "Paul who?" "Never mind."

Sitar Sam hummed a soft note that reverberated beautifully throughout the mausoleum. Pleased with himself, he smiled and encouraged me to do the same. I sang a fifth above him, and it blended beautifully with his note voice, which was still resounding. It went on and on forever, as if I was inside a bell. Transfixed by the sound vibrations spinning around me, within me and through me, indeed I was a part of that bell. Everything twinkled, everything was magic. The LSD was superb!

We spent a good half hour in the tomb and then went to see the adjacent grounds. As we left the inner tombs and came out in the courtyard, we spotted some of our group. Sydney greeted us. "Pretty far-out piece of architecture." (He was really into architecture.) "How's the acid?" and we answered simultaneously "Far out!" One of the girls in the group, Shakti Dev, sat contemplatively against a tree and attempted to sketch the Taj Mahal. Krishna Deva pulled out his flute and experimented with a pretty melody. The sun was hot, but a pleasant breeze was blowing off the Jumna River, and the shade of a banyan tree provided cool comfort.

Sitar Sam put his arm around me and played gently with my hair. This was bliss – I finally understood what was meant by bliss. We spent the whole day there. As evening fell and closing time neared, Sitar Sam found a security guard and gave him some money, explaining that we were newly married and had always wanted to see the Taj in the moonlight. The guard greedily took the money and waved us away. So we spent the whole night at the Taj Mahal, just the two of us, tripping on acid and sitting in the garden gazing in silence at the moonlit Taj. Later we sat by the river and talked through the night. We didn't even need to make love ... our connection was so magical it was totally beyond that.

CHAPTER 10

Hanging Out with Wise Guys

OTHER GROUP EXCURSIONS depended on who was in town and what their interests were. Once we went out to see Babaji. This yogi was reputedly the real Mahavatar Babaji, who was said to be ageless and timeless. The village we went to was reported as one of the places where the amazing Babaji would appear. En route there was much speculation and great excitement, for many of our group were convinced (by reliable sources!) that this was the real Babaji.

When we arrived, we found a strikingly handsome, thirty-year-old guru who sat silently under a tree and seemed not to care about us. This man was radiantly beautiful, and I thought that he didn't look like the images I'd seen but he sure looked like a perfect youth of 30. How could he be hundreds of years old? I didn't quite believe all the hype about this particular guru/avatar. But he was referred to in Paramahansa Yogananda's famous *Autobiography of a Yogi* and many other writings, so I knew he existed. But he was also known to hide himself from people; he did not want to be of the world.

This gorgeous Babaji made no fuss over us whatsoever, even as foreigners. He had no curiosity and asked no questions about why we had come. He mostly just ignored us. But we didn't mind, for everyone knew that just to be in the proximity of such a great saint – allegedly an avatar – brought untold blessings.

The Indian hosts gathered the group for *kirtan* (devotional hymns). Unlike Babaji, they warmly welcomed us as special guests and bade us sit with them near the silent teacher. I felt blessed to be in his presence for a whole afternoon, singing and playing Indian temple bells, as by now I felt comfortable enough to add some music at these sessions.

In classic Indian tradition our hosts kindly offered us chai and sweets. The chai came in little clay cups that you would smash on the ground after drinking. They were made of sunbaked local clay, so smashing them simply sent them back to the earth from whence they came – India's version of disposable vessels. Our lunch was served on banana leaves, and again disposed of by tossing them back to the earth. We sang kirtan all afternoon.

Though I wasn't convinced that this was the real Babaji, I couldn't disprove it either. This guy sure had some magnetism, and after a while I just stopped questioning and came to a place of inner peace. Alternately singing and then just listening, I was in a state of pure ecstasy while the jungle all around teased me with lush beauty and the air sparkled with something shiny. No, we had not dropped acid this time, but I was just as high as if I had – in the presence of this humble saint who just smiled radiantly, eyes half closed in an apparent trance, while we chanted.

NEEM KAROLI BABA

I GOT A TELEGRAM from my guru brother Caitanya (formerly Mental), whom I'd last seen in Bombay. "Arrive Delhi Thurs 4:00 p.m. stop meet me station stop Vrindavan Bound meet Mahara-ji 24th stop come for Holy man Darshan stop Shoshonna comes later stop"

I was excited and told Sitar Sam I wanted to go see the famous guru. Sitar Sam said, "Sweetie, I'd love to come along, but I've got Randy coming into town and we need to discuss some business. You know how it is." Of course I understood, though I felt a bit dejected. "You go anyway, sweetie. Go with your buddy Caitanya. I think it's a great idea. You know Neem Karoli Baba is already an old man. You should get his blessings – he's the real thing."

When I met Caitanya at the station he looked awfully skinny; he had been doing a lot of heroin lately. "Hey sister, you look great!" he told me. I said, "I am sooo in love. I've got this wonderful man, Sitar Sam ... but you, well, I'm sorry, you look pretty skinny, bro'," I replied while hugging him affectionately. "Yeah, I know. I've been using a bit too much lately. Shoshonna said I should go see Baba, and he can help me kick this habit. I've gotta do something, man. This stuff is killing me," he said almost apologetically.

"Maybe some time at an ashram will be good for both of us," I said. "I'd love to meet Neem Karoli Baba; he seems like a real saint. I just spent three months in jail reading *Be Here Now* every day, so it's so cool that now I get to meet the saint."

Caitanya said, "I really need a saint right now. I need a miracle ... a guru with *siddhis* (magical powers)." I replied, "Shoshonna says he has siddhis, and I'm sure he can help you kick the habit."

"Yeah, and I'd like to see the holy city. You know it is a Sacred City to Lord Caitanya Mahaprabhu, my namesake." I didn't know. "I thought it was the birthplace of Krishna," I answered. "Not exactly, Krishna was actually born in Mathura about 10 kilometers from there. But Vrindavan is totally sacred to Lord Krishna; this is where many of Krishna's pastimes occurred in the scriptures. They say that Vrindivan has about 5,000 people and 6,000 temples," Caitanya told me.

So we took a train to Vrindavan. We got there at night so didn't see much of the town, but we managed to find lodgings. My room was sparse, like a cell at a monastery. It was a typical adobe dwelling with recessed, arched niches in the walls for candles – there was no electricity – and no furniture except a rope bed. I fell asleep to the sound of sweet chanting from a nearby temple dedicated to Krishna, like most sacred temples in Vrindavan. But this one was special: it had a twenty-four-hour-a-day chant that had continued without interruption for hundreds of years. After awakening to the same sweet melody the following morning, we went to check out the temple and inquire about Neem Karoli Baba's ashram.

Not finding anyone who spoke English, we hung around for a while. I gazed around at the beautiful simple peasants gathered to sing their love to Krishna. They were not shy, they were not egotistical ... they just sang like little children. Soon I was so captivated I glided into the room, and Caitanya and I found ourselves seated in the circle of all-Hindu devotees and chanting the Maha Mantra. At least two hours went by. I couldn't believe we'd been at it for that long, but we had to resume looking for the ashram.

There was no phone or even a phone book for finding such a place, so we began by asking people. At the time, Vrindavan was not a big town and since foreigners rarely visited it was easy to find the ashram: all the locals knew that if you were a foreigner and especially a hippie, you were looking for Neem Karoli Baba's ashram. This was even before

Neem Karoli Baba reclining and having his legs massaged.

the ISKON (International Society for Krishna Consciousness) people –
the Hare Krishnas – had begun to build a temple there. Vrindavan was
off the radar and of no real interest to tourists, except to Hindus who
especially loved Krishna. We got directions for the ashram and found
it was only a few kilometers away, an easy walk.

We went to eat breakfast and purchase fruit and flowers (one
never goes to a holy man without offering at least fruit and flowers).
In those days you never had to pay to visit an ashram and it was pretty
casual: you could just show up and they would accommodate you.

At the ashram the first thing that struck me was the giant statue of
the famous monkey-god Hanuman at the entrance. It was twenty feet
high, and gaudily painted in typical Indian style. A handful of Indian
devotees and a few Westerners were at the ashram at the time, mainly
because Neem Karoli Baba's main ashram was in Nainital, near the
foothills of the Himalayas. But the great guru's Indian devotees here
had begged him to visit Vrindavan, so he was here for a few weeks.

We were greeted warmly, and offered chai and a room. We were
told that Neem Karoli Baba (whom his devotees called Baba), would
greet his *chelas* (devotees) after lunch. Beautiful Western women
dressed in sarees were preparing food, sweeping out the rooms and

carrying out various tasks of labor they called "karma yoga," the yoga of selfless service. I spent some time reading, and Caitanya played his *dotara* (two-stringed drone instrument) and sang *bhajans* (devotional songs) all morning until lunch. The food, always vegetarian, was simple but delicious: dal, rice, chapatis and yogurt. In those days people didn't have – or at least dared not mention if they did – food allergies or sensitivities like lactose intolerance. You simply ate what was given to you or you didn't eat.

Finally lunch was over. We chanted for half an hour in anticipation of the great guru coming out to greet his devotees, and the excitement was palpable. Finally Neem Karoli Baba emerged. The first thing that struck me was how fat he was. I had seen pictures of him in *Be Here Now* and on Shoshonna's altar. Still, I expected a holy man not attached to anything to be skinny. He hobbled out somewhat unsteadily, as he was an old man and it was not easy for him to carry around his own body. Wrapped in a blanket, he sat down on a divan, and two female devotees immediately began to massage his feet. It is considered a great honor to touch a guru's feet; it is believed that one can get his blessings that way. Neem Karoli Baba smiled at his little group of devotees, about twenty-five people. One by one they began offering salutations and fruit to the guru, bowing down in full prostration at his feet.

The guru was feeling playful that day. Each time someone offered him a mango or other piece of fruit, he playfully threw it out to the group and burst out laughing as his chelas ducked and dodged his fruit missiles. Soon he was throwing oranges, mangoes and bananas at his devotees, laughing while saying, "Why offer this to me? I don't need it. You eat it! You are the ones who are always hungry."

When Neem Karoli Baba tired of this game and spotted Caitanya and me as newcomers, he asked us in English, "What is your name?" "I am Caitanya," my friend said, and I answered, "My name is Diksha."

The guru looked at us with curiosity and said through his translator, "But these are Sanskrit names ... how did you get these names?" Caitanya answered, "A teacher in Bombay initiated us and gave us these names." "Which teacher?" Neem Karoli Baba asked.

I answered this time. "Bhagwan Shree Rajneesh," but the guru did not seem to recognize this name. One of his Indian devotees whispered, a little distastefully, "the sex guru."

Neem Karoli Baba said, "Tantra? Tantra yoga?" and some of his

MEMOIRS OF A HIPPIE GIRL IN INDIA

devotees nodded yes. He continued, "But why do you come to see me? You have a teacher."

Caitanya answered a bit bashfully. "Master, I was hoping you could help me get off heroin." In puzzlement the guru asked, "Haroun? What is haroun?" Another Indian devotee translated "Opium." The guru looked at Caitanya with deep compassion and said, "Opium no good. No good." Then he laid his hands on my friend's head and said a silent blessing.

Mahara-ji turned to me and said, "You, no opium ... I think you are chillum baba, yes?" He laughed as I blushed for my naughty habit.

Then he surprised me and said, "Charas okay ... chillum baba okay." Then he made the gesture of smoking a chillum, saying "Bom Bom Bolay," and pretended to throw a chillum at me. Everyone laughed. Then he moved on to the next devotee and asked some questions.

After another ten minutes of dialogue with devotees, the guru clapped his hands and said, "Kirtan, kirtan," for he loved hearing his devotees singing hymns. In no time I found myself singing Sanskrit hymns I didn't know the words to. But they were mostly repetitive so easy enough to pick up, or at least the chorus. The group really got going with the "Hanuman Chalisa" devotional song, and I thought I never knew such ecstasy. I was not high – it was the presence of this great saint and all his loving devotees that lifted my spirits so divinely. And of course, being in this ashram in this beautiful town devoted to Krishna. The ashram was a peaceful place. I did not detect any jealousy amongst the devotees, which often happens as people vie for the teacher's attention.

In this ashram it seemed everyone worked together harmoniously. So many people were softly chanting or silently smiling while they worked. I liked the fact that women were valued equally. Life seemed so peaceful in the ashram, and my only regret was that I didn't stay there long. In fact, I had only that one day with the famous Neem Karoli Baba – but it was enough to last me a lifetime.

Neem Karoli Baba sat with his devotees all afternoon. We chanted and chanted for hours. Finally, he silenced us and said, "You have seen me now. I have seen you. Go!"

And that was that. He made a move to stand up and immediately several women assisted him to his feet and guided him to his private chambers. Everyone else bowed down prostrate as he stood up to leave. Then some devotees stirred a little, stretching and walking around, while others remained seated and the music continued. Many chillums were lit and smoked as the music continued. Caitanya wanted to leave to get some more substantial food. At least that's what he told me. Although the food at the ashram was delicious it was sparse, so after the chanting he was gone. But that's not all he was craving. The following morning he was gone, back to New Delhi. I suspect he was in search of heroin.

STRANGE ENCOUNTER WITH A BABA

I stayed behind and had an interesting adventure. On the day of my visit, Neem Karoli Baba had announced to his devotees that he wanted to be alone in the ashram the following day, so they were all to leave. He simply announced that everyone had to go away. His devotees gossiped among themselves. What happened? Is Baba upset with us? But soon we found out why.

There had been a problem with a newly arrived American devotee who was doing yoga nude on the roof. In spite of their general acceptance of foreigners, Indians do not tolerate public displays of nudity. The guru had to do damage control and wanted his Western devotees out of sight, out of mind. Krishna Das, Kabir and other principal devotees organized a hiking tour of the countryside outside the ashram for all those in attendance. I understood we were all to meet at the ashram gate at seven o'clock in the morning.

But I woke up at nine and found Caitanya's note saying he'd left on the early bus to Delhi. So my friend was gone and all the devotees were on this group outing; I was alone. I was upset that I woke up too late and didn't know what to do. I decided walk over to the ashram anyway to see if anyone was around.

Sure enough, the one guy there was the new devotee who had offended the Indians with his naked yoga. He too had slept late and missed the hiking. He was walking out of the ashram gate when I ran into him. He smiled and said, "I guess we missed the tour." I nodded. He asked me if I wanted to hang out and see the town. I said, "Why don't we walk away from town and do our own hike into the wilderness? As long as we stay on this foot path and don't wander too far, we should be okay."

He agreed and off we went. His name was Nathan, he was from Philadelphia, and he had arrived in India just two days ago. I asked him what had happened the previous day. "I was just doing some yoga, and some people got upset ... 'cuz I was naked. Seems they had a problem with that. I was kinda surprised. I honestly thought the Indians were more liberated."

"You know what, Nate? I've been in India for only six months myself, and I can tell you it's an honest mistake. They're a strange bunch! First you think they have all this sexual liberty because they have tantric yoga, and all these temples with orgies and stuff. But really, that's a very small element of Indian culture, and it really has more to do with the past. Modern Indians are very prudish, almost Victorian. They're really uptight about nudity and public displays of affection. Indian society is very polite and they find total nudity offensive."

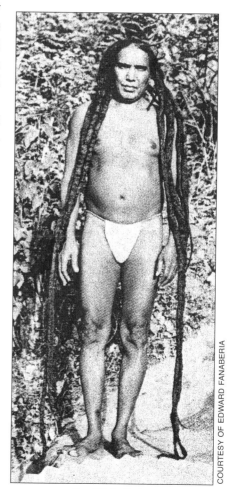

Soon we walked in silence. It was beautiful to do so with someone and not feel uncomfortable; in effect it was a walking meditation. After about two hours we paused. It was eleven o'clock by now and getting hot; we would need to take shelter from the sun. We were both a bit hungry and thirsty and had foolishly set out without food. We paused under a neem tree, and Nate pulled out of his cloth bag a large juicy apple. I hadn't seen an apple in months. It looked so good, so shiny, red and tempting. I was practically salivating.

Just as Nathan searched through his bag for a pocketknife, along came a wanderer. Until this point we had met no one on the

Tat Wala Baba

path, but now an old man in dirty rags appeared with a walking stick. He was barefoot, but the remarkable thing was his massive hair, matted and twisted into dreadlocks, culminating in one massive dreadlock draped like a rope over one arm. This sadhu's hair was longer than the length of his own body. He might have been a Naga Baba from what I could tell. Sitar Sam had told me about Naga Babas: they never cut their hair and put ashes all over their bodies.

The sadhu walked right up to us and gave us an uninhibited, toothless smile. His eyes were shining with light and piercing. We gave each other the Indian greeting "Namaste" ("I see the Light within you"). He smiled and pointed to our apple, gesturing for us to give it to him. I couldn't believe it. Just as we were about to eat our apple, this guy comes along and wants it.

But we could not refuse him. If a saint, a holy man or a hungry wanderer asks for food, it is impossible to say no in India. It just isn't done. Besides, this dirty sadhu could have been our own Neem Karoli Baba in disguise, maybe wanting to teach us a lesson. A lesson about attachment, whatever ... you never know.

So we handed over our precious apple, which the sadhu took and stuffed into the folds of his robe. He was searching for something to offer us in exchange and sure enough, from somewhere in his robe he pulled out a small handful of cashews. These were stale, dirty and dry-looking cashews. As I looked at the cashews in his outstretched dirty hand, I noticed a flea was crawling amongst them as he offered them to us. In fact two fleas were in his handful of cashews. He just smiled at us with this outstretched hand, and all I could do was accept his offering. Was this supposed to be an exchange? If so, I wasn't very happy with the deal. Still, one cannot refuse a gift from a sadhu, and even if the cashews were stale, dirty and flea-infested, food from a sadhu is considered *prasadam* (blessed).

We didn't know if this guy was a real sadhu or just a clever beggar. Either way, we had lost our apple, and with nothing but our pathetic cache of six cashews we spent the rest of the day hungry. Yet we felt fulfilled. It was such a blissful walk we didn't even think about food anymore. The sadhu's gaze stayed with me all day. I kept wondering if it was Neem Karoli Baba playing a trick on us.

Anxious to see Sitar Sam, the next day I returned to Delhi.

DR. KAUSHIK'S PLAIN WISDOM

One day we went to visit a doctor who had become popular as an author and kind of pseudo-guru in certain hippie crowds. Sitar Sam had met Dr. Rajeshwar Prasad Kaushik a few times and had become enamored of him. He told me the doctor was a very wise man. "What's so special about this guy? And is he even a real doctor?" I asked.

"If you mean a medical doctor, yes, he is a real doctor," Sitar Sam said. "He's practiced medicine for many years, but he is also a philosopher. Apparently he was devastated by the death of a friend early in life and went looking for answers, but couldn't find any by the traditional methods: religion, prayer, meditation. So he embarked on a study of the human condition, and has been at it most of his life. I think he's got some wisdom. Anyway, I think he's worth checking out."

Shanty, one of Sitar Sam's friends, wanted to visit the famous doctor for counseling, and soon others decided to come along. Once again we had a sizeable group, so we hired a few taxis to take us to a village fifty kilometers out of Delhi where the doctor lived. It would be unannounced like most visits in India, as telephones were rare and telegrams took time to arrange. Surprise visits were pretty standard and acceptable, and we were confident that the doctor would not be put out. We brought flowers, fruits, nuts, sweets and other gifts befitting a visit to a man of his stature. We also brought along a load of LSD.

The doctor greeted us with open arms and welcomed us graciously into his home. He introduced us to his wife, offered us chai and seated us. After polite enquiries with Shanty and Sitar Sam about common friends, the doctor asked in puzzlement, "What have you all come here for?" What do you want of me?"

Speaking in Hindi, Shanty briefly explained that he longed to be in the doctor's presence and missed his association and his wise counsel, and that the others just came along. The doctor smiled politely and nodded quietly while digesting this, but I got the impression he was trying to sense what was going on. The doctor's wife came into the parlor in that graceful glide that Indian ladies have, and unobtrusively served tea and sweets. In the silence that followed we were invited to chatter among ourselves and while the doctor and Shanty left the room for a brief, private dialogue.

Shanty had a delicate situation regarding a beautiful young girl from Assam (in northeastern India) whom he had recently met and fallen in love with. Shanty being Italian, a foreigner and raised Catholic, while Chui Chui was a young Hindu girl with little education and no world experience, there were major cultural differences to overcome. Shanty had come to India to study yoga and didn't expect to fall in love. Chui Chui declared she was in love with him, and left her village against her parents' wishes. Shanty wanted to make sure he was doing the right thing; he needed the doctor's advice mainly because he had been practising *Brahmacharya* (a yogi's total celibacy) for nearly two years, and wasn't sure if he was ready for a romantic relationship, let alone a serious commitment like marriage. There was no alternative to marriage, as in those days young Indian woman didn't have sex outside of marriage. It was truly unheard of; hence the discreet dialogue.

After tea and sweets were finished, dishes removed and pillows doled out for everyone to relax on, I noticed some turquoise-and-blue parakeets and budgie birds in the trees. In Canada, of course, we saw these only in cages. It suddenly struck me what a different world I was in, with exquisite tropical beauty all around and the smell and taste of cardamom lingering on my tongue after the heavily spiced tea. Somehow it all felt natural, like I belonged here. I loved it.

When everyone got settled, we eagerly looked to the doctor for a morsel of real gospel.

The doctor caught Sitar Sam's eye, and Sitar Sam spoke up. "As you know, dear doctor, many of us are seeking and wondering what we can do to attain personal enlightenment. Could you tell us your views on the path of yoga and renunciation, and wherein lies our social responsibility living in the world? I see so much suffering here in India and feel frustrated that I can't help or even imagine how to begin the enormous task of creating social equity."

Dr. Kaushik leaned back in his chair and pondered a long time before answering. "Of course, the degree and intensity of peoples' suffering is very obvious in India. And I am always touched at how you foreigners look at us and want to help. But the first thing you must understand is the prevalence of insidious cultural beliefs that is our great downfall. Our culture is defined by flawed belief systems that hold us back in so many ways. It is absolutely necessary that we in India get rid of the caste system. India has a very strong class mentality that has been here for thousands of years."

The doctor's wife and a young servant girl busied themselves with our gifts of fruits and flowers, and scurried about making sure the blinds were closed to keep out the hot sun. Fans whirring, birds singing and the smooth steady clip of the doctor's precise English had me spellbound. I was grateful that the doctor's house, unlike most in such a little village, had electricity.

For a total transformation to take place— freedom has to be discovered. And freedom means the freedom from self, freedom from the ego.

YOGA JOURNAL

Dr. R.P. Kaushik circa 1973.

The doctor continued. "I won't address problems elsewhere in the world, but here in India we confront the class mentality every day. When there is such an overwhelming need as we see here, all we can do is try to address what is immediately in front of us."

Sitar Sam interjected, "You mean that when the universe throws something in your path, like a hungry man, you have a moral obligation to deal with it?" "Exactly," said the doctor. "You do whatever you can in the immediate circumstances to correct the situation. But you don't fret over the bigger picture; that is for politicians. Life is as it is … there is no point in losing your peace of mind over what you cannot change. Just change what you can."

I looked around me at the intense faces of our little group of devotees. The doctor's house was indeed quite modest with its bare walls and lack of décor. He had little furniture or other visible possessions – but the room had a wealth of books in Hindi, Sanskrit, Persian, English and other languages. Our doctor appeared to be well educated.

One member of our group had thoughtfully provided some LSD. Sitar Sam had a secret desire to try the now-famous Ram Dass test of a guru. When Baba Ram Dass had given a psychedelic drug to Neem Karoli Baba, it had no effect and the guru was able to deflect the high back onto his devotees. Although Dr. Kaushik was pleased with our visit he politely declined the drug, assuring Sitar Sam that he did not need such stimulants to experience "what you young folks call 'the psychedelic plane.'" But he invited us to go ahead and partake ... he would find it amusing, I thought, to see how an entire group of crazy foreigners would behave under the influence of a psychotropic drug. Some of us dropped the acid and some declined; as usual there was just enough to go around.

Shanty's girlfriend, Chui Chui, was named after a flower, and certainly she was as beautiful, softly mannered and delicate as a wild flower. She told me that she had never taken recreational drugs, and I believed her. Back at the commune I noticed that she always declined invitations to smoke hash or take stimulants, even coffee or cigarettes. But this time, contrary to our expectation, she took the drug. It was evident that she felt comfortable in the presence of the guru-doctor and her beloved hero, the exotic Shanty.

After a lengthy, roundabout discussion on the meaning of the renunciant's path and the meaning of action in a dualistic world, I had enough of this intellectual dialogue. My back was sore and I wanted to move. Fortunately, the doctor paused in his discourse and excused himself from the room (we assumed he went out to the lavatory). We were offered water and fruit, and a chance to stretch our legs or go outside for a smoke. After visiting the bathroom I wandered around outside. A white peacock walked past me, but I was tripping on the acid and saw it transform into a beautiful, full-feathered male peacock. His beautiful multi-colored tail fanned out and I was fixed on its dazzling colors. Then I saw a light around him grow brighter and brighter. I heard a flute playing and suddenly the peacock transformed into Krishna in his glorious and gaudy guise. He just smiled at me and said nothing.

When I came back into the house, Chui Chui was sitting cross-legged in the lotus position, eyes closed. She was humming with her arms swaying to the melody of a flute being played by Lily, a beautiful petite English girl in our group. Following the melody, Chui Chui began shaping her hands into various yoga hand symbols called *mudras* as Shanty beat out a rhythm on a drum. She was entranced with her own movement, and soon began freely wiggling her arms and shoulders in sensual, snaky motions. Someone else began a chant and brought out a harmonium, while others chimed bells and banged sticks. Soon the timid Chui Chui stood up – dancing furiously to the increasing rhythm, like one possessed, amidst a vibrantly chanting musical circle. The music intensified, and Chui Chui danced up a storm; soon she was out of control. The doctor

Once your mind is carrying the idea of immortality, it must carry the idea of the opposite, death. And therefore death must take place.

YOGA JOURNAL 1980

smiled in approval at the music, the dancing, the clapping and the wild spontaneity.

Another girl with us was the beautiful Tanya. I didn't like her. Gorgeous as she was, she had caught Sitar Sam's eye as soon as she arrived at the commune a week earlier. A Californian of Danish descent, she looked every bit the classic beauty: tanned, long-limbed, shapely and pretty, with silky blonde hair, magnificent blue-green eyes and large breasts. I couldn't help being jealous. I had no reason to be so, because Tanya was the sweetest person you could meet. That's what made it so hard. She had given me a beautiful ivory bracelet when I hardly knew her, but I still didn't like her: she was too perfect. Strongly independent, she'd been traveling on her own for two years. She seemed to have money, and was educated and an avid reader. She and Sitar Sam discussed so many books that I felt totally left out. I remember them discussing the teachings of Krishnamurti once, and I didn't even know who Krishnamurti was. I was determined to find out, and asked Sitar Sam to give me something of his to read. But I could never keep up. Tanya was older, more confident and sophisticated, while I was just a dumb kid from Toronto.

After the chanting and the impromptu dance, poor Chui Chui suddenly stopped, realizing that she'd made a spectacle of herself. She blushed profusely, very embarrassed. She immediately sat down, eyes downcast and waiting quietly for the doctor to start speaking again.

I listened intently to the good doctor for a while, and then began tripping more intensely on the LSD. Then I turned around and noticed that Sitar Sam and Tanya were absent.

"Oh my god, they've disappeared. Together!" was all I could think. I had to keep my thoughts and emotions in check, however, for fear of dampening the party spirit. But I felt like I could burst into tears at any moment. The doctor noticed too and knew what I was thinking; it was as if he could see right through me. He looked straight at me and said, "We must be very careful about forming attachments. Attachment implies possession. And possession is pain."

So I asked the doctor, "Tell me, sir, how do you not get attached when you are in love with someone? Isn't the whole idea to get attached? Isn't that why we have marriage? Sex? Bonding?"

He laughed and agreed that was true. "But, my dear, ultimately all attachments must be broken. Even the attachment to this very body, as you well know – we must surrender it one day. It is one of the most difficult challenges facing humanity, this business of attachment. Certainly our need to bond, our need to socialize and form groups, gives us a certain comfort and security ... security in numbers and all that. So we form couples and families and tribes and social groups, and bond out of necessity. And that's why we get so caught up in our attachments."

He paused to drink some tea and survey the silent room, with everyone hanging onto his every word. I think he was a bit amused at all the fuss we made, treating him like a guru. He continued: "But this is all just common sense. I don't know what you kids are looking for ... what kind of answers. It is only a question of a little introspection. Maybe a little critical thinking, maybe re-thinking some of our belief systems."

He always gave us time to digest his words. As the afternoon progressed to early evening, the time most Indians ventured outside, he invited us to go outdoors and sit under a tree. I needed a break. I was distressed about Sitar Sam's absence and thought of the lyrics to the pop song "It's my party and I'll cry if I want to." My jealous girl's heart was quickly breaking.

Besides taking a break from all this dialogue, I wanted to smoke a big chillum and figure out why Sitar Sam had left without me. It was so humiliating. But soon enough Tanya and Sitar Sam returned from their little walk and acted as if nothing was happening. Quickly Sitar Sam began talking to the doctor and I had no chance to approach him. I told myself, "Don't be jealous, don't be childish. He still is my boyfriend." But why the fuck did he run off with her?

Right then the doctor invited us to go for a walk. Sitar Sam walked next to and talked to anyone but me. I gave up. Soon I was walking next to Tanya, who smiled at me radiantly like the goddess of love and beauty. I had to smile back and admit to myself there was no competition: she was perfect.

When we got to a bridge over the nearby river, we sat down in the shade and some paused to smoke. Dr. Kaushik asked us how we liked India. "And why do so many hippies come here? What do they want?" He was a humble man, and like most well-bred Indians possessed an honest dignity. My brain was still adjusting to the effort of hearing and understanding his English, which required intense concentration. Although his grammar was perfect, the accent left me struggling; often I'd find my comprehension lagging a few words behind.

The doctor continued. "As we were discussing attachment earlier, I think you should know that in Thailand, for example, when a young man becomes a monk it is naturally considered a great honor for the whole family, and most of all for the young man. But no matter how young they are when they take their vows, as soon as a young man becomes a monk he must promise to never again hug or kiss his mother. Never! No touching the mother ever again. Only bowing before her. This is how they understand the need to break attachments. And the mother attachment is one of the biggest."

As he continued to speak and others asked questions, I began to tune out. Anyway, I didn't dare ask questions for fear of giving myself away. I was falling to pieces mentally while tripping on acid and thinking how I must appear such a fool. As we were walking I noticed an ancient fig tree, the kind with strange long roots that hang down from the branches but eventually touch the ground, take root and form a kind of jungle jail cell. Yes, that tree really looked like a forest prison.

I realized that I was deeply in love with Sitar Sam, and that for me was indeed a prison. The doctor was right: I needed to learn to love with detachment and have confidence in my own unique self. Well, that was the whole problem. No matter what the doctor said, I couldn't let go of my attachment. I didn't even want to – I wanted Sitar Sam all for myself. He was so perfect for me. Somehow he said and did all the right things, and seemed popular wherever he went. It made me mad with envy, partly because I was not sure about his feelings for me. On the one hand he made me feel special and interesting, even though I was a pretty unsophisticated kid from Toronto. I lamented that I did not posses the suave worldliness of others in the group, but he assured me that I was beautiful and complete just the way I was. I wanted to believe him. And I did believe him.

For a minute. But why was he always flirting with other beautiful, sophisticated, educated women? It tormented me no end. I was in fact quite jealous and only pretending to be cool about "free love." When I looked into my girlish heart, I wanted to marry Sitar Sam. But Sitar Sam was not the marrying kind. He had even confessed to me that he was "hopelessly attracted to *all* women" and "that would never change." He said it shouldn't concern me because most men are like that. And he reminded me that he was especially attracted to me, and that's why we were together. But then he said he was not sure he could really love me and was a bit afraid he might hurt me.

Whoa! Too much at once. Perhaps picking up on a needy vibe in my fragile sense of self, he had qualified that with, "I'm not sure I *can* love you, sweetheart, the way you need to be loved." He had problems with the classic definition of love. I thought that was an intellectual cop-out: what's so complicated about love? You either love someone or you don't, right?

After we returned to the commune, I put up a brave facade and pretended that everything was okay. In fact, I never told Sitar Sam how I felt about him disappearing with Tanya that day. I made up my mind to accept whatever Sitar Sam had to give and force myself not to get attached, no matter how difficult that was – though secretly, I was determined to win his love.

I decided that if I could not be an Intellectual, I could at least see if I had any creative talent. Deep inside me I felt some kind of artist was eager to come out. Ever since I discovered Joni Mitchell's music I'd wanted to play guitar; now it was time to learn. At the commune I approached David, a beautiful Californian musician who took the yoga path seriously. He'd been at the hotel for a few days and had a really mellow vibe. I noticed that aside from Chui Chui, he was the only commune member who did not smoke hash or take any drugs. He said he was in a state of spiritual bliss from deep and intense yoga practice, so he didn't need further inducements into altered states; yoga was about all he could handle and he was already flying high. He was so different, and didn't mind my stupid questions. And although he did not use artificial stimulants, I noticed that he was not the least bit sanctimonious about it, and did not judge others for their drug use. He simply declined invitations to partake, and smiled lovingly.

I found it intriguing that David could be so much a part of the scene while still remaining apart. He was also the warmest and least snobby of the whole bunch, at least towards me, and I felt I could trust him. A few days earlier he'd played and sang the entire ballad of "Alice's Restaurant," and I was impressed with both his musical skill and that he remembered all the words. (It has about 18 verses.) His entertaining and fun rendition of Arlo Guthrie's song captivated the whole group.

I meekly walked to his room and asked him, "Can you teach me to play the guitar?" He smiled and said "Sure," and began my first lesson on the spot. I took to the guitar with the the enthusiasm of a new student and practiced hard. For about a week. I had a goal: I was determined to become an Artist. Then Sitar Sam would have to love me.

That evening I asked Sitar Sam, "What did the Doctor tell Shanty? It seems like they are sleeping together now … so he's not celibate any more? That seems pretty serious."

"The doctor initially told him that he couldn't advise him on 'affairs of the heart' and basically just told him to trust his instinct. But then Shanty pressed him for more, and finally the doctor told him that although he believed Shanty's desire to live the life of a Brahmachary (monk) was obviously quite sincere, he reminded him that this is not usually the path for a young man. He said, "In India one must first live in the world as a householder. That is, to marry, have a family and a job and to be a productive member of society in one's youth. However, later in life when one becomes an old man and has done his duty as a householder, then he may become a renunciant.""

One day a new couple arrived at the hotel, friends of Sitar Sam. They had become recent devotees of the up-and-coming Guru Maharaji. Then only fourteen years old, he was said to possess great knowledge and insight; another guru who had become a sensation in parts of America and certainly in India. I got some of the inside story from Sitar Sam, who was practically the guy who "discovered" him.

We heard that Guru Mahara-ji had been to America and was coming back to India with eight jumbo jets of new devotees. There would be a massive gathering, and Sitar Sam asked me if I wanted to go. "I dunno. Does this guy have anything new to say?" I asked. "Not really," said Sitar Sam, "but he is a bit of a celebrity now and there's sure to be a party. Randy's got a tape deck and we thought it might be fun if we kind of went 'underground' and pretended to be journalists and interviewed some of these kids. Just for a laugh."

And that is what we did. Randy Crazyhorse was a friend of Sitar Sam who was travelling with a professional tape recorder and a microphone. He had been involved in some kind of media or journalism back in the States.

We went to the gathering and Randy interviewed kids, who were all wide-eyed wonder and amazement. The big question at this gathering was "Do you have the 'knowledge?'" Apparently, Guru Mahara-ji dispensed to each individual disciple what he called "the knowledge." I didn't want to be left out, so I waited in line with hundreds of other kids and was given a secret mantra and some techniques to do. That was it: suddenly I had 'the knowledge."

One girl who had just arrived had the audacity to tell me I wasn't dressed properly for India. Little did she realize that I had already

been there more than six months, and she only a day. I looked at her with pity and said, "You don't have to overdo the modesty thing. We don't have to dress like nuns just because we are in India." She looked at me dumbfounded as I said a few words in Hindi just to prove I was an old hand.

Bored with the scene, I left the gathering and flagged down a taxi. Sitar Sam stayed behind to talk with Guru Mahara-ji's mother, whom he knew from two years before. He told me she was the real power behind the kid, that the kid himself was a bit confused

"India has a sadhu on every corner."

with all the fuss being made over him. But I saw the fourteen-year-old fat kid was basking in the glory of his devotees. He might have been the guru for some people, but I didn't connect with him at all.

Sitar Sam was also a bit jaded. Although he considered himself a past devotee and a bit of a skeptic, he still enjoyed the company of others who shared the blissful state. So he stayed on for the entire event.

One day another American couple arrived at the hotel/commune. Baba was a handsome 23-year-old Italian-American, and Sha Sha was a pretty, petite 20-year-old with some Hispanic blood. Although both were from New York they had met in Amsterdam. Both dancers, they were a striking couple with intense good looks. Now they were into massage and yoga, eating healthily and keeping their bodies beautiful forever. They had come from Dehradun in northern India, and Sitar Sam was excited to see them again.

I could not help but feel attracted to Baba. He was downright gorgeous, and it was obvious that he felt attracted towards me – sparks were flying. From the beginning it was also glaringly obvious that Sitar Sam had eyes for Sha Sha, and she for him. So in the communal spirit of "free love" it seemed that a couple exchange was inevitable; it was just a matter of when. But I was not sure how I would deal with it. I was far too attached to Sitar Sam, and knew I would be jealous. I had a hard time feeling this 'free love' thing.

One day at a spontaneous nude 'happening,' Sha Sha performed a belly dance. She had studied the dance in Afghanistan and was quite good. And she had a perfect body for belly dancing: tiny waist, generous hips, strong shoulders and large breasts. Her moves, beauty and sex appeal had everyone captivated; I was mesmerized. Sha Sha transformed into a love goddess, and soon everyone was aroused. Sitar Sam was totally smitten. I was a bit jealous, but on the other hand thoroughly enjoyed her performance. Now I was sure that the gorgeous Sha Sha and my beloved Sitar Sam would end up making love. I was determined that if they did, I would have to go with Baba – the hell with fidelity and true love!

My Bombay friend Shoshonna, who had arrived in Delhi the day before, entered the room to announce that she was going shopping and asked if anybody needed anything. Dressed in her usual modest saree, she opened the door without realizing there was a happening. At first she seemed taken aback to find everyone nude, and I was sure that our motherly Shoshonna – so prim and proper – was much too straight and shy to participate in this scene. She stood fully clothed, taking it all in without embarrassment.

Someone asked her to join us and she replied, "Actually, I do have to go to Amex and then to the post office, and then to the market to pick up some groceries. Then I wanted to see if I could find a certain book and ..." – surveying the room full of happy nudists – "oh, what the heck!" To my surprise, she tore off her saree and ripped open her blouse, and out tumbled her enormous breasts.

Baba was banging on a drum, and others were strumming guitars and shaking various percussion instruments. The guy who'd asked Shoshonna to stay began to dance frenetically and invited her to join him. Soon Shoshonna did so, peeling off the rest of her clothes bit by bit with everyone cheering her on. In no time the two were on the floor in a wild and passionate embrace, practically making out right in front of everybody. I was flabbergasted. Is this what happens at a nude-in?

But the couple exchange that seemed so imminent never happened, at least not quite the way I expected. The morning after our "love-in," I awoke to find a note on my pillow from Sitar Sam. He'd gone with Baba to Amex to see if any money had come, and would be back later. I was hungry but had nothing to eat. So I wandered into Baba and Sha Sha's room, finding Sha Sha lazing in bed with a book and a bowl of fruit. I hesitated, but Sha Sha smiled and gestured for me to sit on the bed. She kissed me on the forehead and offered some fruit.

"What are you reading?" I asked. "The *Kama Sutra*," she replied, and gave me a dreamy look I wasn't sure how to interpret. I said, "That was quite an amazing dance you did yesterday, sister. It was so damn sexy you looked like a goddess. Where did you learn to dance like that?"

The beautiful girl just smiled and said nothing. She picked up a mango and asked me, "You know the best way to eat a mango?" and without waiting for my reply demonstrated how.

"You need a really ripe mango, like this one – real juicy. Then you bite a little hole in the skin like this, and suck out all the pulp while squeezing the mango." I watched as her beautiful, generous mouth kissed the mango. Then her lips locked on it, and she bit a tiny hole in the skin and spit out the peel. Then she sucked long and hard, and I clearly saw the mango lose volume as she sucked the pulp out. It looked erotic. "Sort of like a baby sucking the mother's breast," Sha Sha added, smiling at me naughtily. "Try it!" I tried it and discovered that indeed it was the perfect way to eat a mango. You just suck out the juice and there's no mess. And squeezing the squishy mango did remind me of babies working their mother's breasts.

Sha Sha sat up, and both her beautiful brown breasts showed above the crisp white sheets. I couldn't help but notice how lovely they were. Sha Sha caught my eye and said, "Come here." I came closer, and she put her arms around me and gave me a kiss. But not a friendly peck or a sisterly kiss. Oh, no! This was a passionate, loving kiss, and I was afraid.

"Relax," said Sha Sha. "You know you enjoyed the dance yesterday. I saw you looking at me. And you know what? I think you're gorgeous too!" I was stunned. She found me attractive? I kind of froze. "So what are we waiting for?"

Before I knew it I was being kissed all over and enjoying it! Sha Sha was tender and gentle with me, realizing I was a pretty uptight girl. I had been unaware of any innate lesbian tendencies, but soon I relaxed and accepted that I enjoyed making love with this woman, this sensual creature. It was a beautiful experience for us both, although clearly Sha Sha was more experienced. I had no shame in this encounter.

Afterwards we stayed in bed, smoked a chillum and ordered tea. We talked about our backgrounds and our ambitions in life, and I found that we had a lot in common. I asked her if she could show me some of her belly dancing moves so that I could be sexy too. Sha Sha said sure, but then told me, "You are already a very sexy lady. Belly dancing will come naturally to you." We cuddled up together now in our newfound bond of sensual love, and Sha Sha read aloud from the *Kama Sutra*, pausing periodically to explain things.

And that's how Sitar Sam and Baba found us, two ladies in bed together flushed and fragrant with fresh sex and fruit. Though surprised, they correctly concluded what had happened. We didn't say a thing but just smiled at them. "Far out!" was all that Sitar Sam said, although I thought he looked a little miffed at being thwarted by the two of us. I got to her before he did, whoa!

CHAPTER 11

To the Himalayas

AFTER SEVERAL WEEKS IN NEW DELHI, Sitar Sam decided he'd had enough of that scene and proposed going to his country house in Simla. "You have a house? Here In India?" I asked, incredulous. "It's not much of a house; I guess we should call it a basic shelter. It's a little two-roomed affair with no electricity. And no running water, of course, but it is right in the foothills of the Himalayas with a magnificent stream running just below, and we collect fresh water. This is in some of the most beautiful country you'd ever wanna see. Even the British had their country places in Simla back in the day."

"Let's go!" I said gleefully, and hugged him tight.

We traveled by train to Chandigarh, and from there took the bus to Simla (now called Shimla). On the train Sitar Sam overheard a conversation in Hindi. He mostly understood the language and sometimes found it amusing to listen to people, especially when they were talking about hippies. Sitar Sam leaned over to me and whispered in my ear, "Shh, they're talking about us ... I wanna listen for a bit."

"What are these foreigners doing here? Why are they here in India?" one asked. "They are hippies" another replied. "What are hippies?" a third person piped in. "Hippies, they are very dirty. I heard someone say they must be outcasts from America. Look how ungroomed they are, with their long hair and beards, and their dirty clothes." Sitar Sam gave me a running whispered translation of the conversation, and we both giggled.

"Do you think they are rich? They are, after all, foreigners. How could they get here if they are not rich? You know some rich people like to dress like they are poor." "They had to get here somehow ... so

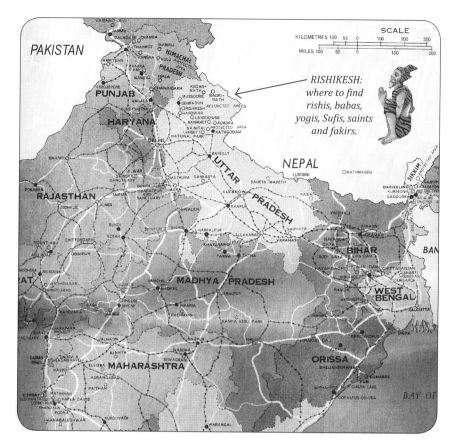

RISHIKESH:
where to find
rishis, babas,
yogis, Sufis, saints
and fakirs.

they must be rich. But they are not at all like the British of recent times.
Oh, no. The British were always so clean and proper."

The dialogue continued among three Indian men behind us on the
train. I couldn't say what caste they were, but they were workers. "Look
at these hippies: they smoke hashish and walk barefoot like peasants.
They can't be rich. Why would they be travelling second class?"

"Maybe they are spies?" said another one. As Sitar Sam whispered
this latest comment to me, we both laughed so hard that the men
suddenly became quiet as they realized we understood. Sitar Sam answered back in Hindustani "yes, we are spies," and rolled his eyes. The
Indians stared at us with a mixture of fear, distaste and wonderment.

In spite of cockroaches, funky toilets and discomfort, the train was
fine, as I had gotten used to travelling this way. But the bus ride following that was a horror. We boarded a rickety old bus that looked like its
axle would break from the load: sixty human passengers, several goats

and boxes of live chickens, suitcases and bundles, even a mini-motor-cycle. The roof was piled to nearly double the height of the bus. As we boarded I noticed the bus was missing its windows and doors, and was tilting badly. The motor was working hard, the muffler was broken, and who knew what else was falling apart. This vehicle was supposed to traverse narrow ridges of dirt roads snaking along some of the highest mountains in the world? I was quite alarmed, but Sitar Sam assured me it was safe. He'd made the journey before. "Besides, when it's your time to go, it's your time to go, right? So what are ya gonna do about it? Anyway, what can you do about it?" Great, I thought; he's getting philosophical again. Some comfort. What if you're afraid of heights?

For the entire three-hour trip I sat on the edge of my seat, pray-ing I'd make it alive and dying a thousand times. As the hills became steeper and steeper and the bus motor strained to its limit, I peered out the window only to see that the outer third of the front wheel on my side was actually over the edge of a cliff – with a drop of several hundred feet below!

I lost it and started screaming at the driver, which caused several heads to turn ... including his! This brought me to near-hysteria, and Sitar Sam screamed at the driver to keep his eye on the bloody road while attempting to calm me down. For the rest of the journey I kept my eyes closed and chanted the Lord's name earnestly. (Sitar Sam had told me that the *Vedas* say if you die with the name of the Lord on your lips you will be eased through suffering and go straight to Nirvana/heaven.) While the other passengers found my nervousness and fear amusing, I passed some of the most exquisite scenery in India with my eyes closed. Well, I saw some of it.

In the end we made it safely to Simla just before nightfall, and Sitar Sam showed me his house. As he had promised, it was a basic two-roomed dwelling plus outhouse with no indoor plumbing or electricity. He lit a few candles and proceeded to start a fire to make chai. Know-ing that we'd have no food until morning, he had picked up a small bottle of milk and a lump of sugar to go with the tea and spices he knew he had at the house. I watched him make the fire and wandered around the darkening house as the sun swiftly went down.

It got cold almost as soon as the sun set, but Sitar Sam had a fire going and a lovely cup of chai. In fascination I watched him making it. He was slow, methodical and like a monk completely absorbed in the task at hand. I noticed a little cove where he had a few small clay jars containing spices and tea. Deftly he assembled ingredients on a brass tray as if to perform a ritual. Then he began to pound the various spices with a rock, chanting "Om Nama Shiva" over and over again.

"What is that?" I asked. He gave me the Hindi and English names of every spice: ginger, cinnamon, star anise, black pepper, cardamom. To boiling water he added the milk and sugar. Then he began chewing black pepper and spit it into the mixture. "Why'd you do that?" I asked. He nonchalantly threw some cardamom in his mouth. "Do what?" he responded. "I saw you spit that into the chai mixture."

"That's right, sweetheart. There's no other way to grind them right now. I don't have a mortar and pestle. Some are easier to chew than to pound with a rock. The peppercorn bits go all over the place. So I just find it easier to chew them."

"But Sam, don't all those pepper corns set your mouth on fire? How you can you handle it?

He looked at me with a glint in his eye and said, "It's a yoga trick. You really don't taste the pepper." He chewed and chewed, and I could hear the sound of peppercorns being ground in his mouth. I was amazed at how long he kept chewing them; it must have been at least five minutes. Then he spit the whole mass into the milk/tea mixture. "We'll need to get a few items in town tomorrow," he said. "Remind me to get a mortar and a pestle, and some dhal and rice. There's some paper and a pencil over in that corner ... wanna make a list?"

"No," I said. "I wanna know why you are spitting ground-up spices into the chai. Isn't that a bit unhygienic?"

Sitar Sam laughed heartily. "You're kidding, right? You can't be serious – we kiss and make love, and we exchange bodily fluids all the time. And now you're freaked out about a little bit of saliva?"

He then explained that in the yogi tradition not only is it not un-hygienic but a great honor if your guru or teacher personally chews the spices for your chai: you are receiving his *barakah* – a blessing or benediction. "But really you are getting the guru's energy." I wondered if Sitar Sam was my teacher now.

We sipped our chai under a nearly full moon, and it was some of the best chai I had ever tasted.

I awoke the next morning and did a sun salutation yoga sequence for the privilege of breathing the crisp, clean mountain air. The place

DON'T WORRY —
BE HAPPY.
— Meher Baba

Meher Baba's mantra, later made famous in a Bobby McFarrin song.

felt utterly peaceful, isolated and almost sacred. Nothing around for miles, only the sound of the river below us. Sitar Sam was right: his house was just an adobe shelter. But it was enough to keep out the rain and shade us from the sun, and it had a spectacular view into the valley and river below us. We spent a good month at Sitar Sam's country place. I would later recall those days in Simla as the best times of my journey in India, maybe even of my whole life.

We spent the days roaming through the hills gathering wild flowers to decorate our altar. As a practicing Shaivite, Sitar Sam had to have his altar and his ceremonies and various rituals. He was a pretty serious devotee.

He had several bowls of ritual substances, sandalwood, colored powders and *ghee* (clarified butter), and little bells, incense burners and a Shiva lingam, and always fresh flowers and rose water to offer to the deities. Pictures of saints were all over the house. In fact, the only kind of décor was pictures of holy men. He had Papa Ram Dass, Meher Baba, Sai Baba of Shirdi, Hariakhan Baba (his own guru), Babaji and a couple of others I didn't know. My favorite picture was the calendar image of the beautiful, blue-skinned Shiva sitting peacefully on his tiger mat with serene eyes, the third eye glowing and the Ganges spilling out of his topknot. By now I knew most of the significant gurus and major deities in the Hindu system.

In spite of the temple-like atmosphere of his home, Sitar Sam, I learned, was not always such a saint or even a good yogi. He had brought along quite a bit of the fabulous LSD we had taken at the Taj Mahal, and we dropped acid almost daily. So the ceremonies were sprinkled with psychedelic awareness and were all the more beautiful. And so was our music, which seemed almost celestial.

We bathed Indian-style (not quite in the nude) in the river below, and though it was cold it was wonderfully refreshing. We would sit on a rock and dry off in the sun. Then we dressed each other's hair in the afternoons just before our afternoon *puja* (ritual offering to the Hindu saints).

In our simple existence we lacked even a mirror for self-grooming. A large rain barrel collected our drinking water, which Sitar Sam assured me was pure – but we boiled it anyway. Sitar Sam cooked up wonderful meals and taught me a few things about Indian cooking. I was amazed at what could be done with practically no kitchen utensils and only a small propane burner. Sitar Sam often read to me from one of the sacred books and explained Sanskrit terms to me. I was getting quite an education.

On our third day at his house, Sitar Sam and I began to make love, as we did every day. I said, "Sam, shouldn't we be careful? We haven't really got any protection. What if I get pregnant?" Sam looked at me and said, "Haven't you noticed, my dear, that I never come? There's no way you can get pregnant." He was right. So far our lovemaking consisted of him either not ejaculating or pulling out just in time. "Well, I'm concerned," I said. "What are we gonna do about it?"

He stopped caressing my shoulders and looked me square in the eye. "When we practice Tantric yoga there's no way you can get pregnant. What are you worried about?"

"Sam, how do you do it? How do you manage to not ejaculate?" He smiled at me and said, "It's called 'holding back the yellow river.' When I have the urge to ejaculate, I simply pull it back and force the kundalini up my spine"

"Isn't that hard? I mean, you're going against your natural impulse and it's a pretty strong impulse, I believe."

"Yes, it is." Sam was preparing a little bed for us. He unrolled several blankets for padding on top of his prayer mat, lit some incense and began a yoga breathing technique called *kapalabhati*. "It takes great effort and concentration, my dear."

"Isn't it frustrating for you? Don't you want to come?" He said, "The path of yoga is never easy. It's all about overcoming our natural desires in order to experience a higher ecstasy. I've had lots of training."

And so we made love, and once again he did not come. He was totally pre-occupied with my pleasure, and it seems it gave him great pleasure just to do that. "You are a goddess. Enjoy my offering " as he caressed and stroked my buttocks and entered me. I was amazed but it was true. He either never came or he pulled out in time. He had absolute control.

We had our usual dinner of lentils and rice and then went outside to watch the sunset. We smoked a chillum and sat in perfect silence for the rest of the night. No need for conversation. We were perfectly at peace with each other.

The next day, after our breakfast of hot milk and spiced tea, we went for a walk. Sitar Sam pointed out the ruin of an ancient palace, some crumbling walls overgrown with weeds. He was explaining the history of these parts, but I wasn't listening. I was gathering flowers for our afternoon puja.

Later that day I came to Sitar Sam and asked what we were going to eat. He was busy tuning his guitar to sound like a tamboura and practicing a rift. "I'm afraid the animals got into our food and there's nothing left," he told me.

"Sam, I'm hungry." "So what?" he said nonchalantly. Sometimes I felt like such a child with him. "I said, I'm *hungry.*" "So what?" he replied, totally unconcerned. "So is half of India. Get used to it."

"Why are you being so mean to me?" "I'm not being mean, sweetie. I'm just saying it wouldn't hurt you to fast for a day."

I couldn't believe what he was telling me and got pretty upset. "Look Sam," I said, "I didn't sign up for this yoga thing. I don't want to fast. I'm really, really hungry. What are *you* going to do about it?"

He was having trouble with a string that wouldn't stay in tune and seemed irritated with my pestering him. "The question, my dear, is what are you going to do about it?"

I said, "I've got money. I'm going down to the store and get some food." He laughed and said, "It's pretty late in the day for that. It's already four o'clock and it's a two-mile hike. I doubt you'd be back before dark." He was right, of course, and I was afraid to go alone. I'd heard that tigers were out there.

"Sam, won't you come with me? Please?" "No, I'm busy right now." "But aren't you hungry?" I asked. Brushing hair from his face and sighing, he said, "not really" and continued tuning his guitar.

I was mad as hell. "What am I supposed to do then?" He said, "just meditate. Sit with your hunger and experience it."

I went outside and tried to meditate. I couldn't let go of my anger. Sitar Sam was so uninterested in my needs; I couldn't understand why he was being insensitive. I sat cross-legged on the ground observing all the beauty around me. I thought we were coming here for a vacation and felt ripped off. How can I enjoy myself when I am so hungry,

I thought. I went back into the house and started searching frantically through all his little jars in the kitchen. All empty ... nothing but a few hard, dried-up raisins. I ate them anyway and went back outside.

Just then a beautiful butterfly landed on my knee and stayed there. I watched it fluttering for some time and thought about my situation. There really was nothing I could do about it – there wasn't a scrap of food in the house. And so I spent the rest of the day experiencing hunger. I walked down to the river and bathed and came back to the house just before dusk. Sam had a nice fire going and I sat with him trying to understand this yoga thing of overcoming desires. I went to bed hungry that night and thought about all the people in India who went to bed hungry every night. It really sucked.

The next morning I woke up early with the sun warming my face, and Sitar Sam was doing his morning puja. There was no milk or tea or anything for breakfast. I told him, "I'm going to get some provisions," and went off by myself for the first time. Sitar Sam called out, "Hey would you pick up some biddhis for me?" I said, "sure." But on the way I thought I would forget the biddhis. If he wanted to teach me about non-attachment to hunger, then I might teach him about non-attachment to smoking.

Every day we had a two-hour puja session that included smoking several chillums of hash, always offering to Shiva: "Bom Bom Bole, Hara Hara Mahadev." Then Sitar Sam would smear on our bodies ashes that had cooled from his sacred fire plus holy water from the Ganges. Next he read from the *Upanishads*, lighting incense and throwing flowers and rose water on the pictures of the saints.

Under Sitar Sam's tutelage I was fast becoming steeped in Hinduism. Daily I honored the various saints and gurus on the altar and learned to pronounce all their names and learned all their attributes and *siddhis* (miracles). I became increasingly comfortable with Sanskrit words, and pretty soon had a basic vocabulary. In the evenings Sitar Sam serenaded me with his guitar under the moonlight, and we talked of philosophy and the meaning of life.

I really blossomed in this environment. Sitar Sam pointed out that I was becoming calmer and learning to quiet my mind chatter. I also learned how to be silent, realizing one does not always need to talk. We don't always need to fill the void with conversation, I thought; we can just be in one another's presence.

One silent night when the moon was full, Sitar Sam looked at me and said, "You know how I told you about a month ago that I wasn't sure if I could ever love you?" Sure I remembered, and answered cautiously. "Yeah...?" "Now I'm not sure that I could *not* love you." He drew me into his arms, and I was ecstatic: Sitar Sam was mine.

The days passed smoothly as we two lovers became more and more entranced with each other. Soon I was convinced that Sitar Sam and I were the Divine Couple, as Richard had told me about in Bombay.

After several weeks of bliss we decided it was time to return to Delhi to check the mail and see if Sitar Sam had received any money from his friends in Amsterdam.

MEETING KRISHNAMURTI

When we got back, Sitar Sam got a written notice that his visa had expired and could not be renewed. He'd managed to bribe his way through two years of living in India, although an American's visa was good for only three months. It seemed that the visa official would no longer extend his visa for fear of arousing suspicion; Sitar Sam would have to leave the country. But he was not ready for this: he did not want to leave, and didn't have the money to do so.

"Shit, this is really a bummer. I guess I should've figured it would happen sooner or later, but I was hoping we could go to Goa together," he said as he prepared a chillum. "I think you've been pretty lucky so far with getting the visa renewed," I offered.

"You're lucky, being Canadian," he countered. "You don't even need a visa. You can stay as long as you want." (Though independent, India was still a member of the British Commonwealth, along with Canada.)

Sitar Sam ordered some chai from a chai wallah, and as we drank our lukewarm tea a giant cockroach scuttled across the floor. Sitar Sam didn't budge. I grimaced as usual, and he said, "You get used to them. Don't worry."

"Yeah, right," I replied. "I've been on boats with cockroaches and trains with cockroaches and seen them in every restaurant and hotel, and even in taxis, for God's sake. They're everywhere – this is the land of fucking cockroaches." Sitar Sam laughed and gave me a hug. "That's what I love about you. You're so ... honest." I melted in his embrace and mumbled something like, "I'm not gonna pretend I like them."

We made passionate love, and it seemed each time we had sex it was better than the previous time. We had a magical connection that was almost telepathic, as if he could read my mind. Sitar Sam was practising tantric yoga, wherein the man does not ejaculate, and I think it helped. At least it prevented unwanted pregnancy.

As I lit up a cigarette I asked, "Can't you just go away for a week or two and come right back?" He said, "Yeah. I'm just not sure where to go." Sitar Sam had ordered some hot water, towels and soap from a hotel servant. He wrapped a sarong around himself and proceeded to bathe me. He always washed me first and then himself; he was thoughtful that way.

Later that day Sitar Sam said: "I've got a plan. Remember my friend Irish Patrick? The one with such a lovely accent who was at Shanty's happening a few weeks ago when that film crew came by? I ran into him today, and he said we should go to Nepal. He said we'd fit right in and there's a happening scene there and we'd love it. And that it's a nice break from India."

Nepal was the closest and safest neighboring country. "What's up in Nepal?" I asked. "First of all, it's way up in the Himalayas, and secondly it's right next to Tibet – well, China-occupied former Tibet, to be exact. Lots of Buddhists are up there, and Patrick knows some cool people. He gave me a contact so we can send them a telegram and let them know we might be in town soon."

"Wouldn't it make more sense to make a long distance call?" I asked naively. Sitar Sam answered, "Do you have any idea how remote Kathmandu is? Nobody has a phone there except maybe the king and some government officials." "There's a king?" I asked. He said "Yes, that's' why it's called the Kingdom of Nepal. I'll tell you more later. We need to read up on this."

We discussed it briefly, and in no time I agreed. "I'm looking forward to meeting some Tibetans, and it might be a nice change from India." So I gave him the money we needed and he arranged for us to fly to Kathmandu. We had a week to leave the country. Sitar Sam hoped his friends would arrive from Holland and bring him the money he was owed. He assured me that he would reimburse me for the cost of the tickets to Nepal, and I always believed him. But his friends never came.

The commune in Delhi had dispersed, though a few people were still hanging around. It had gone from a core of about two dozen people down to seven or eight. Someone mentioned that the famous Jiddu Krishnamurti was in town and would be giving a lecture the following Friday. Sitar Sam was a big fan and was eager to go. I was barely familiar with Krishnamurti and therefore unimpressed by what I thought was just another guru, though in this case one who didn't want to be treated like a guru.

Because of Sitar Sam's connections we were fortunate to get a front-row seat. I loved sitting close to this wonderful man, because I saw how sincere he was. Though at times I didn't follow what he was saying, it was really nice to have him speak right in front of me and look at me. Sometimes he seemed to be speaking directly to me. But I knew that was ridiculous: the auditorium was packed with maybe five hundred people. His dialogue was intellectual and sometimes Byzantine. Once again I had trouble following what a famous teacher said, but listened politely with undivided attention.

After Krishnamurti's address, the host organization put on festivities that naturally included food, sweets, music and dancing. Indians love to dance, and at most occasions they find a reason to dance. I noticed that it was almost always women with women and men with men. I saw a circle of ladies dancing and was enjoying the lively up-tempo music. When they beckoned me with outstretched arms, I jumped into a circle of dancing lady devotees. I knew the chant and the movements to this folk dance from my time in jail.

The women were surprised that I knew the Sanskrit words and movements, and laughed and pointed to me with encouragement and joy. They threw garlands of flowers on me and clapped in time as I fell in step with the simple folk dances. When I didn't know the next dance they taught me, and I managed to pick up the steps and even the words to the song. Sitar Sam saw that I was the center of attention of these delighted women, and his face beamed with pride.

Later he introduced me as "his woman" to a dear friend. He told me, "Diksha, you've grown so much in such a short time. I've witnessed this transformation, and you are becoming even more beautiful to me than when I first saw you. I don't know how that's possible." Now I was in seventh heaven. Finally Sitar Sam saw something of value in me. All I could think was, "Sitar Sam, could it be like this forever?"

CHAPTER 12

To Kathmandu

THE FLIGHT TO NEPAL WAS HAIR-RAISING. In a tiny aircraft seating approximately 25 passengers, we rattled through turbulent air and bumped our way across the Himalayas. "Look at the magnificent view," Sitar Sam coaxed. But as on the bus to Simla, I was too frightened to look out the window. I sat on the edge of my seat, terrified and praying earnestly that once again God would spare me a horrible fate like crashing in the mountains.

It was a short flight but Nepalese Royal Airlines kindly provided food. I received a small cardboard box with dried meat and cold rice, which I could barely look at. "Is this for real?" I wondered. "Am I supposed to eat this?" We were the only Westerners on the flight, along with one or two Nepalese, the captain and the pilot. Every now and then I glimpsed the glorious Himalayan landscape below me, snow reflecting sunlight like a thousand little diamonds. But then we'd hit another wind shear and drop, and my heart would again be in my mouth and I'd cover my eyes and hold on to Sitar Sam for dear life. Soon enough, though, we were on the ground again and taking in a new and different country.

Kathmandu in 1972 was quite a place for a young hippie girl like me. The city was filled with colorful characters from all parts of the world. Indeed, it seemed as if hippies were half the population in Kathmandu. They came from America, Europe, even Australia. They came to smoke great hash, legally. They came to study Tibetan Buddhism, or to trek in the mountains. Or just to hang out in one of the freest, coolest places on the planet at the time.

I soon discovered one of Nepal's main attractions. Our first day

One of many legal hash shops on Kathmandu's Freak Street around 1972.

there was sunny and we strolled down the main street named, believe it or not, "Freak Street", which until 1968 had no name. We browsed in various shops and then came upon Eden Hashish Centre. I couldn't believe my eyes. I 'd heard that hashish was sold legally here, but now I was actually standing in front of that shop. And there were many others just like it. How I wish I had a camera then – but who traveled with a camera in those days? By the time you'd gotten to Nepal it would have been lost or stolen or even sold, because so few people actually had such a luxury. We sampled a few different types of hash and finally settled on some nice local stuff. Sitar Sam sure knew his hash, and you could obtain any form of ganja or hash you liked there.

As we left the hash shop, Sitar Sam pointed. "Look, there's Wavy Gravy. And Dr. Larry Brilliant and Tent Tom. Remember them from Woodstock?" I didn't go to the Woodstock Festival" I said. "Yeah, but you saw the movie, right? Wavy Gravy and Larry Brilliant were there, man, doing the free food and medicine tent. And Wavy Gravy was one of the emcees, remember?" I recalled a scene from the Woodstock movie. "Yeah, he's quite a crazy character," I answered. "But what are these guys doing here?"

MEMOIRS OF A HIPPIE GIRL IN INDIA

As we walked down the street Sitar Sam, who seemed to know everything, told me, "I heard they were on their way to Bangladesh to help out after hearing about the disaster there from George Harrison's Concert for Bangladesh. Tent Tom drove their bus all the way from Europe to India, but then they got railroaded 'cuz a civil war had broken out in Bangladesh and they couldn't even get near the border. So they diverted and came to Kathmandu – they heard there was a happenin' scene here, I guess."

I was impressed. "Wow. You never know who you'll meet on the hippie trail." And I realized I was there. I had arrived.

As we walked along Freak Street, Sitar Sam pointed out shrines and places of importance. I couldn't believe how primitive, even medieval, the city looked. There were hardly any cars, and most roads weren't even paved, just dirt roads with pedestrian traffic, animal carts and the occasional taxi. The buildings were ancient, often wood

Available as Always:
Different Varieties;
1. Parwati Charesh (HASHISH)
2. Arcant (HASHISH)
3. Attar (HASHISH)
4. Temple Ball (HASHISH)
5. Ali Bamm Ganja
6. Tarai Flower Tops
7. Green Ganja
8. Mountian Flower Tops and Cookies
9. Tiger Tail
10. Hashish Oil

A menu and promotional cards from some of the government-licensed hash shops.

OVT. REGD.   Phone No. 14658
-: PLEASE VISIT :-
CENTRAL HASHISH
STORE
389 MARUHITY TOLE, KATHMANDU 14
NEPAL
FOR BEST NEPALESE HASHISH & GANJA.
WE ARE ALWAYS AT YOUR SERVICE.
S. M. BASNYAT

construction with once-colorful peeling paint. Very few places had electric lights or any kind of modern technology. Kathmandu was the most primitive city I'd ever seen.

Tent Tom

"Hey, you wanna get something to eat? I heard there's a neat restaurant nearby that's in a cave. They are totally cool" – which to us meant friendly to hippies. I believe it was the Yak & Yeti, and everything on the menu had cannabis in one form or another. Hash tea, ganja soup, breads made with ganja ... everything. And it was all vegetarian and tasted pretty good. We got blasted that day.

Another time we went to the Rosy Mushroom cafe run by Afghan Ted (who was really an American) and Tory (Victoria), who started this little hippie cafe. As soon as you walked in you were greeted with a complimentary chillum. In fact, everywhere we went, hash and free chillums were abundant. A *chillum* (clay conical pipe) was the common way to smoke hash. The cafe also had some amazing music, and I remember dancing there among curtains of sarongs and garlands of flowers. Afghan Ted and Tory became legends as the first couple of the hash trail. I don't know if that's true, but they were definitely innovative and ran a really cool place right in our part of town.

Most such places had no electricity so lighting was minimal, consisting of oil lamps or candles. And the only music available was on cassette players that the hippies brought and provided tapes for.

Hippies openly smoking chillums on a stupa.

These were run on car batteries or other improvised batteries. At night the city got pretty dark and the only street lighting was from dim oil lamps and, if you were lucky, moonlight.

Kathmandu was a crazy and free place

– sometimes I really felt like Alice in Wonderland. We stayed near the Swayambunath Temple, where Sitar Sam had found us a place through Paul G., known as the Hippie King of Nepal. He'd been there so long that he knew all the local feudal lords and important lamas, and even members of the royal family. He spoke Tibetan and Nepalese, and understood the culture like one born to it. He had also converted to Buddhism. Paul's own large white house was the only one in the area with electricity and proper plumbing – rather luxurious compared with the standard dark hovel typical of Nepalese dwellings.

I instantly liked Paul. He was kind enough to escort us on the long hike uphill on our first day there, and I noticed he was cheerful and said hello to everyone he met. He spoke to some in Tibetan ("Tashi Delek"), some in Hindi ("Namaste") and some in Arabic ("Salaam Aleikum"). The first time I took that climb I thought there was no way I could do this more than once a day. It was a very slow walk. We were several thousand feet above sea level, and I wasn't used to such altitudes.

After an hour of hiking uphill we finally got to the temple. It was known as the Monkey Temple because so many monkeys lived nearby, although that was not its official name. Paul paid his respects to the lama, and although we were invited in to tea, he declined in order to settle us into our new house before dark. Paul pointed out various plants and animal species, and then we mostly walked in silence. It was so remote-looking I was a bit worried. I remember asking Paul, "Are there any stores up here, or some place to get supplies?" He looked at me as if I was some pathetic child and laughed. "Up here?" stretching his arms to point out the vast wilderness. "You're joking. No, I'm afraid you have to bring your own supplies."

The hill was named after a Hindu goddess, Saraswati. I couldn't figure out how the Hindu goddess's name reigned over a hill occupied by mostly Buddhist monks, but with the way various cultures over-lapped in Nepal I didn't query it then. Then Paul said, "Turn around." Snaking away behind me was Kathmandu Valley, and the entire little city of Kathmandu began to vanish. Clouds were moving in and soon the whole city disappeared; all we had to look at now at was the Himalayas.

Off in the distance I saw magnificent snow-capped peaks against a violet sky. "There's Mount Annapurna," Paul said. "It's one of the highest peaks you'll see from here. Almost as high as Mount Everest." I asked eagerly, "Can you see Everest from here?" Paul replied, "No, we've got the wrong vantage point. But from the other side you can see it just fine on a clear day."

Our brief time on this mountaintop was another of the very best times in my travels. Sitar Sam and I used to awake for early morning meditation and observe the comic antics of the cute monkeys. On my first day I saw a couple of Buddhist monks chasing the monkeys, cursing them and beating them with sticks. "I always thought Buddhists were pacifists," Sitar Sam exclaimed. "But look at these guys go. These monks are positively vicious."

Indeed, they were. I could hardly believe that Buddhists were so mean. Only later did I understand that the monkeys were notorious thieves and stole food from the temple stores. It was necessary to be harsh with the monkeys, for they could rob you blind.

With the complete absence of motorized traffic or 'city noise' atop the hill, we heard only the wind and temple bells or the monks chanting, or sometimes monkeys walking on our tin roof. But there was no radio or television or even a phone for miles, and it felt like not only another place but another time – like Middle Earth in *The Hobbit*, which I had just read. There wasn't much to do. We made simple meals on dung-fueled fires, and kept water in a clay pot with a lid. Like so many other houses in Kathmandu, ours was not much more than a

The valley of Kathmandu in the early 1970s.

MEMOIRS OF A HIPPIE GIRL IN INDIA

wooden shack, a basic shelter with no glass windowpanes or any such luxury. In case of rain we had shutters to close, but then it would be dark inside. And if we lit a fire inside we'd choke on the smoke. So if it rained we stayed in bed, dropped acid and made love.

Nepalese houses were built for the short people who resided in this little kingdom; ceilings were generally about five feet three inches high. That meant most foreigners had to duck their heads to enter a typical Nepalese house or business – very humbling. Really tall people had to sit down immediately, because like Lewis Carroll's Alice they were simply too large for a doll-like house. But by now I was used to these types of houses. In any case we spent most of our days outdoors and really only slept in the house.

There was no plumbing anywhere on the mountain. We did our toilet in an outhouse. Like the monks and our neighbors, we purchased water from a water bearer who hauled it up the mountain for pennies a bucket. This barefooted little man carried five-liter buckets on the end of a long pole straddling his upper shoulders and neck. I used to see him bouncing up the hill and noticed he had a special way of walking, a certain cadence or rhythm. I wondered at how such a slight man carrying all that weight could fairly run up the mountain, and thought he must have tremendous stamina and amazing lungs. After several days of watching him I discovered his technique. Like a rickshaw wallah, once he had a certain momentum he could not stop. The water

A typical Nepalese house (note the short door).

bearer never spilled a drop and always delivered water on time. I decided to pay him a lot more than double for the water he brought me.

In a typical Nepalese house, candles, oil lamps or gas burners served for light. There was no firewood to speak of, so cow dung was used as cooking fuel. Surprisingly, cow dung was a great odorless fuel, and I soon got used to it and always associated it with good cooking. Once a week we went into town for a real treat: a hot shower in Kathmandu's only public bathhouse. It cost 10 Nepalese rupees (about 75 cents) for 20 minutes. But it often proved disappointing: the water was rarely hot but mostly lukewarm for the first 10 minutes, and downright cold after that.

Otherwise we bathed in a nearby river. The Tibetan and Nepalese ladies, just like the Hindu women I had met, didn't bathe in the nude. Their modesty could be attributed to the fact that most people did not have the luxury of private bathing facilities. They used the river, pond or whatever body of water was around. And of course they bathed in broad daylight, at the sunniest and warmest time of day. I joined the women and learned how to bathe partially dressed.

The river was also the place to wash clothing. There was no washing machine nearby that I knew of, so I had to learn how to wash my clothes in the local fashion. This consisted of soaking them in the river, then rubbing a bar of soap into them to lather up. In lieu of an agitator we rubbed the soapy wet clothes against a rough-surfaced rock (like an old-fashioned washboard) and then rinsed again. To extract the excess water we manually twisted the clothes and then beat them against the rocks. This worked marvelously well. Finally the clothes were laid out on the ground to dry.

The women were impressed that I washed clothes with them, and nodded with approval as I copied their technique. They had strong arms and could really beat those clothes and wring them nearly dry. We had no language in common but a lot of sign language and laughing, as they tried to teach me their language. Sometimes they sang as they worked away. I loved the sweet innocence of their heartfelt singing, mingling with the sound of the water rushing as we splashed and waded ankle deep in the sun-warmed river. High noon was the only time to do the laundry, because if you waited too long there wouldn't be enough sunshine to dry the clothes, and the water you were wading in would not be at its warmest.

Clockwise from top centre: Ira Cohen (waving) Petra Vogt,
unknown Australian (peace hat), unknown (Canadian Lynn K.?),
Andy, Margo, Paul G. (Hippie King), Svetlana, and Sitar Sam.

Nepalese food was also new and interesting to me. At our favorite little restaurant, Sitar Sam ordered *buff tupka* for us. I had no idea what this was. "Well, they don't have cows here, and they don't eat beef. But they do have a lot of water buffalo, and they eat the meat and drink the milk the same way we do with our cows." Buff tupka was water buffalo meat cooked with noodles and yak butter. I was surprised to learn that Tibetans were big meat eaters. But I had no hesitation about consuming meat in Kathmandu, for the Nepalese offered the freshest meat possible: lacking refrigeration, they often slaughtered and ate the animal the same day. In the Brothers Café I witnessed a live goat being brought in the restaurant's front door and coaxed past incredulous Western onlookers to its inevitable doom via the cook's knife. This would be dinner tonight.

The Brothers Café was a meeting point for Westerners. Amongst the monks who frequented it were also a lot of hippies, students and backpackers eating, drinking tea and smoking chillums. Many a trav-

To Kathmandu

eler had left a memento in the form of a photo or a note, so the café's walls were covered with pictures of hippies from every imaginable part of the world and walk of life. It was a kind of message board for travellers. A typical note might read: "For Danish Parvati – change of plans. Goa bound. Write until Nov 15th c/o Thomas Cook, Anjuna, Goa. After 15th heading to Madras ... J. & B."

Sitar Sam took to hanging out at the Brothers Café daily, smoking chillums while thinking and networking. One day I found him talking to an interesting guy I'd seen at Paul's house. "Diksha, meet Ira Cohen." I nodded politely and allowed the two to continue talking. They were discussing the Kumbh Mela, a Hindu pilgrimage that culminates in mass bathing in a sacred river, and the possibility of filming it. After Ira left, Sitar Sam said, "Ira's a really cool freak, man. He's organizing a poetry reading at the white house tomorrow, and asked us to come."

Blowing on my chai to cool it, I noticed skin on the hot milk beginning to form while Sitar Sam gazed at the community message board where people left notes. He seemed to be networking all the time, getting desperate to make some cash. "Maybe next Khumba Mela we'll film it. It would be so cool – no one's ever done it before. And the next Mela is just next year."

"Isn't Ira staying with that strange woman at Paul's house?" I asked. "You mean Petra. Yes, they are a couple. She's an actress, and Ira is into photography and film and stuff. They make a nice couple, don't you think?"

I wasn't sure. "She's kind of aloof, I find" was all I could muster. Sitar Sam prepared a chillum as we drank our chai. "He's a pretty heavy dude. He did some nice photos of Hendrix and then started a magazine called *Guoung* and basically launched William Burroughs."

"William who?" I wondered. Sitar Sam, startled, gave me a condescending look and said, "I keep forgetting how young you are."

Sitar Sam had bought me a beautiful pair of Tibetan boots of black cotton and felt. They looked a lot like the 'Eskimo' boots in Canadian souvenir shops. He unwrapped the newspaper-bound present and gave it to me with a kiss. Then he pulled out a beautiful sterling silver snake belt with turquoise eyes. I loved it, and jumped out of my seat to hug him tight. "Sam, these are so beautiful ... but can we afford presents right now?" "Don't you worry your pretty little head about that" he said. With what I've got in the works we'll be flush soon."

So Sitar Sam worked at developing a friendship with Paul, hoping to get a deal going. Having been referred by a good mutual friend in Delhi, Sitar Sam knew Paul had the best connections and the credentials. Though his title as the Hippie King of Nepal is disputed, Paul was one of Nepal's oldest foreign residents and had apparently been there since 1967. He told Sitar Sam, "You've gotta understand that this place just came into the twentieth century five years ago. There was no electricity anywhere in the entire kingdom until just five years ago." Paul knew everything that went on in town, and he was generous and tolerated just about everything – except heroin. At the time, amazingly, heroin use was unknown in Kathmandu; at least, I didn't see any street junkies as I had in India. Paul and the mellow hippies who started the hippie scene intended to keep it free of hard drugs. Chillum babas were always welcome because they smoked only cannabis. Kathmandu had a very laid-back vibe, and the Nepalese and the many displaced Tibetans living there graciously tolerated the hippies in their community.

Paul had amazing influence with the lamas at the various temples, and knew their personal lineage and various sects and subsects. He was almost forty – which to me and other younger folk seemed old. A gentle, gracious, graying hippie, he had the charm, poise, power and purpose of living a nice quiet life in Nepal, and he wanted to keep it that way. Sitar Sam told me that Paul was an American kid whose parents had been in the diplomatic service. Born in Bombay and living in Nepal in recent years, he had actually spent most of his life in the States. Paul had been a cab driver in New York City for some years, and in the late 1950s had hung out in Greenwich Village and personally knew people like Andy Warhol and Allen Ginsberg, which gave him a major cool factor. I was not really impressed with any of this, but everyone else practically revered him. Sitar Sam, in spite of himself, was deeply impressed.

Christmas was coming and Paul was planning a party. But before celebration there was obligation. As a practicing Buddhist, he needed a blessing ceremony before embarking on the holidays and a new year. I guess he also wanted to bless whatever business operations were currently happening. A good friend of Paul had recently been busted and thrown in jail in Kathmandu. This shocked the whole community, as the guy had been in business for a long time and there had never been any trouble. Paul felt it wouldn't hurt to pull in the power of the lamas and arrange a ceremony to help the brother in jail, and to bless Kathmandu and all the hash makers. And so we were invited to attend a gathering of a twenty lamas and at least thirty monks who would perform a puja on request. It was understood that Paul would make a significant donation to the temple.

The tiny temple hall, lit only by candles, was really dark compared with the bright afternoon sun outside. Prayer flags and other symbolic gadgets were strung up, and the smell of incense and yak butter was ever present. Also the strangest instruments I'd ever seen: something like an alpine horn about twelve feet long. There were massive hanging brass gongs, some maybe four feet in diameter. There were prayer wheels, brass *dorges* (hand-held Buddhist implements) and other instruments used in Tibetan rituals.

As my eyes adjusted, I saw the monks and lamas in full costume and headdress. It seemed a great ceremony was about to begin. There were offerings of incense, garlands of flowers, fruits and nuts. Once a dedication to His Holiness the Dalai Lama was pronounced, the head lama began reading from a sacred text, one of the Tibetan *sutras*. Then he began to chant in the fabulous, deep, almost groaning voice that Tibetans are now famous for. Soon there was a kind of call-and-response chanting; at times he chanted alone and at others the whole gang joined in. When they all blended their voices with the continuous ringing of a gong I heard layers and layers of overtones, and the sound became so powerful I felt we were moving into another dimension. What is it about real music, spiritual music, that transports us into the realm of the soul?

I didn't understand a word of Tibetan and certainly understood little about the whole ritual, but apparently it was a real blessing to have that many monks and lamas chant for a specific purpose. Paul, Irish Patrick, Ira and Petra, and Sitar Sam and I were the only foreigners at this special puja, which took more than two-and-a-half hours. The lamas were going all out for Paul and, based on what I knew, it sure seemed that his life was blessed. He was very respectful of the lamas and the monks, and in their own way they respected him too.

Every Saturday afternoon it was customary for several of the hippies and many locals to go to the *chyang* shop. Chyang is a kind of rice beer, a much cruder form of fermented rice than the well-known Japanese sake. This stuff was milky, sour and bubbly, and had the most revolting smell. I certainly never drank it and couldn't understand why it was so popular. Paul had taken to hanging out with some of the local folk who liked to drink chyang. The most popular shop in town was at the Boudhanath Stupa in the center of town. It was easy to spot because its dome had two stylized Tibetan eyes painted on and could be seen from anywhere in the city as no buildings were more than two stories high at the time. It was in fact a major temple complex, and every day you could see several devout Tibetans perambulating the *stupa* (mound) with a prayer wheel chanting a sacred mantra.

Many of the hippies in town lived in the area and gathered at this particular chyang shop. All afternoon they would drink the foul rice beer and smoke copious quantities of hash. Endless chillums went around, and everyone got drunk, happy and chatty. Again I was surprised to see Buddhists consume alcohol. Some of the Sherpa women, at least in Nepal, even drank the foul chyang. Sitar Sam pointed out that one woman was flirting with a foreigner. "The Sherpa women can have more than one husband" he told me. "I had no idea. That sounds pretty liberated." "Yeah, it's rare, but their culture allows for polygamy for both sexes."

As Christmas approached, Sitar Sam was getting antsy. He wanted to contribute to Paul's big party and get gifts for me and some friends. In spite of repeated long distance calls and telegrams, he still had no money from his partners. One day a letter from his parents came with a gift: a ticket to Israel. Sitar Sam's parents were concerned that their son had gone to India two years previously and hadn't come back. They didn't like this yoga/Hindu stuff, and wanted him to explore his Jewish roots. Sitar Sam had no desire to go to Israel at that time, but saw an opportunity. He called his folks and asked them to change the ticket ... he would come home for a visit! Of course, they were delighted to hear that and immediately changed the ticket. So now Sitar Sam had a single ticket to California. I thought he was waiting for a special order of hash oil, but minded my business and never asked Sitar Sam about his business dealings. By now I knew any business dealings by hippies would surely be illegal. Sitar Sam planned to go home the day after Christmas and stay in the U.S. about two weeks. He was waiting for some Tibetan carpets and other art stuff to take back.

Paul's Christmas party was fun and full of colorful people, but not the romantic event I expected. I was secretly upset that Sitar Sam did not invite me to travel with him to California, which I had always wanted to see. Besides, I would have traveled anywhere just to be with him – I was concerned that he might fall in love with another girl and abandon me. I was hoping for a romantic evening at the party and some promises under the moonlight. Promises like: "I still love you. I'll be back. Please wait for me ... it's only two weeks. Don't worry ... Of course, I'll miss you." Most of these things were in fact said, but I still felt I was losing him.

And I didn't fancy being alone in Nepal for two weeks. It was winter and cold, and I didn't have proper warm clothing. Houses had no heat, no hot water and hardly any wood was available for a fire. Evenings got really, really cold.

After Sitar Sam left, I missed the warmth of his body to sleep with. To stay warm I drank a lot of tea and ate butter cookies. I heated a rock on a fire to sleep with the warmth of the rock wrapped in a towel. It worked. And I stole every chance during the day to warm my body and my face in the sun. I had a routine morning meditation and practiced a sun-gazing exercise Sitar Sam had taught me. Then I'd meditate on the mountainside, gazing at the snow-capped peaks of Annapurna in the distance, while the temperature would gradually climb up until the sprinkle of morning frost melted, the mist from the valley lifted and the whole of Kathmandu appeared. The sun and its reflection from the snow-capped mountains all around became blindingly bright, and the dissipating mist was exquisite. I breathed in this glorious mountain air with joy.

The scenery was beautiful, the place was magical, but my lover was gone. Sitar Sam my love, had abandoned me. I couldn't get over the fact that he was so excited about going back home. All kinds of parties were lined up for him, and he'd see some old friends. California would be warm and fun. Meanwhile I was left in a little unheated shack in Kathmandu's freezing-cold mountains with hardly enough money for groceries. Albeit with explicit instructions that Paul would take care of me if I needed anything. He and Paul were partners now.

Before he left, Sitar Sam had suggested I could sleep at Paul's house if I wanted. But the white house was like a commune of intellectuals, artsy-fartsy types, and had some weird people I didn't feel comfortable with, so I declined. I wasn't afraid of staying alone in our little house on Saraswati Hill, surrounded by monkeys and the Buddhists. And I felt pretty safe next to a temple too. Even though I couldn't speak a word of Tibetan, I had come to know some of the monks by face , and they certainly knew who I was.

But I had mixed feelings. I had been both excited and fearful about staying alone on the mountain. In the heart of the Himalayas with none of the intrusions of modern civilization, moonlit and starlit nights were spectacular. But when there was no moon or too much cloud cover, it got so dark you couldn't see your hand in front of your face. Sometimes I was afraid to go out to pee in the middle of the night, so I used a typical Indian/Nepalese solution: a chamber pot.

I was still annoyed at Sitar Sam for leaving me in this situation while he was off partying in California. Why couldn't he have taken me with him? He could have borrowed the money and I would have provided a nice cover. I got the distinct impression he really didn't want to take me. Lately he had been getting more and more distant. We'd had a good three months together, but what had gone wrong? It seemed that as soon as my money was gone, so was he. I didn't like that thought, but it was true. Still he'd left me with promises; why was I so fearful?

The first evening after Sitar Sam departed I sat alone in my little house trying to play some *tablas* (hand drums) someone had left. I had nothing else to do and couldn't read at night in the oil lamp's weak light. I kept thinking about events in recent weeks. Sitar Sam had grown distant from me just around the time a new lady, Barbara, had appeared on the scene. Barbara was a bit strange. She was an American writer, and had lived in Spain for some time and learned to speak passable Spanish. She claimed to be a devotee of Mahara-ji (the fourteen-year-old wonder boy) and called herself a *premie* (devotee). She was also little older, maybe pushing thirty, and had an air that was at once aloof, mysterious and, well, quite seductive. It didn't take her long to work her way into Paul's little commune and even to charm Paul. Meanwhile, Sitar Sam had been spending a lot of time with her as well and I was jealous. What was it about Barbara that attracted men? She wasn't even a great beauty, yet she had a powerful way with men.

Naturally I didn't like her. When she first came on the scene I noticed that Sitar Sam was losing interest in me, and spending more time with her and the others at the white house. The hippies at Paul's place were a nice bunch but I never really felt comfortable there. A pretty sophisticated group they were: an English actress; a renegade

Irish lord; a dope dealer from Holland named Dutch Bob; a beautiful, independently wealthy English girl named Margo; Svetlana, a Russian-born, American-raised classical dancer; a German mountaineer/explorer; an Australian Sanskrit scholar; Pamela, a lovely slightly older lady from New Zealand; and Heti, the acclaimed niece of Aldous Huxley who became a Buddhist nun and shaved her head. Also living there full-time was a Swedish artist who had become an impressive painter of *thankas* (sacred Buddhist paintings), such that many of the monks said he was surely a re-incarnated Buddhist monk. His paintings looked exactly like those of the monks ... it was truly astounding.

They were all friendly enough towards me, and called me 'the kid.' But they were older and well traveled, and so sophisticated I didn't always follow their conversations. I was off in my own little dream world ... observing it all, taking in but without fully participating. Of course Sitar Sam was fascinated with all these trendy folk and fit right in with this crowd. I didn't, and I knew it.

At Paul's Christmas party everyone else had fun – someone produced some whiskey and other treats – but I was gloomy. Sitar Sam ignored me most of the night, charming all the beautiful women, and no one was much interested in a young provincial girl from Canada. I felt so out of my element that I sat outside for a long time, alone, confused and crying. I communed with the night sky and said the Lord's Prayer in earnest. I sat silently for a while and then lit a chillum and offered it to Shiva. And then to the moon. In the Himalayas the night sky is exquisite, especially when it is cold and crystal clear. I sat there for a long time, but no one missed me or even noticed I was gone.

When we got home and Sitar Sam said he wanted to make love, I said I was too tired. The following day Sitar Sam said we needed to talk. Sensing my insecurity, he wanted to make sure I was alright. We talked a bit about our relationship and my fears, and he promised he was coming back. He said he'd return soon with money, and then we could leave Nepal and head back to India, maybe to Kerala or elsewhere in south India that I'd never seen. I believed him. Oh how I wanted to believe him.

The first couple of days after his departure I did not fare well. I didn't know what to do with myself. I didn't particularly feel like hanging out with folks at the white house. On Saraswati Hill I had met a girl who was renting a little house, the only other foreigner nearby.

She was a student of anthropology from University of Michigan, staying in Nepal to study the monkeys. She was polite but a bit shy. She didn't hang around the scene much, as she wasn't really a hippie and didn't smoke hash or do drugs as far as I knew. When I went out early one morning to meditate and catch the sunrise, she was out as well. We sat together and she told me all about the monkeys. She had names for them all, knew which was the dominant male, and which ones were couples, brothers, sisters and families. She even identified some gay monkeys. I was surprised – gay monkeys? But she said there are some and homosexuality does occur in the animal kingdom, maybe more frequently than we'd like to admit.

THE MONKEY AND THE MONK

The second day after Sitar Sam's departure. I had no more food and headed down the mountain to purchase groceries. It was a long walk, several hundred feet down, taking about forty minutes to descend and a little over an hour to climb up again. There was a little footpath from the temple down to the village and I began my descent anticipating breakfast. I had very little money and didn't think I should waste it in a restaurant, so I bought an egg, a piece of bread and some butter. I had a cup of chai to warm myself against the morning cold and dampness, and then started to make my way up. As the air was thin and it was quite a hike, I usually did it in three stages. I'd walk about a third of the way up and then catch my breath for five or ten minutes and then continue another third of the way up. I still hadn't adjusted to the rarified air.

To get into a walking rhythm I practiced a Buddhist chant. When I got to my second stop, I sat down winded. Distracted by the beauty of the early morning sunlight sparkling on the dewy leaves, I suddenly heard a noise behind me. A monkey was running off with my package – my whole breakfast! I tried to chase him but he was too fast. I begged him to give it back and then sat there crying in frustration. The monkey just made fun of me and ran away with my hard-earned breakfast.

Out of nowhere a monk appeared. He was not one of the regulars from the temple, as by now I knew most of them. How did he just appear like that? I would have seen him coming down the path as I walked up. And he certainly was not there a few moments ago. I was astounded. He gestured to me that he had seen what happened and said in broken English: "Monkeys very bad. Thieves, thieves." He tried to comfort me but I was in tears and inconsolable. I explained that this was all the money I had left and I wanted to eat that day. He then asked me how much I had paid for my purchase, and when I told him it was three rupees he dug into his robes and gave me exactly that amount. It was strange because I thought renunciants weren't supposed to have money. Also, I was sure I'd never seen this monk before; I never did find out who he was.

I thanked him for his kindness and trekked back down the mountain, purchased another egg and bread, and once again climbed up – this time carefully guarding my purchase. As I had taken such trouble and more than two hours to obtain it, I really enjoyed my little breakfast that day.

Later I went down to see Paul, a bit reluctantly, but now I was completely tapped out and needed money. Paul was out, but Pamela invited me in for tea. We chatted for a while and then she asked me what was up with me and Sitar Sam. I said he was my boyfriend and that when he got back from California we were going to leave Nepal and go south to a warmer climate, maybe Indonesia or Bangkok.

"What if he doesn't come back?" she asked. I hadn't really thought of that possibility. She added, "If he gets busted or falls in love with someone else, what will you do?" Again, I hadn't even thought of it, as I was sure that Sitar Sam would come back and take care of me. I had been mostly supporting both of us for three months, and my money was gone. Pamela thought this was a bad situation for me.

Then she asked me about Barbara ... how well did I know her, and so on? How did she and Sitar Sam meet? Then she asked how well I knew Paul. It became obvious that Pamela had fallen in love with Paul and had had a brief affair. Paul had many ladies but no wife or steady partner, and he seemed to prefer it that way. Now Barb was working on Paul and Sitar Sam both. What was her agenda? Pamela thought she was not to be trusted. She gave me some money and said she would collect it from Paul later.

The conversation with Pamela lingered in my mind. Now I had serious doubts and couldn't sleep that night, so I read by candlelight until my eyes hurt. All I could think about was Sitar Sam having a great time in California and me lying here in misery ... cold, broke and with no real friends. My options weren't looking good: there was a distinct possibility that Sitar Sam might never come back. I knew I was in love with him and probably much too attached.

Irish Patrick, who'd seen me moping around and knew I was Sitar Sam's girlfriend, suggested some introspection. He recommended going to a beautiful and ancient monastery high in the mountains far from town, where you could sign up for a week-long silent retreat. It provided one meal a day (rice and vegetables) and a room with a clean cot. No reading material was allowed, no writing or musical instruments, no distractions. So I went.

Black Kali in a Kathmandu square.

It was a long walk to Kopan Monastery and there were no roads so it took me several hours to walk there. I left early in the morning and arrived just after noon.

The residing lama, Thubten Yeshi, gave me a mantra and I spent the next four days attempting to understand the Buddhist concept of suffering: desiring what we don't or can't have. I had read the Buddha's teachings and knew a bit about the Noble Eightfold Path to end suffering and achieve self-awakening. But I couldn't get past the idea of spiritual detachment. Instead of profound revelations and deep meditation, I spent too much time crying in loneliness and worrying and wondering about Sitar Sam. Against the rules I started to do some writing. I knew I was cheating and not really following the program – I just couldn't do it. I got bored with meditating all the time and decided it wasn't fair to others who might really benefit from the retreat space. And so, with apologies to the presiding lama, I left.

The walk back to town was about five miles. Along the footpath into the hills I passed tidy homes with beautiful terraced gardens; a farmer tending his few vegetables waved and gave me a broad, toothless grin. The local people were always so friendly and greeted foreigners with a mixture of curiosity and respect. I'm sure they must have wondered why these strange foreigners, these hippies, came to their humble hill station in Nepal? I'm sure they couldn't figure out what attracted us. Nepal had no fancy hotels or resorts or activities for tourists; there was little to do but hike in the mountains or study Buddhism.

My walk through the mountains lifted my spirits, and by the time I got to town I was hungry and thirsty so I paused at a chai shop. I ran into Pamela sitting with – wouldn't you know it? – Barb. I said I had just come down from a four-day retreat at Kopan Monastery and told them I didn't like it.

"Any news from Sitar Sam?" asked Pam. "The last I checked was Monday and I've been at the monastery since then, so no news. But I'll go to the post office on the way home, and maybe there'll be a letter from him. Or maybe even some money," I said, full of hope. Pam and Barb also wanted to check their mail, so we went to the post office together. They were all chummy now and seemed to have forgotten their mutual distrust. They were busy plotting and trying to figure out Paul's next move. Paul had recently taken up with Svetlana, the beautiful but aloof dancer. Who could blame him ... she was gorgeous.

I picked up my mail and sure enough, Sitar Sam had sent an aerogram. But no money. He said things were going really well in California; his flight was easy, and he and his carpets had gotten through customs without a hitch. He seemed happy and excited to be back in California and seeing old friends again. After two years of austerities in India living like a renunciant, he was now enjoying the luxuries of his Beverly Hills home and going to lots of parties. But he wrote that he might stay another week to attend some lectures with a specialist in brain research using biofeedback. Scientists were beginning to study yogis and Buddhist monks in deep meditation by measuring their brain waves. His father had been involved in some of these studies at the Menninger Foundation, and Sitar Sam was also interested. He had spent many hours in deep meditation on his Himalayan retreat, and now his dad was doing this neat stuff. It was a great way to reconnect with his father. He said he missed me and that I should hang tight and wait for him to return.

Oh God ... he'd been gone only ten days and I could barely stand it. Now I'd have to wait another two weeks for his return. I didn't care about biofeedback or brain waves or anything like that. I suspected it was just an excuse to stay longer in California. What if he had a girl-friend there? I was starting to hate Nepal. It was very cold at night, and I didn't have heat or proper clothing or bedding. I didn't fit in with Paul and his intellectuals, and had no money. Once again I felt hopeless, forlorn and trapped.

The next day I ran into Pamela at the Brothers Café. Pam said she needed to go into town and invited me along for a chat. It was a pleasant morning and only about a mile, so we decided to walk instead of waiting for a taxi. A friend had suggested an alternate route through the hills with a picturesque, pastoral view.

Little did we realize this route also involved traversing a gorge of several hundred feet on a flimsy rope bridge. I had never been on a rope bridge, and this one spanned a huge expanse with a raging rocky river below. The drop must have been at least four hundred feet and, scared of heights, I could barely look. In addition, this flimsy-looking construction had a tendency to undulate as you walked. On a rope bridge you have to walk so that the undulations created by your own steps don't come back at you and throw you off balance. It was a weird feeling. And because it was single-file pedestrian bridge, if someone else was coming towards you, you had to either back up or squeeze by in an awkward embrace. I held the rope handles tentatively until I learned the proper rhythm.

A Tibetan woman with a bundle of grasses and a broad smile waited patiently at the other end. She laughed openly at my awkward-ness. "Tashi Delek," she said. I had learned to say the Tibetan greeting as well and responded with it. Pam was right behind me, and once on solid land again I confessed a terrible fear of heights. She too had been frightened, but we had both done it and felt proud of overcoming our fears.

We paused on a hill, and to celebrate our little victory Pam pulled out a chillum and began preparing a smoke. She said that she saw Bhagavan Das , the famous chanting hippie from *Be Here Now*. He was already a bit of a local celebrity, and the buzz was that he was staying at the Rosy Mushroom Cafe. Perhaps we could go down there and do some chanting. I felt much more comfortable with Hindu chanting than the more complex Tibetan Buddhist chants, so I said, "Let's go."

Pam also told me she wouldn't be staying in Nepal much longer. "I'm pretty fed up with the scene here, and especially with Paul and his two-timing shenanigans. By the way, how are things going with Sitar Sam?" "Terrible," I told her. "I just got a letter from him and he says he is staying in California longer than expected. He seems to be having a great time partying and hanging out with old friends. But I think he's completely forgotten about me. He was supposed to have sent me money, but it hasn't showed up yet."

Pam said she suspected he and Paul were partners, and that Paul had also been antsy lately with no word or money coming from Sitar Sam. She said Paul was having doubts about Sitar Sam, and that wasn't good for me. Paul would ask me a lot of questions I probably couldn't answer. Anyway, Pamela said she didn't like Paul's games and ego trips. Sure, he was generous, charming, talented and intelligent – but he was still a drug dealer and, according to Pam, not trustworthy because he "mostly just used women."

Pam became adamant. "Don't they all? I mean, just use us? Who needs these men? Why don't we split the scene and go somewhere warm? Have you ever been to Bali?" I hadn't, but it sounded good. I was tempted.

"But Pam, how can I travel to Bali without money? Besides, Sitar Sam will be coming back soon and he'll be loaded. Then we can go to Bali together."

Pam looked at me with concern. "You're really hung up on this guy, aren't you?" Taking the chillum, I took a long draw and blew out the smoke thoughtfully. "Well, I'm in love with him ... " I said, and nearly started to cry again. Pam said, "But what if he doesn't come back? How long will you wait?" In my young girl's heart I almost said "forever," but I knew that would have been a fairy tale.

I wanted to leave Nepal. My short stint at the monastery proved that I was not suited to meditation or Buddhism or self-reflection. I had been invited to go hiking in the Himalayas, but declined the invitation because I did not have proper clothes or shoes. Now I regretted not going ... possibly someone could have lent me some gear. The scene in Kathmandu had become boring for me, as it focused mostly around Paul and his artsy-fartsy, oh-so-cool friends. I still felt marginalized.

I was ready to go anywhere. "Okay, say we want to split. How do we do it?" Pam smiled almost condescendingly, like a loving mother talking to a dumb kid. "We'll do a dope run, of course! You did say you've done it before, right?" I nodded. "So what's the big deal?" she asked.

Pamela explained that she and Barb had worked out a deal. They figured that since Paul was playing them both for fools, they would get their own sweet revenge. Barb had some connections in Europe that Paul really wanted access to and never got. She had been playing him all along. And Pamela had an influential family in New Zealand and knew some pretty heavy people in Australia. As a little surprise they would both leave Paul at the same time, with no goodbyes and with no forwarding address.

Both Pam and Barb had been mules before, for some well-known drug dealers, and made a lot of money for some of these guys. They got to talking and found themselves asking: "Why couldn't we just do it ourselves? Who needs them? And really who needs men?" Pamela said she had contacts in Australia and Calcutta, and Barb said she could put up seed money to buy the goods. They needed a third person to help carry the suitcases and both agreed on me. It sounded so simple ... they had it all worked out.

Impulsively I agreed to go, mainly because I was bored and wanted to get out of Kathmandu. Besides, I stood to make about $3,000, good money in those days. In my heart I still hoped Sitar Sam would come back to me. I figured that if I had some serious bread he wouldn't hesitate to come back, and maybe we could travel to Bali together. He'd been to Indonesia before, and raved about the scene there.

Soon the wheels were in motion and we prepared to fly to Calcutta. The plan was to spend a week there getting the hash and the suitcases. Meanwhile, Pam would contact her colleagues in New Zealand and Australia and see who needed hash. Barb would finance the trip, and the two partners would split the profits after paying me. Then we were each free to go our merry way.

CHAPTER 13

Another Dope Run

SITTING ON THE PLANE LEAVING NEPAL, I was amazed at my own courage. I'd finally had the gumption to leave Sitar Sam and the scene, *his* scene, in Nepal. Pam and Barb left without saying a word to anyone and were gleeful about it. Wouldn't Paul be miffed? We three girls felt empowered and confident that we could easily carry out our mission.

We flew without incident and landed in Calcutta in the early evening. Barb had booked us into the Ambassador Hotel, a classy five-star hotel. I remember seeing the biggest rat I ever saw running along the red velvet-carpeted floor. Like many others, this hotel had a distinctive Victorian look, formal and very English. The waiters wore white gloves; the banisters, chair backs and chandeliers were gaudy and gilded; and there was all kinds of opulent nonsense. But the place had cockroaches, and here's a rat running across the floor. The staff didn't seem to notice these things, or to mind. Hilarious.

Calcutta was as dirty and poor as Bombay but looked interesting, so we decided to go out that evening to see the city. Pam had been to Calcutta a few times but neither Barb nor I had, and we wanted to take in some sights. Barb said she wanted to visit an opium den. Pam had done opium before and was a recreational user. She said she knew one place. We decided to go and I went along, but knew I would not, could not, smoke the vile black gum that had once made me so sick.

Pam looked up her contact, a Muslim art and artifacts dealer named Ali, and arranged for us to visit the following day at his shop. Ali was a *paan* eater, and I never could look at paan eaters' mouths. Their teeth were stained blood red from the betel nut juice, and their excessive spittle also glared blood red. Ali was a particularly ugly man:

too fat and with a greasy and far-too-hairy face, and dark purple circles around his eyes that some Indians seem to have. His little shop was dark and filthy, like most in the local bazaar, but he was happy to see Pamela and two beautiful foreign ladies. He gallantly invited us in and offered us chai.

After formal greetings and questions about common friends, he asked Pam furtively and slyly, "Do you have anything for me?" Pam told him regretfully, "No." I wasn't sure what he was alluding too. What could she have that he couldn't get? She said she would soon travel and return with his desired items. I asked later what these were and she told me, "Pornography. Indians go nuts over *Playboy* and *Penthouse* magazines." She explained that pornography was illegal and totally unavailable in India, and thus much coveted. And he wanted whiskey, real whiskey.

Pamela promised she would bring these items next time she came from home. After some other pleasantries Ali asked her about the purpose of her visit, and she then stated her case. She wanted to buy twenty kilos of the best hash he could procure. She wanted to see and smoke it first. She needed to know his best price per kilo, and she needed the whole amount installed (meaning in false-bottom suitcases). She would have to have these done in a week, but the sooner the better.

Ali listened carefully, bobbing his head from side to side. He agreed with a slimy, red saliva smile and glowing eyes. He was very agreeable indeed. He could certainly furnish the required quantity and quality of hash, and we could discuss the price later. He could let us try some now. In India it was a custom, almost an institution, to offer your clients a sample of your goods. He sent a boy on an errand and began to prepare a chillum pipe. He said he could surely arrange things in the required time frame.

"How long?" asked Pam. "Probably four or five days. But what's the big hurry, Miss Pam? You foreigners, you're always in such a hurry." Pam said she didn't want to spend much time in Calcutta. If she ran into certain people, they might wonder what she was doing there; she wanted to be discreet.

The kid came back with a huge chunk of moist black hash. We all inspected it, feeling, smelling and rubbing it with our fingers and massaging it. As experienced hash runners, we knew our stuff. It looked, smelled and felt like the real thing: Afghan Gold, considered the best hash in the world by some and much loved by international smugglers.

Ali made a great ritual of preparing the chillum. First he soaked a Safi cloth in clean water and wrung it. Then he twisted the cloth and passed it through the conical clay pipe. Then he wrapped the other end of the Safi cloth around his big toe as I had seen Sitar Sam do, sliding the chillum up and down until the cloth came out black with charred gum. He repeated this until the cloth came out clean. Then he put in a stone and mixed the hash with some Gold Flake tobacco and stuffed it in. He lit the pipe, and with a grand gesture offered the chillum to Pam. She nodded respectfully to our host, inhaled deeply and thought-fully, and smiled in approval. Courteously she passed the chillum back to Ali but he declined and gestured to Barb and me. (I noticed that the formality of Indian society penetrated even the criminal element; I myself had met many polite criminals.) Pam had said Ali was filthy rich and powerful, and owned half the neighborhood. Everyone knew that Ali did not make his money selling artifacts. But everyone kept quiet, of course.

I didn't particularly like this Ali character, and prayed for protec-tion. When I received the pipe I said a quick invocation to Shiva: "Bom Bom Bole, Hare Hare Mahadeva." The others looked at me question-ingly and I said, "Sitar Sam taught it to me. It's the prayer to the Hindu god of hash, isn't it?" I was later told it is impolite to invoke a Hindu god in the company of a Muslim, but what did I know?

We had tea, and more chillums were passed around. We looked at Ali's carpets and wood and ivory carvings, discussed politics and the problems in India. As was the custom, doing business also became a social event. Ali looked after our comfort, and we all relaxed. We spent a good part of the afternoon there. After an hour of smoking and chat-ting over numerous cups of tea and sweets, Ali asked, "Ladies, how do you like the *charas* (hashish)?"

"Excellent!" we agreed. We would take twenty kilos.

The price was agreed upon and the deal was done. We were told it would take three to four days, which in Indian time meant seven or eight days. We could now enjoy ourselves and go sightseeing; India has so many architectural wonders and temples that there are always sights to see. Barb wanted to check out a silk merchant she'd heard about in the bazaar, and a quick visit was agreed on although Pam was obviously eager to get back to the hotel. She wanted to see if anyone had called or sent a telegram from Auckland. She'd had no word from her contacts in New Zealand and had even left messages with people in Australia.

Just as we were leaving Ali's shop and heading to the silk merchant, Pam spotted someone she knew and became quite alarmed. "Shit, there goes John. Quick, let's go the other way." We took a detour and quickly left the market. "Who was that?" Barb asked. Pam said, "Australian John. I don't know what he's doing here. He was supposed to be in Sydney. I sure hope he didn't see me."

She wouldn't say any more, but clearly she was disturbed. I knew Australian John as a friend of Paul who was in the Kathmandu scene for a while when we first arrived. He was an artist who painted and had studied Indian singing. I used to hear him singing the scales at the white house: "Sa ri Ga ma Pa Pa Pa," But he wasn't around Kathmandu long, and left before Pam arrived. I still have a lovely watercolor he did of Krishna dancing with Radha (another Hindu deity), which he gave me.

Back at the hotel we got good news and bad news. Yes, a friend in Auckland had called, and a telegram would follow. Pam called back, got hold of her friends and was told, "No, we don't need anything here right now. In fact a ton of goods is available." Pam was stunned. A ton? So much that they would have to lower their prices? It didn't make sense. So she called her friends in Sydney, and heard the same story: the market was flooded. This had never happened before; there was always a demand for hash. She'd done so many runs before and the demand seemed unlimited. What had happened?

Pam speculated that possibly Australian John was moving in bigger circles these days, bringing it in by the boatload. How else could such large quantities of hash be moved? Whatever the case, it posed a serious problem because we had just ordered twenty kilos of hash and now had no buyer or destination. Pam asked if I had any contacts in Europe, and I said no. Barb suddenly couldn't or wouldn't furnish any of her contacts there either. So now we were stumped.

We took a taxi to the bazaar and told Ali our problem. He answered, "There is no problem, ladies. You can take it to Canada. We just sent someone to Vancouver last week and it is easy, very easy. We have a contact for you there. I will contact him right away." I could see Pam wasn't too pleased with this. She knew nobody in Canada and felt completely out of her element, but it was the only solution.

Secretly I was happy. Vancouver was just a hop and a skip from California, and since Sitar Sam was still there, maybe I could go down after I got my money. Also, with my earnings I could visit home. I really missed my family and friends. I had gotten a letter from my mom saying my sister, Edie, had run away from home. My parents were worried sick, and I too was worried. Edie was only fourteen years old; how could she survive on the street? In fact, I felt a bit guilty about my sister, as if I had abandoned her. She had always looked up to me, and my sudden departure to India must have disappointed her – maybe that's why she ran away. Anyway, I thought I could help. Yes, Canada sounded good.

And so it was arranged. To celebrate our business deal we went to a nice restaurant by rickshaw. It was my first time in a rickshaw, and I didn't like the idea of a poor ninety-pound, half-naked guy in bare feet pulling us along the filthy streets of Calcutta. "Do you really think we should be doing this?" I asked. "Taking a rickshaw, using a human like an animal? It's really despicable, don't you think?" Pam answered, "It's tricky. On the one hand you don't want to support this kind of activity. On the other, these rickshaw wallahs need to earn their living too. And if we took a taxi, then they'd be out a fare." We paid the wallah generously (to alleviate our guilt) and proceeded to the restaurant. In India many of the better restaurants have a separate, curtained area for women. I liked having this privacy in our booth.

In the next few days I managed to visit the Kali temple at Dakshineshwar on my own. I remember crossing the Howrah Bridge and the great Hooghly River, and it seemed like a long journey to get there. But the taxi driver waited for me and ensured that I got back to my hotel. I was humbled by the temple's power and beauty. I did the obligatory perambulation, thinking of Sitar Sam and how much he loved Kali. And Shiva, of course. Sitar Sam had become such a devotee that he called himself a Shaivite. I had begun some yoga training with him, and I supposed he was grooming me for life as a Shaivite.

This special temple was dedicated to Shree Ramakrishna who had become the temple priest and had supposedly attained enlightenment there. I spent the afternoon alone, meditating and attuning myself to this wonderful Indian saint. There I found a photo of a strikingly beautiful yoga woman, simply dressed in a white saree with long, loose, silky black hair and no adornments. This was the beloved partner of Shree Ramakrishna, his late wife Sarada Devi. In India she was revered as a saint in her own right, one whom many years later I was to be named after.

I was so smitten by this place I could have gone back there every day. But neither Pam nor Barb had much of an interest in the Hindu religion or their gurus or temples, except as architectural curiosities. Barb wanted to find a casino, and Pam wanted to see some classical dance performances. We never did find a casino, and the only dance troupes worth seeing were not coming until the following month. So there wasn't a lot to do in Calcutta while we waited for our goods.

Pam was stressed and had a tendency to worry. Throughout the week, whenever she had a chance, Pam pulled me aside and shared her concerns, mostly about Barb. "Don't you think it's weird how she died her hair black and tried to pass herself off as Spanish? Remember how when she first came on the scene she was hiding the fact that she's an American? She bloody well doesn't look Spanish. Look at those freckles and her fair skin. Must be of Irish descent; I'll bet she's really a redhead. Don't you think it's odd?" I actually didn't think it odd at all. Lots of women died their hair, and maybe she had a romantic notion that being Spanish was sexier than American.

Another time: "Why do you think Barb is so cagey about her past? How do we know that Barb is even her real name? What do you think she is hiding? Why did she come to Nepal with a typewriter? Who the hell travels with a typewriter?" Clearly Pam had a deep mistrust of Barb. Pam had also taken to visiting the opium den to calm her nerves, although neither Barb nor I accompanied her. If you didn't smoke opium it was pretty boring. In the beginning we shared one suite, but then Barb decided she wanted her own hotel room so she could write.

As the week progressed, Pam continued to harangue me about Barb. "What if she's a spy, I mean CIA? Why did she suddenly decide to get her own room?" I had no opinion on Barb, and thought Pam was being a bit neurotic. Barb had more or less "stolen" Paul away, and Pam never got over it. Why she then decided to do a dope run with her apparent arch enemy I never did figure out. Now we were committed and in together neck deep. Barb had the money to fund our project, and we were stuck with her.

I tried to ignore Pam's doubts and concerns, but then began to have my own doubts. Did it really make sense to go on a dope run with two partners who didn't trust each other? Of course not. In spite of my usual sixth-sense warning system, I ignored the messages coming to me. I thought, "We just have to do this one run, and then both these women can have it out. I'll be back with Sitar Sam and we'll be off to Bali."

Soon enough the suitcases were ready and our flight arranged. Our friend Ali had been unable to reach his contact in Vancouver, and so he gave us a name and a telephone number. Soon we were taking off on a high-risk journey halfway around the world ... It occurred to me that I was flying east to end up west. When I eventually got home to Ontario, I could clearly say I had traveled all around the world.

We arrived in Vancouver and cleared customs without a hitch. Thank God. We immediately booked a hotel and got a taxi to take us there. At the lobby, a kind man who came in just after us offered to help with my suitcase. Before I could refuse he picked it up and exclaimed, "Whoa, that's heavy. What have you got in there?" Pam answered: "Books. Lots of books." When we got to our room she immediately telephoned the number Ali had given us, but there was no answer. All we could do was wait.

It was Thursday night. We didn't know anyone in Vancouver or our way around the city, so we didn't go out. The following day we tried phoning again; still no answer. By Friday night Pam was getting nervous. She didn't like the man who asked about our suitcases and thought that was suspicious. She also didn't like having to sit on twenty kilos of hash for several days.

Our stress levels were high. Pam and Barb had a nasty fight, and Barb was pissed off and decided to get another hotel. Pam didn't want Barb to know where we were and also wanted to avoid the "helpful stranger," so she suggested booking a motel room on the outskirts of town. We quickly moved that night and then Pam said, "I can't stand it any more. Let's go out to a disco and see if we can sell a little bit of hash. At least we'll have some bread that way."

But before we took this drastic action she tried the phone number once more. Finally someone answered, and it was Dave, our contact. When Pam identified herself as a friend of Ali, he said, "C'mon over, let's talk." We took a taxi to his place and brought a sample of our goods. Dave was duly impressed and interested in buying the whole lot. But he didn't have ready cash and tomorrow was Saturday; banks were not open until Monday. We'd have to wait. Bummer!

Back at our motel Pam was fairly climbing the walls with anxiety. She was sure now that Barb was not to be trusted. In fact, she was almost certain that Barb was a CIA agent and probably setting us up. I couldn't stand her paranoia any more and turned on the television. An intriguing movie was on, a murder mystery, and having not watched TV in over a year I was captivated. Pam kept looking out the window, checking the lock on the door and pacing, stewing over her fight with Barb. Now we didn't even know what hotel she was staying at, and she had taken her half of the hash with her. Pam smelled a rat.

We made some dinner and Pam made us drinks. She continued pacing and I continued watching TV. Suddenly, the door burst open violently, breaking the lock. Three big police officers barged in with pistols aimed. "Freeze!" one commanded. "You're under arrest." Pam blurted out: "What for?" He didn't answer. Pam said to me, "Don't say anything at all."

Then another officer came out of the bedroom with our two suitcases, opened them and ripped open the lining, exposing all the hash. "What's this?" he asked. Pam said, "I think you know what it is. I'm not saying anything until I get a lawyer." The first cop said, "Well, ladies, you'll have to come along with us now."

Shit! Busted!

Again.

CHAPTER 14

A Canadian Prison

THE POLICE OFFICERS PROMPTLY HANDCUFFED US, while Pam protested. "Is this really necessary? It's not like we're gonna run away." The cop just smiled and said, "It's procedure, ma'am." We were taken to the police station, fingerprinted and thrown into separate cells.

A little later a female cop brought a doctor to check on me. He asked me to remove my top, and both he and the lady cop seemed startled when they realized I wasn't wearing a bra. It wasn't that common then for young women to go bra-less. He checked my heart and various other functions, and then the lady cop said, "You know you're in big trouble, don't you?" Oh yes, I knew. I started to cry and asked her, "What can I do?" She said, "Get a good lawyer," and left.

I had no idea how to get a lawyer. I was in a strange city where I knew no one. I didn't have any money because I was supposed to be paid after we sold the hash. Now the cops had confiscated all twenty kilos of our beautiful Afghan hash. And my money. And my freedom. Soon misery overtook me again, and I cried inconsolably.

Pam was in the cell next to me. Although I couldn't see her, I could hear her pacing and breathing heavily. She told me somewhat testily, "Get a grip and stop crying over spilt milk. Your weeping makes it hard for me to think." "What can we do?" I asked defeatedly.

"I'll get us a lawyer as soon as I can get to a phone. Also I'll contact the New Zealand High Commission or the British one if New Zealand doesn't have one here in Canada. I think I should at least let them know I am in a Canadian jail and maybe they can help somehow ... I don't know."

"Anyway, just sit tight and don't say anything to anybody. Okay?

Just let me do the talking." Okay, I agreed. That was easy enough. Being all of nineteen years old I had faith in her seniority and sense of survival, as she was so much older than I. I knew she had lots of experience in dealing with difficult situations. She would come up with something. Surely.

Indeed, Pam was able to make a phone call and a legal aid lawyer came the next day. But he did not have good news. "According to Canadian law, possession of any amount over a kilo was deemed to be 'for the purpose of trafficking.'" That alone would carry a two-year sentence. But the amount we had was far in excess of that.

He said, "You gals had twenty kilos ... you weren't fooling around, were you?" There was no doubt our charge would be "importing," which carried a sentence of seven to twenty years. When I heard this I fell to pieces. How could I possibly spend seven or, God forbid, twenty years in jail? I was only nineteen. Pam tried every angle, but the lawyer informed us there were no loopholes because we were caught red-handed with the drug, which under the Narcotics Control Act was a hazardous narcotic.

"Wait a minute. Who said anything about narcotics? We're talking cannabis here, and everyone knows it is a soft drug and certainly not a narcotic." "Of course you are right, technically speaking," said the lawyer, "but some of Canada's laws are quite archaic and backward."

Pam was mad as hell. "How can they possible classify this as a narcotic?" she raged. "What a stupid, barbaric system! I thought Canada was a *civilized* country." And on and on.

I didn't realize the importance of it at the time. But as Pam pointed out, if we were charged with having twenty kilos of a narcotic drug, it might as well be heroin. How would the judge know that we had a much milder drug? Oh my God. Importing 20 kilos of a narcotic and hazardous drug was far more serious than getting busted for a joint. Now I knew we were really in trouble.

Meanwhile, Pam kept asking me "What d'ya think happened to Barb? Do you think she got busted too?" But I really didn't have an opinion. "What if she didn't get busted ... do you think she ratted us out? I think she set us up, I've long suspected she would." On she went with her paranoid entrapment theory. Why hadn't we heard anything about Barb? And how the hell did the cops know where to find us? Most likely Barb told them – no one else knew we were at that motel.

The following day we were taken to the Lower Mainland Regional Correctional Centre in Burnaby, a suburb of Vancouver. And there in the holding cell – along with several young hookers, drunk street kids and junkies – was Barb.

Once we saw Barb locked up, it kind of blew Pam's theory that she was a CIA agent out to set us up, which I never really believed. But Pam did manage to elicit from Barb that she was arrested at 6:40 p.m. – about an hour before we were. Pam figured this proved that Barb had led the police to us. The two began arguing and blaming each other for attracting heat and other fuck-ups. It became a classic accusation-counter-accusation shouting match. I suggested that they should stop fighting and we should all stick together. Barb said, "Actually, I think quite the contrary. We should each fend for ourselves. I won't have anything to do with you guys. You're on your own, kids."

So began the war between these two strong-headed women, which continued for several months during our incarceration. Luckily, jail matrons were acutely aware of relationship conflicts among inmates, and caught on that Pam and Barb were enemies. Barb was put into a separate area of the prison while Pam and I, mercifully, were allowed to share a cell. The first night we arrived we were given uniforms and assigned numbers, and had our medical records established and various forms filled out. Then we were de-loused and showered, shown our cell and taken to the recreational hall, where inmates were allowed to watch TV or play records until 10 p.m.

Because it was still early evening, we were allowed to hang out in the recreational room, which I suppose should have been a way to integrate us into the group. But it was a disaster. I decided that for the moment there was nothing I could do about my situation – I was in jail and that was that – so the best thing would be to trust Ram Dass's advice and just "Be Here Now." Why not enjoy myself in the moment? A Fleetwood Mac record was playing, and I began to dance in my own free-form style.

Soon I felt great and began to spin like a dervish; I was off in my own little happy world. I imagined I had become a swan and moved my arms gracefully as I'd seen Indian ladies do in their classical dance ... at times I felt like Nataraj, the Dancing Shiva. For a few minutes I was lost in the moment and didn't care that I was in jail. Ah, a few moments of respite.

But a couple of tough old dykes off in the corner were watching, and they were not amused. They sent over a young girl who soon got into step with me, and at first I thought she just wanted to dance. I smiled and invited her into my whirling sphere. Suddenly she lunged at me and began to tear my nightgown. I was completely caught off guard and quite frightened, because as she grabbed my gown she also got a handful of my hair with her long fingernails and tore my skin. It hurt like hell. I screamed and she pushed me over and walked away in disgust. As I sat on the floor stunned, my nightgown torn, my chest and my neck scratched from her nails, the old birds by the window were laughing their guts out. Until the matron came over.

The matron was upset and asked me, "Who did this?" Sobbing with hurt and betrayal and without thinking, I pointed to the culprit – a serious mistake. The matron immediately went over and escorted her out. The girl who attacked me, Debbie, was the girlfriend of Marge, one of the senior dykes. Debbie was reprimanded and put in "The Hole," the slang name for solitary confinement. Everyone in prison feared and hated The Hole; I guess it must have been like a dungeon. Marge was furious, and now she hated me. I had no idea of the subculture in Canadian prisons, as my previous jail stint in India was so different. There the women cooperated and lived as in a commune, while in Canada the prison system was a competitive, 'dog eat dog' world.

Marge was typical of some of the older inmates I saw who, frankly, scared me. These women were usually in prison for heroin possession, fraud or prostitution. Marge was about forty years old, thin, with tattooed arms and rolled-up shirtsleeves just like a man. She had a masculine haircut, buzzed close at the ears and neck – way before that kind of hairstyle became acceptable for women. There was nothing feminine about her; she was a classic butch, at least in the way butch was stereotyped in those days. Sadly, she was a hardened, bitter woman, taken away from her kids. Like many women in the jail, Marge was a heroin addict or now a recovering addict. A former prostitute too old to turn tricks, she had taken up dealing heroin to support her habit and her kids. It was really sad. I was surrounded by addicts, poor, lost, tragic souls, mostly women from Vancouver's Gastown area. Also, an inordinate number of native girls seemed to be in prison. I later found out that as a social group they had been so marginalized by Canada's longstanding racism that many fell into criminal activity.

So right from the beginning I was branded a "rat," which is a bad reputation to have in prison. Knowing this, the matron who had rescued me saw to it that Pam and I were kept together in a cell at the end of the hallway near the showers, away from the other inmates. We had been assigned to Ward Six, where they kept the serious offenders: murderers, bank robbers, fraud artists and repeat narcotic offenders. Although we had not committed any violent crime, Pam and I were nonetheless considered a security risk by virtue of our international connections and the U.S. government's newly declared 'war on drugs.' It wasn't fair, but we were locked up with hard-core criminals.

Luckily, we didn't interact much with the other inmates for some time, being assigned separate work schedules, at least until the incident blew over. From the first night Pam suggested we should pretend to be lesbian lovers so they would leave us alone. This became our survival strategy. Without openly displaying anything, Pam let the butches know that I was" her girl," and therefore under her protection. It worked.

WINNING RESPECT

Pam was an experienced older woman who was well traveled and a great deal more sophisticated than I. Next to her I felt young and vulnerable and out of control. Luckily, Pam managed to quickly establish mutual respect among the butches, which proved to be our salvation. Pam understood junkies and hookers, and marginalized people in general. She had spent a lot of time in Australia, and knew some underground criminals there. She told me she had friends among the Greek and Lebanese mafia, and among lawyers and judges. She knew strippers, political agitators, artists, hippies, and of course drug smugglers. Coming from New Zealand – she claimed to be "a direct descendant of Captain Cook" and was a member of the Church of England – she had a charming command of the English language and was a great story-teller and social orchestrator. She came from an upper-class family of landowners who'd been there for centuries, mainly sheep farmers on "the *South* Island," she'd say with a hint of superiority over residents of the North.

She told me her grandparents were trumpet mediums. "What's a trumpet medium?" I asked. She said, "My grandparents were associated with the Theosophical Society, which held séances where they used trumpets to call in the spirits of great saints and avatars, and sometimes even of Jesus' disciples. They were given secret information." "Wow, is that for real?" I asked. She said she had witnessed these séances and they were legitimate. But Pamela had no desire to be a medium herself, instead becoming a hippie/rebel and traveling through Australia to India.

Before she got to India, Pam had spent time in the United States, living in Los Angeles back in 1967. There she sympathized and associated with many radicals, particularly the Black Panthers, and met Angela Davis. Having spent time in racist Australia, she had a passion for equal rights and became involved in underground activities. She told me about her days as a radical, a rebel and a protester. It was fascinating and I learned a lot.

I began to realize how sheltered my former life had been. A suburban kid from Toronto "the good," I was pathetically unaware of most of the social unrest just south of the border. Pam was amazed at my naivety. How could I explain? First of all, I was Canadian and we are known for a certain naivety. Then, with my ignorant parents ... what could you expect? We never discussed political issues or anything like that at dinner. My folks as immigrants could barely read English.

Pam had quite the stories to tell, and pretty soon she was not only accepted but respected by other inmates. In fact, before long we both acquired a certain acclaim, mainly because we were international travellers, a couple of hippie girls who'd spent time in India. And unlike the other prisoners, we got mail from all over the world: exotic places like Kathmandu, Auckland, Singapore, California, Montreal and Machu Picchu. Of course all our mail was opened and censored by the prison staff before we got it. They didn't hide that fact. But there was never anything incriminating in these letters.

It didn't take me long to figure out the jailhouse subculture – I guess it's not much different from any other prison in North America. The older inmates or those doing "hard" time usually ran things. I was amazed to learn that they smuggled booze and even heroin into prison. How could they? This was a medium-security institution, and from all appearances security was pretty tight. I found out later that a certain matron was a closet lesbian and had a brief affair with one of the butches. In 1973, society was not ready for lesbians, and many considered them shameful deviants. I can well imagine this matron would do anything to hide her shame. One of the senior butches (I never found out which) had information on this matron that could compromise her job and reputation. And so she was blackmailed into smuggling things into the prison.

An Anglican pastor, a real character, came in regularly. He was, unfortunately, greasy, hairy, fat and short; an ugly middle-aged man who wore his shirts and pants far too tight. His clothes were much too flashy for a minister and really cheap: think 1970s polyester paisley shirt and stretchy, tight plaid pants, hip-huggers with a big belt and shiny buckle barely visible below his pot belly. Revolting. He was pretty unkempt for a preacher and drooled most of the time. I got a creepy vibe from him.

But he was a great storyteller and I guess he had some charm, for girls flocked around him like flies to shit. Soon enough, Pam figured him out. He always had a major erection, which was hard to avoid seeing with his much-too-tight pants. Pam said, "This guy gets a real thrill out of the concept of the 'bad girl.' He wants to see if he can redeem these 'poor disgraced women.' And doesn't it make him feel superior? Notice how he walks around like a cock with a perpetual hard-on." She was right. I don't know what attracted the girls to him. Maybe he too was smuggling things in for them.

THE NUN AND THE BLESSED ROOM

Over the years some suicides had occurred in this prison, including one in our own prison cell. When we learned this, Pam wanted to purify our cell of any lingering negative energy. She spoke of *feng shui*, a Chinese practice not well known then, but she had had a lot of close Chinese associates. In her inimitable style, Pamela adapted the ceremony using mainly Christian images (this was her upbringing: Church of England and all that), and I was amazed to watch her work. She sat quietly for a long time and then did some weird breathing. Soon she stood up and to me looked really powerful ... like a goddess. Her eyes looked far away, yet she seemed really present. She blessed each of the four directions and invoked Jesus' name by making a large sweeping sign of the cross with her arms and mumbling something I couldn't understand. She burned some sweetgrass we got from a native girl and smudged the whole cell, all the while dancing and chanting in a strange language. Aramaic? Where did she learn this stuff?

Our cell was now blessed, and soon I added an altar with pictures of Jesus, Babaji, Sai Baba of Shirdi, Neem Karoli Baba and a little Buddha. And, of course, Krishna and Radha doing their divine dance.

Every Sunday there was a Catholic service, which Pam and I didn't attend. But I used to watch the nuns who came into the prison. They normally walked gingerly, with great trepidation, as if walking through the valley of death itself. It must have been scary for these innocent women to be walking through the halls of Ward Six – the ward with psychos, druggies, murderers and fallen women. But that was the only route to the gym, where services were held. The nuns usually hastened through, nervously looking straight ahead or down at the floor until they got to the end of the hall, from where stairs led up to the gym and their improvised chapel.

On the Sunday after Pam's blessing ceremony, I watched in amazement as one nun became distracted and approached our cell. From staring at the floor she suddenly looked up and then, as if hypnotized, walked straight into our cell. (During the day our cell doors were wide open, and we could go about freely on our ward.) I was sitting on my bed reading and looking out the open door when the nun entered and declared, "Oh, the Light, the Light! What is this place?" Then she gazed at the strange holy men on the altar next to Jesus, and gave Pam and me a strange look. Stunned, she blinked and looked quite embarrassed and confused, and walked right back out again. We both laughed our heads off. Maybe Pam is a bit of a medium after all, I thought. If the nun saw light, then surely our cell was blessed.

THE GENTLE GIANT

Apart from the junkies, our ward had other interesting characters. Gail was in for drowning a baby. But I could hardly imagine this gentle, timid girl doing such a thing. What was her story? For one thing, poor Gail was quite introverted. A plain, acne-scarred and overweight girl in her teens, she didn't seem to have any friends. She didn't talk much but was always timid and awfully polite when she did speak. She seemed too "goody good," maybe a church girl. Because she was weird, she was mostly shunned by the others and didn't mingle much. Some inmates said she was retarded, and even though she had killed a baby they mostly left her alone because she was obviously "not right in the head."

While she was baby-sitting for friends of her family, I learned, Gail had a strange notion that something bad was going to happen and got really nervous, so she called her parents. Either not knowing anything was wrong with their daughter or in denial about her, they dismissed her urgent call for help. They told her to watch television and not to worry. But something snapped in Gail, and she drowned the baby while bathing her. She had no idea that she had done this. When the baby's parents came home they could see Gail was really distressed and confused. Although heartbroken, the parents didn't want to press charges but the police ignored their wishes. And so poor Gail was in jail on a murder charge.

I watched in amazement one day when she found a wounded dragonfly on the windowsill and spent a long time trying to help it. Fascinated by this delicate insect, she tried to gently lift it without hurting it further. After a good ten or fifteen minutes she managed to slip a piece of paper under the dragonfly, brought it level with the window and then blew gently to encourage it to fly. After several attempts it took off through the bars of the open window. Another inmate would have squashed the insect without a thought, but Gail tenderly nursed it. I wondered how someone so gentle could be a baby murderer. Eventually she was assessed by a psychiatrist, and I think she got off with a lesser charge. Still, I always had the impression she shouldn't have been in jail. Pam said she was obviously "possessed."

Another young girl in for murder was a strikingly beautiful seventeen-year-old with a gorgeous figure, porcelain complexion, deep brown eyes and long silky jet-black hair. Dorothy had a winning smile and a fresh, youthful appeal that was hard to ignore. But she was cocky. She bragged about being in for murdering a girl, wearing it like a badge. I was intrigued ... how could this innocent-looking girl with soft doe eyes be a murderer? She told me that she didn't really kill the girl but it was "an accident" gone bad. And that her boyfriend was taking the rap. She was proud of that, extremely self-assured and certain she would get off.

Here's what she told me. Dorothy and her boyfriend Jake were at a party where Nancy, a girl they knew from school, showed up. Although she didn't admit it, I could tell that Dorothy was jealous of this girl, and the boyfriend had some reason for not liking her either. Dorothy said the girl had done something, and to punish her they planned to beat her up. But not to kill her.

That evening they slipped her some mescaline, and the poor girl was high as a kite when they attacked. They lured her outside and started kicking her, according to Dorothy. At some point the girl stopped breathing. When they realized she was dead, Dorothy and Jake panicked. Not knowing what else to do, they put her body in the trunk of his car and drove several miles to a forest glen and dumped it. But they left a trail of evidence and were soon discovered.

Dorothy said Jake was the one who killed the girl. But after I got to know her better, I figured Dorothy had done it. She let slip that she had orchestrated and carried out the punishment. Oh, she was a killer all right! In her storytelling I saw another side to this girl. She looked absolutely evil as she relished the attention she was getting and the shock she could dish out. Her eyes glazed over and she got a devilish look and a crooked smile when speaking about the poor dead girl. "The bitch deserved it anyway," she said.

Dorothy had no remorse about the incident and was pretty confident that Jake would take the blame. She planned days ahead for her court appearance – you'd think she was going to a fashion event. She carefully rehearsed what she would say, and paid special attention to what she would wear to maximize her "innocent little girl" image. And in fact she did get off, damn it! I couldn't believe it, but one day she was released and we heard no more about her. That was long before I got out of prison. Many years later I saw her on the subway in Montreal. How freaky that was! We looked at each other with instant recognition. She smiled and said, "How are you?" and not much more. She looked the same, as if she hadn't aged a bit. Still beautiful and still evil.

It never ceases to amaze me that some young girls get so jealous that they can viciously kill their rivals. In more recent times a frenzied Vancouver gang of young teenage girls beat up and killed an Indo-Canadian girl, Reena Virk, just because she was different. What possesses these girls to go into that kind of rage? I think one could spend years researching this social phenomenon.

These were two of the more intriguing cases. Pam and I got to know some inmates in our ward and learned about their problems, their sad circumstances, severely dysfunctional families and their path to crime. After a while, I saw that they were just ordinary people who got messed up.

Soon a couple of inmates were coming to visit us for Pam's engaging storytelling, which contained teachings, questions, hidden counseling and advice. We intrigued them because we were world travelers; we knew more than Gastown. We had been to Buddhist temples in Asia, studied foreign religions like Hinduism, and read philosophy. We managed to get a copy of *Be Here Now,* and together reread the entire book and used it for instruction. Ram Dass wrote a lot about prison in *Be Here Now,* and it became the symbol of our attachment to the material world. I had heard that Baba Ram Dass and some Neem devotees were working in prisons to help violent criminals learn self-control, using an early form of anger management through meditation. But the program, the Prison Ashram Project, operated only in California so it was of no use to us. Still, we used Ram Dass's teachings and those of Yogananda and other great masters, and soon we were seen as jailhouse gurus. Girls came and opened their hearts to us, and felt better when they left. Even the matrons noticed we were having a positive effect on the girls, so they didn't mind the informal teach-ins.

Most of the girls in our institution were on medication. Every morning a matron who happened to be a former nun would come around and distribute the various pills. This matron was particularly cold and remote; she seemed bitter and mean, and probably hated her job. She didn't have much sympathy for inmates and seemed convinced that we'd all burn in hell. Because she never smiled and never had a kind word for anybody, everyone said she was miserable because she never got laid. Every morning she'd roll-call the girls' names, and one by one they'd line up and get their daily meds – almost like taking communion. Strange to see these girls lining up, like cows at a feeding stall, to get their daily sedatives and antidepressants.

Pam said, "They're drugging people in here. Nearly all the women here are medicated, have you noticed?" I answered, "Sure. But it seems they want their meds. They seem pretty willing, and no one is forcing them to take these meds." Pam agreed but still argued, "Don't you think this is a brilliant way to control people? How else do you control an institution like this, overcrowded and understaffed as it is?" She had a point. From the beginning Pam resolved – and made me do the same

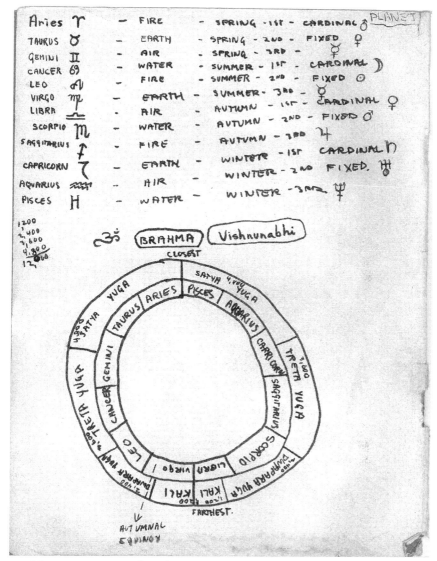

My interpretation of Hindu astrology, done in the Vancouver jail, 1972.

– to never, under any circumstance, take any medicine offered to us unless it was an antibiotic administered by a doctor. She didn't trust the matrons, the nun or any of the prison staff.

The Lower Mainland Regional Correctional Centre already had a bad reputation in the community, and many people were agitating to shut it down. It was a designated prison farm, so it had barns with pigs and other livestock and vegetable gardens and orchards. But it was right in the midst of a suburb that had grown up around it. It was known to be overcrowded and underfunded, and many in the Burnaby neighborhood did not want a prison full of convicts and perverts in their community.

The main building was, of course, for men. It should have had no more than 600 inmates, but was swelling with nearly double that. The women's building was designed to hold 200 inmates, but we were up to 600 at that time. There was no kitchen in the women's building, as it was constructed as an afterthought. So the men did all the cooking and the food was brought over to our unit, which the men called the "cat house." The food was pretty awful, generally overcooked vegetables and meat, boring mashed potatoes and tasteless soups. For Pam and me as vegetarians it was very difficult. They wouldn't prepare special meals for weirdo vegetarians, so we ate what we could and had fish once in a while. For breakfast we always got porridge, except eggs and bacon on Sundays. We got three meals a day and desserts too, so could eat as much as we wanted.

Often desert was like a pudding/cupcake floating in a thick, clear sweet sauce. Pam found most of the food revolting, particularly this dessert. Looking at the sauce one day, Pam said to me, "Men can be such pigs. I don't like them cooking our food. How do we know that some of the cooks aren't having fun with us and masturbating into the food? How would we ever know?" I was stunned. "Oh God, no, Pam. They wouldn't." She said, "I wouldn't put it past them. Look at this pudding – doesn't it look like it is floating in semen?" She had a way of getting me going sometimes, and after tasting the pudding once I couldn't eat it again.

After three long months I was relieved to finally get a letter from Sitar Sam. Not hearing from him or anything about him for so long had me out of my mind with worry. I thought maybe the police were investigating him too, so he couldn't write to me for fear of drawing heat himself. Well, that's what I told myself. Finally, the letter arrived ... and he was still in California! Hurray, maybe he would rescue us! He'd heard that we were in jail in Canada and was devastated. He said he didn't want to contact us until he had a definite idea of how to help. (Bullshit ... in three months, he could have managed a couple of words of encouragement, maybe a testimonial of love for me.)

In coded language he indicated everything was fine with him. Obviously he had managed to off-load the goods he had brought, for he made a point of saying that he was cash flush and ready to help in any way he could. I thought he must have felt guilty for not writing sooner, and was trying to make up for his neglect. He said he was sending us a hot-shot California lawyer he knew, Bruce Margolin, who had defended the Grateful Dead and was now representing Timothy Leary. I was impressed, and so was Pam – Sitar Sam sure had connections. He said Bruce would come on the 18th of April, next week. Wow, Timothy Leary's lawyer ... how cool is that? So we eagerly looked forward to this visit. Did he have some magic trick up his sleeve?

But Margolin's visit was a major disappointment. Because of the great quantity of hash involved, he told us there was no way to avoid jail time, though we might be able to get the charge reduced from importing to possession for the purpose of trafficking. But he said there wasn't much he could do because he wasn't a member of the Canadian Bar. Great! The celebrity lawyer couldn't practice in Canada and was basically useless. Pam was clearly annoyed, and asked, "Is there *anything* you can suggest? How about my status as a foreigner? I'm from the [British] Commonwealth, and Canada is a Commonwealth country. Surely they should just deport me, no?"

Bruce said he didn't know much about Canadian deportation policy. All he could suggest was to get a good Canadian criminal lawyer and hope for the best. He asked if Pam had contacted her embassy and she said yes, she'd received a letter stating the High Commission was aware of her situation and would investigate. By now, Pam had written her parents and they were going to hold a special séance to request divine intervention. Calling in angels, please – that's what we really needed. Man, we were fucked!

So the conversation turned to politics and other things. "What's up with Timothy Leary these days?" Pamela asked. Busted for a large quantity of marijuana, Leary had escaped from jail in 1970 but had been brought back from Afghanistan in early 1972. Bruce couldn't really discuss much besides what was already known in the media. He said Leary had lots of supporters and influential people behind him, and it would be a sensational case whatever the outcome. Pam didn't fail to notice that Bruce stood to make a lot of money on this case. I could tell by the way she composed herself that she didn't much like this high-profile lawyer. He didn't seem to be too concerned about us, and we knew that Sitar Sam had paid him to come up to Vancouver to see us. (We didn't know that the lawyer was planning to come to Vancouver anyway.) Soon Bruce wished us luck and departed.

Naturally we were disappointed with Margolin's visit. Pam said, "Granted, your Sitar Sam tried, but this is not the kind of help we need." Pam had a notion that the boys of our hippie community, our spiritual brotherhood in India and Nepal, should come and rescue us, even help us break out of jail. The Watergate scandal was breaking open, the war in Vietnam was continuing, and politically the United States was on edge. Pam did not like being in jail in Canada, with America just south of us ready to explode. She had been a political dissident in Los Angeles a few years before, and knew how volatile America was. She wrote to everyone she knew, desperately requesting help: leaving secret coded messages effectively saying come break us out of jail ... help us escape, get us outta here. She used some Sanskrit and Tibetan words meaning liberation, service, assistance and so on. Of course, Paul in Kathmandu would be able to figure out the meaning.

Indeed, she finally got a letter from Paul. He was going to engage a hundred Buddhist lamas – full-fledged lamas, not just monks – to hold a puja chant ceremony to remove the obstacles to our liberation. Wow, that sounded heavy! If anyone could carry it off, it was Paul, the Hippie King of Nepal, who had become a Buddhist himself and was influential with their leaders. He financed a lot of temple activities and even drank *chyang* (rice wine) with some of the lesser monks (lamas did not drink alcohol). Paul requested help from the temple, asking a hundred lamas to chant for 24 hours beginning at 12:01 a.m. on May 20th.

I remembered the ceremony I had attended in Kathmandu. It all seemed so far away now, a world away. I wondered about the house on Saraswati Hill and who might be living there now. I smiled warmly as I remembered the friendly monks I used to greet daily at the nearby temple. Pam said, "It's not exactly what we expected, but I guess it can't hurt to have a hundred lamas do a puja. Paul is a darling in his own way, I suppose."

FIRE IN THE PIG BARN

On May 20, the day of the ceremony, the Lower Mainland Regional Correctional Centre suffered a terrible fire. The barn was heavily damaged and several pigs died. It took the Burnaby Fire Department several hours to put it out. Everyone talked about it for days. How did the pig barn suddenly catch fire – was it spontaneous combustion? Arson? And why the pig barn?

Pam had a theory. She said, "Oh, my God, Ann – what if Paul told the lamas to 'get the pigs' and the Tibetans, not realizing he meant the police, targeted pigs! How would Tibetans know that here we call the cops pigs?" We both laughed. Pam wrote Paul telling him of this strange coincidence and inquiring what exactly he told the lamas.

Meanwhile, I received an interesting letter from my friend Shoshonna in Bombay. She said I should get in touch with a young Indian girl in prison in Kingston, Ontario. Malika had apparently been caught smuggling several kilos of hash in Toronto. I vaguely remembered having heard this story while in India, but hadn't paid it much attention. Malika, who came from a middle-class, educated and fairly progressive Muslim family, had been betrayed by a couple of friends, one of them her cousin. The two men in question were also distant cousins of Shoshonna's adopted family in Bombay.

It was a sad story. The Indians, new to international drug smuggling, aroused suspicion on arrival. When their false-bottomed suitcases were discovered, the men turned to Malika and said, "They're hers. We were only carrying them." Poor Malika did not speak much English, and was quickly tricked into a confession while the two lads got away. They shamefacedly returned to India to tell their relatives a lie: there was a terrible misunderstanding at customs, someone switched suitcases, and now Malika was in jail and they could do nothing about it.

Because these creeps happened to be friends/family of Rajiv and because Shoshonna felt a kinship for this poor girl, I felt an obligation to help her if I could. Malika had been sentenced to seven years in prison, which is why she was in Kingston Penitentiary. In 1973 she was the only and possibly the first, Muslim girl in the federal institution. I wrote to Malika, identified myself as a distant acquaintance and discreetly mentioned names and places that only she would know. She immediately wrote back, delighted to have a pen pal in Canada.

We shared stories, being careful to use coded language as we knew our correspondence was screened. "Lakshmi" meant money; "Mouni" meant silence (we don't talk about that); "demons" were police/judges/the system; "Nirvana" meant freedom, and so on.

Malika was only two years into her seven-year sentence, and was desperate to get out of jail. She had been studying English and her writing was pretty good, so she was able to communicate quite eloquently. My heart went out to her. She'd never traveled outside India before, leaving Bombay only once to see the Taj Mahal. Then her cousins Ahmed and Sayeed talked her into going on a trip with them. She was delighted. They said they needed a companion, and it would be easier if they traveled as a group or family and so they would pay for her ticket. They would even give her money to shop. All she had to do was carry a little suitcase.

Malika claimed she did not know the suitcase contained contraband, but I believe she was pretty smart and probably knew and didn't want to ask. Either way, she was still conned. Who would have thought that if they were caught, those two chicken-livered weasels would leave her standing with the bags and claim they were hers? I suppose their logic was that authorities wouldn't be as hard on a girl as on a man. Poor Malika, dazzled and blinded by her adventure, hadn't noticed that the suitcases were all tagged with her name.

Now she was wasting away in the notorious Kingston Penitentiary. It was Canada's most horrible and infamous prison, a stone bastion on the shores of Lake Ontario. When I was a teenager my girlfriend Laura had some family estate near Kingston, and her cousin took us sailing in a little boat. As often happens on Lake Ontario, the weather suddenly turned and we tried to head back to the harbor. But we were tossed about in the choppy water and pulled closer and closer to the prison. Looking straight up at the foreboding structure, I was scared that we might crash and smash up against the walls. It was scary enough outside, and likely much scarier inside.

I could imagine poor Malika gazing out at the cold grey waters and equally dull winter sky, missing her beautiful, warm tropical Bombay. She wrote to me about her home, the garden where her grandmother gathered herbs. Her heart ached for the mango tree, the peacock, and the sound of water running in a brook. Canada was a horrible place. She hated it. She spoke longingly of her sisters and family and friends in Bombay. She heard that one friend had got married, and another was accepted to university in England. She felt alone, abandoned and of course, culturally isolated. She just wanted to go home.

I stopped reading for a bit and shared this info with Pam, who was outraged at the miscarriage of justice. Pamela was by now totally disgusted with the Canadian judicial system and Malika's case proved once again how barbaric and insensitive it was. Malika described Kingston Penitentiary and said she'd got used to things there. But still it was difficult. She hated the food and even though she was not a strict Muslim, there were special times (like Ramadan) when she felt bound to fast and pray. She hid in a stairwell to say her prayers in silence, to have some solitude. Canadian prisons then had chapels for Christians (nothing for Jews) and couldn't properly accommodate Muslims. She was caught praying in the stairwell, and a confused matron thought she was worshiping a pagan god or the devil. The matron said she seemed to be praying in a strange non-human language! Before things were straightened out, Malika nearly got punished just for observing her faith.

Times have since changed, and most prisons in Canada can now accommodate Muslims, Sikhs, Jews, even Native American rituals. But Malika was in prison long before multiculturalism was official policy.

PREGNANT IN JAIL

Pamela kept inquiring about Barb. She needed to know what was going on. She needed gossip. We rarely saw Barb, as she was in a different ward, so we used jailhouse spies to find out what she was up to. We learned that she was being treated well as her pregnancy was progressing and that she was planning to exploit this to get out of jail. "How fucking convenient," Pam said. "Here she is carrying Paul's child, knowing full well Paul was mine! I was in love with him. And if that wasn't enough, she's going to get out of jail."

"How do we know that for sure?" I asked. "Have you ever heard of a woman having a baby in prison?" "Yeah, in India," I protested. "Well, this is Canada!" she said, clearly ticked off.

I hadn't thought about it much. But she was right: as Barb got closer to full term she was released on compassionate grounds. Pam said, "That proves it – she had to be an agent. Now she's getting out of prison because she's pregnant. Fancy that!" I responded, "That's just a coincidence, Pam." And she spewed out angrily, "No! Don't you see? She planned it that way." I couldn't believe Pam was serious. She went on: "That bitch ... she seduced Paul in order to get pregnant so she could pull this stunt. That proves it!"

I couldn't convince Pam that Barb was not a CIA agent, nor that she hadn't planned to get pregnant knowing she would end up in jail and would need a ticket out. It was just too absurd. But Pam was relentless, and with her continued findings and verifications I began to wonder myself. Something sure was up about Barb. Even in Nepal she had always been a little too guarded and remote, while at the same time supremely confident and almost unapproachable. Which I noticed had an appeal to some men.

I wrote about her to Sitar Sam, and he too was concerned about the "premie from Spain," as we referred to her in code. She had been a devotee or premie of Sitar Sam's first guru, known as Mahara-ji, the fourteen-year-old fat boy (as we called him). Why was Sitar Sam now so interested in Barb? Did he too suspect something about her? I couldn't make a judgment on her until I knew more about her mysterious past than Pam's speculation.

Pam was worried about more than Barb. A bigger concern was the Watergate political scandal rocking the United States. It looked like President Nixon was going to be charged in a cover-up and that his administration would fall. Pam was scared to the point of paranoia. She said, "We've got to get out of here. There's going to be a *revolution* in America and we're just too damn close." (The prison was less than 25 miles from the U.S. border.)

"Pam, do you really think it's that bad?" I asked naively. "Yes, my dear, I'm afraid it's going to turn ugly. We're like sitting ducks here in this prison and I don't like it one bit. Remember, I was there during the race riots in the sixties." I couldn't believe that politics in the U.S. were going to have such an impact in Canada. I felt we were in no way more threatened than before. After all, we were in jail ... I couldn't see revolutionaries burning down the jail and attacking prisoners. But Pam was convinced something terrible would happen. And so she planned our escape.

It was classic: Pam inspected a barred window. We were on the first floor so it would be easy to escape ... if we could get through the window. Someone had obviously tried sawing through one of the bars, but all there was to show for it was an eighth-of-an-inch incision in two-inch-thick rebar. Whoa! Sawing through the bars would take months! Every day the news from the U.S. was more terrifying and Pam got more agitated. It seemed imminent that the U.S. presidency was going to fall. It seemed the whole world was standing on edge.

Pam was going crazy. She kept requesting a long-distance phone call or telegram privilege to get a message to Paul. Finally the matrons allowed her one telegram. We were staking all our hopes with Paul; he was the man and her errant lover, Pam said. She managed to communicate "Help, get us out of here!" She was certain that Paul, with all his connections in America, could surely organize an escape. She went on and on about it. I thought Pam's notion was ridiculous. Did she really think that this supposed brotherhood of hippie smugglers were going to suddenly break us out of jail like some radical groups liberating one of their own?

Sometimes Pam confused me. On the one hand she was a smart, independent woman; feminist, brave and strong. And yet here she was playing damsel in distress and expecting the "brothers" to come and rescue us. She figured we were owed at least that much. The cops did not believe that we three girls had done this dope run on our own. And did they pressure us! Several times they called Pam and me up for questioning. But we never revealed the names of any associates, or acknowledged that we knew anyone. Believe me, we knew a lot of people of interest! But we felt honor bound not to reveal anyone's name, so the cops did not get very far with us.

Still, Pam was worried because the police had her telephone and address book. Initially they also had mine, after confiscating it when we were arrested. But mine was returned shortly afterward, I suppose because most of my friends and acquaintances were in boring, old Ontario and seemed harmless. Pam however, had contacts all over the world, exotic names and addresses in Australia, Indonesia, Thailand, India and, naturally California. Pam said, "I'll bet they're harassing me because they (whoever *they* were) know about my past activities, and things are getting really hairy in the U.S. with this uncertain political climate. That's why," she added, "they wanted to make a federal case out of our little crime of bringing a bit of cannabis into the country."

Missing India, I drew tropical birds in the Vancouver jail.

At least in that, I had to agree, she had a point. Because of Pam's involvement in previous underground activities (she didn't elaborate), and her general mistrust of what she called Big Brother, she had written her entire address book in code, switching exchange numbers or writing numbers backwards. And in order to make if difficult to break the code, she wasn't always consistent. Foreign names were inverted so that last name would be first, and the numbers of American friends were reversed. Would the police figure it out?

Pam's worries and constant harping about Barb and the U.S. and Watergate wore on me, and I began to get nervous. Of course, I was grateful that she was there for me. She was a tremendous support; without her I probably would have seriously faltered in the jailhouse scene.

Still, I needed some respite, so I started going to the chapel. I liked the quiet it offered. Although not an observant Christian, I've always felt drawn to churches, temples and holy places of any denomination. I had been corresponding with the Self Realization Fellowship near Encinitas, California, the foundation started by Paramahansa Yogananda. The fellowship was holding a prayer circle for us, and I thought I should do some praying myself.

I sat on the chapel pew and looked up at the makeshift altar: Jesus bleeding on the cross. Why was He always bleeding? I wondered. Why do we always emphasize the suffering of the Lord? Why not show His kindness or depict Him in a peaceful meditative state like the Buddha? Why did Jesus always look tortured? In a few moments of silence I got my answer. Because He reflects the human condition. Internally we are all bleeding; we are all suffering to varying degrees. We suffer the torment of being simply human: conflicted confused and confounded. Well, that's how I understood it.

Next question: "Why me, Lord? Why?" I prayed silently and cried, and prayed and cried some more. The matron escorting me offered a tissue but respectfully did not interfere. I was silent for another five minutes or so but never did get my answer to that question. Kurt Vonnegut brought up the same question in his classic *Slaughterhouse*

Five, when the character Billy Pilgrim talks about a companion being abused by the Germans. This man was forced to remove his shoes, and ended up with frostbitten feet and then gangrene. When his gangrene was beyond hope and he knew he would die, he also asked, why me?

"Why not the guy in front of me or just behind me? Why me?" Vonnegut says something like "that's the whole point. Because to the next guy in line it's the same question for him – 'why me?' – everybody says 'why me?' Really the question should be 'why anybody?' but there is no answer to that ... it's just sort of random."

Pam got a letter from Paul. Trouble was brewing in Kathmandu, as the U.S. government was putting tremendous pressure on the Nepalese government to stop the legal sale of cannabis. Being right on the border with China led to a lot of American interest; the CIA was everywhere. Paul, a long-time citizen of Nepal, had no desire to leave his beloved kingdom. According to Pam, Paul was actually born in Nepal although his parents were American, and he grew up mostly in the United States but had lived in Kathmandu for nearly a decade as an adult.

I remembered walking along the dirt road that led to the bridge into town, with Paul the charming and informed host telling Sitar Sam about changes he had witnessed. "This place is so off the map. Nepal just entered the twentieth century, in a manner of speaking, like five years ago," he said. "Kathmandu acquired electricity in 1967, and it was a big deal for the little valley to be lit up." It was the first time I had lived in an environment that primitive – in 1972 many places still had no electricity.

Paul said the lack of many modern comforts was a fair trade for peace of mind. Nepal had no television or radio stations that I knew of, few modern conveniences like hot water, and certainly no major paved roads – people got around pretty much on foot or on pack animals. A few cars navigated the Kathmandu Valley on dirt roads, but it was challenging, even nerve-wracking. Paul pointed out that the only other foreigners we saw in Nepal were serious mountain climbers or backpackers who were keen on the remote country. It was almost "accidental" that hippies spilled over from India and Afghanistan to land in this little Himalayan kingdom, he'd told Sitar Sam.

"I guess they grooved on the mellow Buddhist vibe and found Nepal a cool place to hang out. More and more people are coming to Kathmandu. I don't think our little secret will last much longer."

Now Nepal was going to criminalize cannabis in order to stem the flow of hippies, according to Paul, who had connections to the royal family. Why? I wondered. Who cared about a bunch of peaceful hippies living in Kathmandu? King Birendra, newly installed, surely knew about the hash trade in his kingdom and perhaps even saw a tourism opportunity. The previous king had always tolerated hash-smoking hippies. Birendra and his ministers must have been convinced that it would only be a matter of time, Paul theorized, before heroin users followed the hash smokers, and then crime and corruption. In fact, that was beginning to happen in Kabul, Bombay and New Delhi. Certainly the new Nepalese king would not want a bunch of foreigners creating a hard-drug culture and its attendant horrors in his peaceful Himalayan kingdom. Paul was upset that some foreign agents were becoming interested in his little piece of paradise. He and the existing hippie community had managed to some degree to keep junkies out of Nepal.

Paul also felt that the hashish shops were a tourist attraction. Everyone who came to Kathmandu with a camera in those days had their picture taken in front of one. Nepal was one of the few places in the world where you could buy hash, legally, from a government shop. And with only a handful of peaceful hippies, Tibetan scholars and mountain climbers – totaling maybe a few hundred – it wasn't hard for the Nepalese government to keep track of foreigners. Indeed there wasn't much crime in Kathmandu, and Paul had had his secluded little paradise for many years. Why wouldn't they leave well enough alone?

I didn't know it then, but this was more or less the end of the hippie scene in Kathmandu. With a big fat bribe from the United States, the king effectively threw out all the hippies; in a matter of a year most moved to Indonesia.

I was dreaming, lying on my cot staring at the ceiling. Kathmandu seemed far away. The annoying sound of "Tie a Yellow Ribbon on the Old Oak Tree" played on a scratchy radio. The radio was set on one station and piped in over a speaker in each cell. It was god-awful music, but we had no choice in the station or volume. How I longed for the days when I'd wake up early in the perfect stillness of a cold morning and sit on the mountain to watch the whole valley under cloud cover as the sun came up behind the Annapurna Mountains. I'd watch monks involved in their daily work suddenly chasing thieving monkeys out of the temple kitchen. I'd watch the water bearer rhythmically dancing up the mountain. I remembered the peace and tranquility of the Nepalese terraced gardens of countryside and the always smiling Nepalese farmers and Buddhists. I couldn't believe that I once said I hated it there.

Now, stuck in jail, all I could do was dream about gorgeous Nepal. I was sick of the prison's pale green walls, sick from the lack of fresh air and longed to feel the sun on my skin. It had been five months already. Aargh! Pam was agitated. I fervently wished she would take a Valium or something. She read voraciously and wrote profusely: letters, her diary, anything. When she wasn't reading or writing she was ranting. I decided we should try a craft that the prison system offered. We both picked macramé, a great craft to keep us busy. I found it calming to tie the knots and create a pattern.

Our only other regular activity was house-cleaning. Every week we had to polish the hallway floor of old-fashioned linoleum tiles, in alternating fourteen-inch brown and white squares. I remember that floor well. In order to polish you had to remove the old wax. So on Thursdays we spent the whole morning stripping the floor, which actually looked fine from the previous week since there wasn't that much traffic in Ward Six. In the afternoon we applied a layer of fresh wax and polished the damn floor again. It seemed like such a stupid, make-work kind of task: polishing, stripping, polishing, stripping. Was the point to keep us busy?

HOSPITAL CORNERS AND DARNING SOCKS

Before fitted sheets were common, a young woman had to know how to make a bed with hospital corners. We prisoners had to do the same. Luckily, my mom had been a nurse and taught me the knack. And as female prisoners we had to darn the men's socks too. Can you believe it? At least the socks came clean, in large laundry bags. Each prisoner was given two socks to mend. Again, I already knew how to do this as my mom taught me when I was a kid. It's a bit like weaving. You put a wooden darning egg inside the sock so that the egg shows through the hole. Then you create a warp by mounting woolen threads lengthwise over the hole, and weave over and under horizontally until you the hole is filled. Having spent many an evening with my mom mending socks, I was quite good at it.

Before the advent of cheap goods from Asia, whether it was cheaper to buy new socks or mend the old ones was debatable. And these socks were prison issue and good-quality wool, so could not immediately be replaced. Like most practical-minded women of the old world, the nuns and the matrons in our institution believed "a stitch in time would save nine." Anyway, it was policy and practice: the women had always mended the men's socks.

But now some of the gals were questioning and even protesting this sexist duty. Couldn't the men also learn how to darn? After all, they learned to cook. Pam grumbled and complained about having to do all these stupid and sometimes useless tasks, but at least it earned us privileges like access to the library ... so we conformed.

For my part, I got into the yoga concept of divine service, that is, not being attached to the outcome or results of my actions. That was the trick: dedicate all my actions and the fruits of my labor to God. Stripping wax and polishing floors, stripping and polishing, I sang and sang my heart out, and offered all my labor to the Lord. Stitching, weaving, darning, waxing, polishing ... I sang with abandonment. I remembered the words of Krishna in the *Bhagavad Gita*, who said, "Be not attached to the fruits of your actions." What else was I to do? I might as well be in the moment and love what I was doing. I got into the Zen of selfless labor ... polishing and stripping and polishing and stripping.

A LITTLE PROGRESS

Finally our legal case began to move. We got a local lawyer through the provincial Legal Aid Society. He was nice but seemed overworked and unable to visit us often, and we felt abandoned and frustrated. Still, he managed to move the case forward, working for a plea bargain. We were finally charged with possession for the purpose of trafficking – a less serious charge than importing, which carried a minimum seven-year sentence. As our court appearance approached, the lawyer was certain our judge would be considerate.

But on the day of our hearing we didn't get the judge our lawyer expected. The judge we got had an imposing presence I didn't like:

hard, mean, a little bored, and quite severe. Before pronouncing judgment he scolded us harshly, saying this was a "very serious" crime. He went on that he was "tired of seeing young girls being tricked and used by criminals to carry drugs." He said he needed to make an example of us, set a precedent. Since the crime's seriousness was in the exceedingly large quantity of "narcotic" we possessed, and the rising use of drugs in Canada posed problems of related crime, he felt he had no choice but to sentence us above and beyond the usual two years.

"I impose ten years on Pamela Henderson for being the instigator, and a five-year sentence on her accomplice, Ann BeCoy, because of her lesser involvement. Case dismissed."

We were devastated. Oh my God! I started to cry like a helpless child. I couldn't believe it. The lawyer had said it would be two years or less. How could this be?

Pam looked sick, literally sick, as if about to throw up. She went green. The lawyer shook his head in disappointment and said, "I'm so sorry, girls." Pam freaked out, yelling at him. "Sorry? What the fuck! Can't we appeal?" "Sure you can," he said. "But I don't do appeals. You'll have to get another lawyer. And it'll cost you, and I'm afraid it will take time."

Pam was furious. I was scared. A penitentiary – what would that be like? From the gossip I'd heard, and from my own memory of the fort-like stone behemoth in Kingston and the letters from poor Malika ... I didn't really want to know. Five years. Gosh, I was not even twenty years old and already had two stints in jail: three months in India and ten months in Canada. Now I was facing another five years. I was scared and depressed.

And my first thought? Now I would not see Sitar Sam for five whole years. Five fucking years ... I couldn't believe it. Would he wait for me? I doubted it. Could I really expect him to? I was beginning to feel that Sitar Sam did not love me the same way I loved him. Sometimes I felt he considered me sort of cute and maybe amusing, but that he didn't take me too seriously. I feared in my heart that I had lost him, and wept forlornly for weeks.

Pam sent a telegram to tell her folks the bad news and that she planned to appeal, immediately. She asked them to send money and meanwhile contacted the Law Society and the human rights commission and God knows who else, searching for a good appeal lawyer.

We finally found Sydney G., reputedly the most expensive and best criminal lawyer in Vancouver.

Sydney said he would try to arrange something under a special clause in the appeal procedure. He wanted a lot of money up front, which Pam was able to come up with. He said he was pretty certain he could get the charge reduced to two years less a day. In fact, it was really quite simple because the maximum sentence was supposed to be two years. The judge exceeded the maximum in order to set a precedent, to make an example of us.

Pam kept complaining. She had never really wanted to plead guilty to anything, and felt betrayed by the legal aid lawyer. By now she had made our case into a political issue. She figured we were political prisoners because we were promoting the use of cannabis as an alternative to the evils of alcohol. I know that's stretching it, but in her mind it was a question of freedom of choice. Shouldn't people be allowed to choose their recreational stimulants?

She began furiously researching the history of drug legislation in Canada. By now she knew all about the Le Dain Commission into the Non-Medical Use of Drugs, which in its interim (1970) report recommended decriminalizing marijuana. Why had it not been implemented? Why were the laws enforcing archaic views? (In fact, the Le Dain recommendations were never enacted.) Pam wanted to argue the point. But Sydney told her we didn't stand a chance if we tried to argue that the law is flawed; we'd do better to focus on getting the sentence reduced. Pam had to relent and follow the lawyer's advice.

Pam asked me, "Can you write to your parents and ask for money to help pay our new lawyer?" Ashamed, I said, "You don't know my parents. I seriously doubt that they would come up with any money or want to help me at all. They'd just say, 'it's your own fault' and beg off." Pam looked bewildered. "What kind of parents wouldn't help their kids? My parents would *mortgage* the house, if they had to, to help me out." I couldn't explain, nor could I accept this kind of refusal, so I lamely wrote a letter asking my parents if I could borrow a thousand dollars. I didn't receive any response for two weeks, and finally requested a phone call to talk to my mom. I had to phone twice because the first time my father answered and wouldn't accept the reverse charges, which was the only way I could call long distance.

I asked my mom point blank, "Can I borrow the money for this lawyer?" Mom hesitated and then said, "I got your letter and talked it over with your father. He said, 'No, absolutely not. Let her rot in jail.'"

I asked why? "I can pay you back!" Mom responded, "You know damn well why. You get yourself in trouble and now you come crying to us for money? You have a lot of nerve. You go running off to India against our wishes and get yourself mixed up with all kinds of drug dealers ... and now you want us to help you out? You must be joking. Anyway, we don't have that kind of money, so there's no point in discussing it."

That was that. I knew she was right. It was terribly selfish for me to think that they would mortgage their house or go into debt for me.

I told Pam and she was incredulous. I fell to pieces and wept bitterly after that phone call. How I ached and longed for an understanding mother. Pam, taking me under her wing, was beginning to understand that I came from a screwed-up background. "Don't worry about it. My folks can cover for both of us and you can pay me back later ... whenever you can. Don't worry about it, kiddo." And she hugged me.

Then I broke down and whimpered and cried like a child. It wasn't so much my parents' denial of money that hurt – I more or less expected that. It was the lost hope that my mom might have some sympathy and understanding, an inkling of my pain. Maybe she could see that I was only human, I make mistakes; maybe she would give me a second chance. But that was against their nature: with my folks you never got a second chance.

I'd read about a journalist who penetrated a puritanical religious community in Ontario, a Mennonite or Amish sect, to get an insider's view. Sect followers lived on remote farms and, as if in another century, without modern conveniences like tractors. For example, they used horses and wagons to deliver vegetables. The children were brought up to believe that their elders knew best and had absolute authority. Living in their insular community, they had to accept that the sect's way was right and that the outside world was full of evil and temptation with nothing good to offer. If an inquiring adolescent or young adult ventured off to discover the world outside, he/she would never be allowed back into their community; this 'errant' child would be mourned as if dead.

I think it's pretty severe to stifle a person's natural curiosity ... to enforce your authority over every aspect of kids' lives, to dictate that they must accept their parents' word no matter what. My folks were like those religious fanatics. If ever you strayed, you were ousted for good. Not very Christian, I'd say.

Talking to my mom upset me and made me feel guilty. How could I be so stupid? How did I let myself get roped into this mess? What had I hoped to accomplish? She was right about one thing. I knew better, and yes, she had indeed warned me. How had she predicted that if I went to India I'd end up like this? Was she psychic?

I spent the next day brooding, and came to the conclusion that I was a complete idiot. If you believe in angels or intuition or guidance, or just plain horse sense, sometimes you get a feeling that something is not good. I'd had lots of intuition about the dope run, lots of signs that it was not going well. First, Pam and Barb fought all the time. Second, the hash market was flooded in both Australia and New Zealand. Third, we couldn't connect with the contact in Vancouver. Why did I ignore the obvious signs of bad karma? In later years I discovered that because of a psychiatric disability, part of my natural defense system shuts down. Because of this disability I was unable to make intelligent decisions. Something was malfunctioning, which took me nearly a lifetime to figure out. But that is another story.

I kept analyzing where we had gone wrong. Why did I do this stupid dope run? One reason was because I was in love with Sitar Sam and felt I was losing him. I was sick of India and Nepal, and thought that if I had enough money he'd come with me to Bali. I was trying to buy him back – what's a girl in love to do?

A letter from a friend in New Delhi said the famous Dr. Kaushik had had a heart attack. He was okay for the moment and recovering, thank God. Dr. Kaushik had been aware of my predicament, and kindly sent me some letters of encouragement and counsel. He said, "if you make a mistake once, it is forgivable. But if you make the same mistake twice, then there is serious karma." Okay, okay, I got the message. I had done precisely that, making the same mistake twice. Now I had disappointed not only my parents but Dr. Kaushik, my guru, Jesus and all the saints, and even God himself. I felt I had to do serious penance. I wrote to Dr. Kaushik and asked if I should make penance by cutting off my baby finger. He wrote back, "Of course, not!"

I realized that I did this stupid dope run because I had no money and felt trapped. Why else would someone do something like this?

I was stuck halfway around the world in a foreign country with no money or ticket home. My lover had abandoned me, returning to California with a promise to come back – but I didn't trust him any more. After my money ran out so did he. How could I know whether he would come back? He was having too much fun in California. Meanwhile I was stuck in Nepal in winter with only cotton clothes and sandals – no warm bedding or heat – and I was tired of the damp and cold. I was hungry most of the time, lonely and miserable. When you are stuck in survival mode you take risks.

So now I was in prison for smuggling hash, for the second time in my life. Clearly I'm not very good at smuggling, I realized ruefully. How could I get out? I looked at the partially cut bar on the window, and remembered that salt makes metal rust faster. I started applying salt and water to the incision, let it sit a few hours, dried it and began sawing again. Pam managed to sneak a metal nail file from a grooming station that we used. The salt did assist the rusting process, but this method would still take months. Our enthusiasm for escaping this way diminished day by day.

Finally Sydney G. our lawyer had some good news. The appeal was accepted so our sentences would be reconsidered. What a relief! This meant we could avoid the dreaded Kingston penitentiary. However, we would face the maximum provincial sentence of two years less a day, and likely the judge would not count the eight months that we'd been in jail. Dead time, they called it. Shit. So we might still face another two years of incarceration, though in the provincial system you could apply for parole for good behavior after eight months. It was the best we could hope for. "Let's do it," I said, and Pam agreed.

Barb, whose case was tried separately, was released from jail in July with no explanation other than that she was in her ninth month of pregnancy. We were not told where she went, simply that she had been released. The Bitch. Would she contact anyone on the outside to help us, I wondered. Pam said, "Of course, not. Barb only looks out for Barb." Pam was more concerned that Barb might go back to Nepal with the baby and lodge a paternity claim against Paul. This was driving her around the bend, but it seemed unlikely. Why would a woman with a newborn baby who just got out of jail travel all the way to Nepal? Barb disappeared and we never heard about her again. We never even found out her real name.

The next few months went by painfully and slowly. Pam and I took up pottery and beading in addition to macramé. I also took a correspondence course in Music 101 and tried my best to understand it ... but without an instrument and teacher it was pointless.

Eventually, on appeal, our sentences were reduced to two years less a day. Pam and I were enormously relieved that we didn't have to go to the federal penitentiary and that we could serve our time in the provincial institution we were familiar with. Lower Mainland Regional *Corruptional* Centre we called it. Better the beast you know.

Meanwhile, the Watergate scandal had blown wide open and it looked like President Nixon would be impeached – and nothing terrible happened in Canada. At least nothing major that I knew about. But Pam was working another angle. She had a notion that because she was not a Canadian citizen she should not have to serve her time in a Canadian prison. She found a loophole that would allow her to serve her time under "house arrest" so long as it was within the British Commonwealth. As a New Zealander (a British descendant of Captain Cook, remember), she could plead "compassionate grounds" to serve her house arrest in her home country. Her well-connected parents had enlisted the help of the British High Commission and some New Zealand diplomats they knew. Although it took some time to arrange, Pam succeeded and was scheduled to be released in a month.

We had been in jail for 10 months, time that the lawyer working with the New Zealand diplomats were able to get counted as "real time served," so Pamela would go home basically a free person. Now Barb was gone, and soon Pam too would be. What about me? I had no idea whether my sentencing would take account of my served time. It didn't look good. Because unlike Pam I was Canadian, maybe I would get the brunt of the stick. It seemed unfair, and I was worried.

Meanwhile, I was getting tremendous support from friends abroad. People were holding prayer circles, and my cousin in Amsterdam wanted to come and rescue me (break me out of jail, he later told me).

But my parents were completely unsympathetic. Occasionally I talked to them on the phone, seeking normalcy despite their distancing. But if I started crying and saying I was sorry, they'd just say, "It's your own fault. Don't expect us to feel sorry for you. You have to obey the rules." Only later did I find out from my sister that Mom hung up the phone and fainted on the floor.

I was hurt and felt that they had no real compassion for my suffering. Indeed, they were ashamed (I found out later) to talk about me amongst relatives and even themselves. I was like the Mennonite kid: I'd done something wrong once, and was gone as if dead.

Oh, my burden was heavy. Sick of jail, I wept in misery and feared I would be stuck here forever. How could I possibly serve another eight months in this hellhole? I longed for some fresh air and to be outdoors. I longed to stand under the night sky and look at the stars. I longed for my siblings and my friends; I longed for India, Nepal and the peaceful life I once knew. I longed for fresh food. But most of all I longed for Sitar Sam.

A few weeks later, Pam was liberated and I was devastated. I still had no idea if my appeal would take into account my time served, which was now nearly a year. So I still didn't know when I would get out of jail. I kept writing to Malika, and I kept up correspondence with friends in India.

One day I received a telegram from my good friend Caitanya, in Delhi. Neem Karoli Baba had died on September 11, 1973. I wasn't surprised at his passing but felt weird when a priest formally delivered the telegram to me. He was so damn solemn he looked like a mortician. I guess prison authorities had to do things with decorum and so they sent a priest. He handed me the telegram and said, "I'm so sorry for you." I read the telegram: "Neem Karoli Baba left his body last night. Stop. His last words were 'Now I am leaving central jail.' Stop. Make puja for Baba."

The typed words attacked my eyes and I was dumbstruck. Was the jail reference a personal message for me? In any case, I had no sense of real remorse or sadness, only great joy; I felt the guru had sent that message especially to me. So I jumped up and said, "Hooray, now he is free." The priest looked puzzled; probably he'd never seen anyone jump up and dance to celebrate a death announcement. But I knew that Mahara-ji was in a good place, and at the moment I got that telegram I heard him laughing joyfully and felt his presence. I knew that for such a great master, the physical body is truly like a jail. Perhaps it was a sign.

The weeks dragged by slowly. I read a lot, everything from *Jonathan Livingston Seagull* to Anaïs Nin. I read all the newspapers, now closely following the Watergate scandal. A letter from the Self Realization Fellowship said they were continuing to pray for me. A letter from Pamela back in New Zealand said she was delighted to be home and sorry to hear I was still incarcerated; she would have her folks do a special séance for me.

But I was a nervous wreck. I wasn't sleeping well and must have lost a lot of weight. I lived for letters from friends and loved ones. I waxed and stripped those damn floors for weeks on end. I cried bitterly until I had no more tears. There was no more news from Sitar Sam, and I was sure that I had lost him.

One night I had an intriguing dream. After a lot of confusing scenes I saw myself amongst a flock of white birds, and someone was throwing golden seeds to the flock. Suddenly a presence appeared and the whole flock of birds flew away. I was one of them.

The next day I got the news: I would be released within days. Hallelujah, I would be free at last! My release conditions stipulated that I had to go home to my parents and finish my two-year term on parole in Ontario. What would home be like? I wondered. Whatever, it had to be better than prison.

Sprung at Last

TO HELP ME "INTEGRATE" INTO SOCIETY, I was accompanied – for one brief day in Vancouver – by a social worker from the Elizabeth Fry Society. A nice lady, she took me to Stanley Park and later to a movie. We saw *The Way We Were*, a Barbra Streisand/Robert Redford film about a failed romance, which made me cry and cry. Later we had dinner in Vancouver's Chinatown.

As I sat on the train taking in the gorgeous sights of British Columbia's mountainous interior and moving through Alberta, I was told to watch out especially for Jasper. When we got there I was amazed: it looked like a picture postcard of a Swiss Alps village. After India and the Himalayas, it was interesting to discover that at home in Canada were magnificent landscapes, equal to any in the world.

I went to the bar car for a cigarette and my first alcoholic drink in over a year. I was not much of a drinker then, but I really wanted to catch a buzz and ordered a cognac. There sat a long-haired, velvet-clad, hippie with a guitar, drinking beer and smoking. He smiled at me and gestured for me to sit down. Guy was from Quebec; he didn't speak much English.

Oh dear! The cute hippie, the only cool guy on the train, and we can't talk to each other. Communicating was amusing at times, and sometimes frustrating, but I gathered that he was a poet and musician. He had been out west and loved the geography, but couldn't adapt to an all-English environment and so was heading back to Quebec.

During our overnight journey we hung out a lot. He knew all Neil Young's songs, some Creedence Clearwater Revival and interesting French songs. Nothing is more fun than riding a train, getting high and making music. I imagined that it must have been like this for the Festival Express people a few years earlier. Janis Joplin, the Grateful Dead, Mountain and The Band lived for two weeks on a train crossing the country and doing concerts in several cities. I had been at one of their concerts and reminisced about that time; a film was later made about it.

I reflected on my life since I left Canada in March of 1972 – now it was February 1974. How my life had changed: from an innocent eighteen-year-old girl to a wild child partying her ass off, and finally to a jailbird going into deep self-inquiry and finding some degree of self-awareness. And yet I felt I hadn't changed that much. I was not bitter about my experience. When I thought about it, it was more like, "Wow ... that was pretty fucking freaky. Now what?" I had no idea what I would do with my life.

What puzzled me still was how we got busted. I never did quite figure out why or how, but in the end it didn't matter. I went through that experience and it gave me enormous strength, strength to endure almost anything. And indeed my future life would throw me more curve balls, but that is another story.

After I returned to Ontario, one last letter came from Sitar Sam.

Next we passed through the prairies, and I'd never seen so much flat land. It sure is a trip. Guy, my French-speaking buddy, managed to procure a joint. We hid in my private cabin and blew smoke out the window. We were careful to put a towel at the foot of the door to prevent its odor from escaping. Because we couldn't talk much, Guy went back to writing poetry and I to reading and looking out at the landscape. Although they were covered with snow, the endless prairies were still beautiful to behold.

In the last two years of my life (or by the time I got to Toronto), I had literally circumnavigated the globe. Was I any wiser? I doubted it. But I did learn a few things that have been helpful survival tools. I learned to try to understand situations and not judge. I learned to Be Here Now. I learned to find the Zen of just doing a task. I discovered that I am not so important. I learned about Bhakti yoga, the yoga of devotion. And I learned that I don't practice those learnings all the time – but that is my constant goal.

I learned that there are times to surrender and times to listen to the unsung whispers around your conscience or gut instinct. And I learned the hard way to never do business with two partners who do not trust each other. Especially if those partners are two head-strong, competitive women. Moreover, two women in love with the same man!

JAIL WRITINGS – VANCOUVER

Analysis of Headspace – May 1973

1ˢᵗ Impression of Sitar Sam: Compassionate, loving, selfless, tranquil. A humble person. (Also: charming, attractive, intelligent)
MY FEELINGS: Love and attraction, Respect and Awe.

2ⁿᵈ Impression: Super-Freak, talented, flower child, yogi, Guru, but serious, religious, aesthetic, humorous combination Yogi and beach bum.
MY FEELINGS: Humour. Love, more attraction, more respect and awe.

3ʳᵈ Impression: Pleasantly dominating, his head's together, strong, wise. (Also: eccentric, nutty, crazy.
MY FEELINGS: Satisfaction, love, humour and respect.

4ᵗʰ Impression: Super-hip guy, always been "where it's at", exciting life style, affluent background, California cool, a bit lazy, lot's of chicks.
MY FEELINGS: Resentment, slight jealousy of his background. But I really look up to him.

5ᵗʰ Impression: Selfish, self-centred, unsure of self, super perfectionist. Flirting, charming and successful.
MY FEELINGS: Fear (of losing him), insecurity, great dissatisfaction.

6ᵗʰ Impression: Rotten bastard! No letters for three months! Selfish, egotist, hung up, lost Sitar Sam.
MY FEELINGS: First hate, then hurt. Second: Compassion

DO I LOVE HIM? Did I Ever Love Him?

Write: a) a nice casual, impersonal letter?
        b) a mean, bitter letter?
        c) an honest letter telling him how I feel?

Letter to Sitar Sam – *May 15, 1973*

Your two recent letters came as a surprise to me and also the information your letter contained was indeed plentiful. I can't understand why I didn't hear from you for three months. Surely, you had heard that I was in jail.

You say you have worked hard "business-wise" and I say that work is good—but it is not good that the fruits of one's labours must immediately go into the hands of others. So that your debts be fulfilled. I can't understand all your financial debts. How much did you pay this lawyer Bruce? If the money you paid Bruce exceeds the money that WE gave to donald then I will certainly try to pay you back. However, that would be at a much later date as I myself am now in debt a fair amount. Also, did you ever get any returns on the money we invested in Donald? Also you imply that friend in Kathmandu have "ripped off" and exploited you? Can you elaborate on that? I am completely unaware of the trips that have gone down for the last eight months and you've always been secretive about your business dealings. I don't really need details but since my money was also invested I would kinda like to know what went down.

Before continuing I will answer your question about Bruce. While you were overseas we telephoned and wrote to Bruce regularly inquiring as to when he'd be here. He finally came on may 7th one day before our trial of May 8th. We realised he could not defend us as he was not a member of the B.C. lawyers bar unless of course he had an international license or a paid a fee of something like $1,000. Surely he should have known this. So now we were stuck with our hopeless legal aid lawyers and Bruce said he would co-defend us and advise our legal aid lawyers. He concluded that we should plead guilty and he said that we should expect at least six months as it were. If we decided to plead not guilty we'd have to wait about nine months for a trial in a high court as they were booked up and backlocked and this would all be dead time. We had already done three and half months dead time and did not want to waste any more time. The three lawyers would approach the prosecutor with the following proposition: if we would pleade guilty to "possession for the purpose of trafficking" the prosecutor would drop our "importing" charge (minimum sentence of seven years).

The deal was made. Then they changed judges. The new judge hear the case and remanded us for a week to study the case. Bruce left and the next week we were sentenced to five years penitentiary time for me and ten years for Pam. It was all so disorganised and confusing. The lawyers were really rude to Bruce and disliked him immensely because he was telling them how to run the show and I think they suspected we were paying him and yet we did not pay for them but took them through legal aid. Of course, we had no bread. But that's not how it looked to them. So that's the whole trip summarised.

I should inform you that both Pam and I are certain that the premie from Spain was directly responsible for our arrest...indeed for the whole affair and the numerous heavy trips (interrogations) following our arrest. She has proven herself a very clever con-woman and a very evil entity, completely lost in her self. She has been up to untold dirty work with her money, manipulating and blackmail. I could write ten pages on the trips we've been through with her. She has just been sentence to "two years less a day" which means no penitentiary time for her. AND she had nearly double the quantity we had. Well so much for the past experiences.

Now we wait to have our appeal date set. But still nothing is clear as we are waiting for premies circumstances relating to our appeal, to clear up. Both Pam and I have our heads together in here and we seem to have managed to "transcend" the jail atmosphere...if one really can do so. On a spiritual level I have increased my psychic awareness and my perception is clearer and I have overcome many illusion. This experience though the physical conditions are difficult, has proven itself a form of Sadhana and I can see my learning and spiritual growth has been remarkable. It has thus far been a time for learning for myself and perhaps for Pam a time to teach. She is a very high and pure soul with a good heart and between us the bond of friendship is eternal. I am so grateful to have her here with me. I myself even, have done some teaching in here. Many lost souls with absolutely no concept of the consciousness. The irony of it is that essentially this jail structure was meant to turn people like us off. Instead, we have turned the jail on!

Originally we were rejected by the inmates mainly because we were different and they couldn't understand us. Now, joy of joy, we have finally "made it" in the jailhouse sub-culture of tattooed lesbians whose status symbol is being a junky, being tough and butch. Yes, we have been elected group reps for our ward.

I am happy to know that you are also fulfilling your role of teacher or guru by lecturing the University circuit. Giving discourses on Sadhus and Tantra...sounds pretty cool. I guess they pay you for this? Certainly, this is right up your alley and your knowledge of the subject comes from direct personal experience. Without a doubt it will go over well.

Remember though to open yourself up to the divine and allow the words to glow through you that the projection of the thoughts will be clear coupled with the manifestation of a sadhu and the related subject matter which is of course yourself. I think the students' curiosity and interest will be aroused. The time is right for the teachings of India to come to North America. There is only the subtle trickery of the ego, particularly when one is teaching, to overcome the flattery that naturally puffs up the ego, of having so many devoted students looking up to you. So, my love, we must continually realize that we are in fact only tools. Tools designed for the work of a higher power and that we are actually only puppets and all that we egotistically think we know is in fact the knowledge of another and that knowledge existed before we did. This is what I have come to realize anyway enough of that. I find this letter already too long but as you said we have three months of catching up to do.

You wanted the time of my birth so that you could do a chart. But this is impossible. I have no birth certificate (as my parents lost it). I was not born in a hospital but in a little country shack with a midwife. My mom after bearing six children even confuses our names sometimes and certainly cannot remember my time of birth. I've always wanted an accurate chart done but alas it is my fate that I shall never have it.

I was interested to hear that you bumped into Tony and Rene … as I have lost touch with them. I wish to contact several people. Perhaps you can fill me in on the current addresses of Tony and Rene, Baba and Sasa, Dr. Kaushik, Daniel and Dawn, Valeria and Pierro, Bernard (from our house in Kathmandu) and remember Richard from the commune in Delhi? He was going to write a book called Dialogue with the Himalayas. I wonder if you have his current whereabouts? Also, why did Shoshonna not write back to me? I am very disappointed in her and I wonder just what the trip is there?

So now to close this letter I send you all my love and mehta,

Diksha

Made in the USA
Charleston, SC
04 April 2014